THE
Devil's Doctor

THE
Devil's Doctor

Felix Kersten and the Secret Plot
to Turn Himmler Against Hitler

John H. Waller

John Wiley & Sons, Inc.

Published by John Wiley & Sons, Inc., New York
Published simultaneously in Canada

This publication is designed to provide accurate and authoritative information in regard to the subject matter covered. It is sold with the understanding that the publisher is not engaged in rendering professional services. If professional advice or other expert assistance is required, the services of a competent professional person should be sought.

Library of Congress Cataloging-in-Publication Data:

Waller, John H.
    The devil's doctor: Felix Kersten and the secret plot to turn Himmler against Hitler / John H. Waller.
       p. cm.
    Includes bibliographical references and index.
    ISBN 0-471-39672-9 (cloth : alk. paper)
       1. Himmler, Heinrich, 1900–1945—Friends and associates. 2. Kersten, Felix, 1898–1960—Biography. 3. Nazis—Biography. 4. Physical therapists—Netherlands—Biography. 5. Germany—Politics and government—1933–1945. I. Title
    DD247.H46 W35 2002
    943.086'092—dc21
    [B]   2001045452

Printed in the United States of America

10 9 8 7 6 5 4 3 2 1

To those who died or suffered
as a result of Nazi tyranny in World War II

Contents

Acknowledgments

IN RESEARCHING THIS BOOK, the extensive documentation of World War II intelligence activities held by the U.S. National Archives and Records Administration (NARA) proved to be particularly valuable. The declassified Office of Strategic Services (OSS) documents cataloged in Record Group 226 was dramatically augmented by the release in June 2000 of some four hundred thousand heretofore classified documents. These documents from the OSS and its temporary successor, the Strategic Services Unit (SSU; 1945–1946), were declassified as the result of the Nazi War Crimes Disclosure Act as implemented by a Nazi War Criminal Records Inter-Agency Working Group (IWG) and the mandated actions of the National Archives and the Central Intelligence Agency. The senior National Archives executive associated most closely with wartime intelligence documents is Mr. John Taylor, who has for many years enjoyed the admiration and gratitude of researchers, including myself, interested in this aspect of history.

I also wish to thank Miss Maria Waller, the talented researcher who combed the National Archives for valuable source material for my project. Another volunteer at the National Archives who has been most helpful to me is Mr. Burton Gerber, whose knowledge of Nazi intelligence activities during World War II and command of the German language also proved valuable.

I wish to express my deep gratitude for the editorial help and online library searches for material on my subject provided by Ms. Stephanie Robinson.

For illustrations I am deeply grateful for photos and other documentation of the Kersten story provided by Mr. Arno Kersten, son of Felix

Kersten, and his widowed mother, Mrs. Felix (Irmgard) Kersten. They were both most gracious and generous.

Other sources of photographs appearing in this book to whom I am exceedingly grateful are Ms. Diane Tachmindji, Mr. Angus Thuermer, and the talented author of two books on the OSS, Ms. Elizabeth McIntosh.

For translations from the German and Swedish I have been fortunate in having available to me the skills of Dr. William Haskett, Ms. Larilyn Andare, Mr. Karl Richter, Mr. Angus Thuermer, and Mr. Andreas Zellhuber. I offer my thanks and gratitude to them all.

Prologue

CONFLICT—TOO OFTEN, ARMED CONFLICT—seems to be always with us one way or another. It is only a fortunate few, blessed with luck and endowed with a will to survive, who emerge relatively unscathed by the horrors of war when caught up in the violence of its storm. Rarer still is the person who struggles to survive war's adversity yet finds courage to help his fellow beings despite the risks this entails.

One such Samaritan was Felix Kersten, a skilled masseur and physical therapist of Finnish citizenship and Baltic German origins, who served the Dutch royal family until it was obliged to find safety in England as Hitler's panzers invaded the Netherlands in World War II. Kersten then had the misfortune of being pressured by Heinrich Himmler to resettle in Germany and continuously administer to his debilitating attacks of excruciating stomach pain. Kersten's story has faded with time, but memories and archival records survive to tell the strange story of how he saved the lives of countless victims of Nazi inhumanities—victims of atrocities perpetrated by Himmler—and helped convince Himmler that he should overthrow Hitler as prelude to making peace on the Western Front with the Western Allies at the expense of the Soviet Union. His collaborator in this plot of high treason was Walter Schellenberg, well positioned as chief of Nazi foreign intelligence, who was convinced that Hitler could not win the War and that Stalin, if allowed to share in the victory over Germany, would dominate Eurasia unless a deal could be made with the United States and Britain to stop him.

Kersten exploited his talent as a physical therapist to influence Heinrich Himmler who became progressively dependent on his therapeutic massages. H. R. Trevor-Roper, Lord Dacre of Glanton, a British intelligence expert on Nazi Germany during the War and a respected postwar author and academician, phrased it well when he wrote in an introduction to *The Kersten Memoirs:* "Kersten, holding as he did the keys to salvation, became to Himmler the all-powerful confessor who could manipulate at will the conscience as well as the stomach of that terrible, inhuman, but naive, mystical, credulous tyrant of the New Order."[1]

With an insider's knowledge of the plotting and conniving by various Hitler henchmen, particularly Himmler, Kersten would prove to be a valuable secret informant for the U.S. Office of Strategic Services (OSS). In secret discussions with Kersten's OSS contact in Stockholm, Abram Hewitt, Kersten and Schellenberg described their special relationship with Himmler and tried to convince the United States through Hewitt in mid-1943 that the Western Allies should secretly support him in ousting Hitler and taking the reins of power himself, as prelude to concluding a peace with Germany—but continuing the war against the USSR.

At the same time Kersten secretly served Finland, the country of his citizenship; the Dutch underground movement, out of sympathy for the country of his adoption, now in thrall to the Nazis; and the government of Sweden, which benefited from Kersten's position and had been particularly impressed with the fact that the masseur was able to talk Himmler into saving the lives of Swedish nationals arrested by the Gestapo in Poland and Germany. Himmler shared many confidences with Kersten, who kept these governments well informed with a variety of important secret information.

Perhaps one of the secrets of state of particular importance that Himmler shared with Kersten was Hitler's worsening health. While the medical evidence collected secretly by Himmler was not accurate as to diagnoses, the very fact that Himmler believed it and was worried by it was important. The *Reichsführer* used his "Hitler dossier" as rationalization for his treasonous plotting against him. As early as August 1942, if not earlier, Himmler had convinced himself that the *Führer,* his idol and inspiration, was losing the War and was no longer fit to rule Germany. But his deeply ingrained admiration for Hitler remained in conflict with his instincts for self-survival—reinforced by Kersten—which demanded he replace his Führer and repel the Russians as prerequisite for earning the confidence of the Western Allies.

Himmler saw in Kersten an aide who could prove useful as a go-between with representatives of the Western Allies via neutral Sweden. Ignoring the agreements implicit in the "Grand Alliance" between Russia and the Western Allies and the specific commitment to the principle of unconditional surrender, Himmler deluded himself that the Western Allies would welcome his plan. Himmler also underestimated the hatred and contempt felt toward him by the West; his name had become a metaphor for inhumanity even before the full dimensions of the Holocaust horror had become known. He fantasized that he could save himself from punishment, if not find favor with the Western Allies, if he were to remove Hitler from power and reach a peace agreement with them. But his divided psyche caused him to vacillate, much to the exasperation of Kersten and Schellenberg, whose own fates could have been jeopardized had he ever felt compelled to make them scapegoats in order to protect himself if Hitler learned of his treasonous proclivities.

Heinrich Himmler, followed by his physical therapist, Felix Kersten, debarks from an aircraft. The Reichsführer insisted that Kersten be near to him much of the time, even on important, sometimes secret business trips in order to treat him should another very painful intestinal spasm occur. (Courtesy of the Kersten family)

Himmler was typical of most rabid Nazi leaders whose basic loyalty was in fact defined by motives of personal survival, however ardently they seemed to pay homage to their Führer. Nazism had become Himmler's religion despite his Roman Catholic upbringing; hence, he was guilty of apostasy to his Nazi cause as well as high treason against his godhead, Hitler. Himmler's character defects were many and complex. It is difficult to reconcile his fundamental personal weaknesses with the power he achieved and the evil he caused by its misuse. Kersten understood the flaws and foibles of his boss well enough to exploit them with signal virtuosity.

If Himmler is the heavy in this drama of a devil's dilemma, Felix Kersten plays the lead as a mitigating influence in the devil's domain and agent, helping certain of Germany's Western enemies. Kersten may not have found a place in World War II's pantheon of heroes, but his adventures—indeed, his very survival in the miasma of intrigue enveloping Himmler's headquarters—qualifies him for recognition. Credit must be given where credit is due, even by his most skeptical critics, for the role he played in this "theater of the absurd," as Kersten himself once described Himmler's court.

Kersten's partner in manipulating Himmler, and arch-plotter in this scenario of high treason, was *Brigadenführer* Walter Schellenberg, who served as head of the powerful Nazi foreign intelligence apparatus, the Sicherheitsdienst (SD), Amt VI. Schellenberg's motives seemed to have combined fear of ultimate retribution as a war criminal by the Western Allies if he did not somehow redeem himself and aspirations of personal power if he did succeed in his efforts to achieve for Germany an "honorable" peace. If he could propel Himmler to the top by ousting Hitler, he would want to take Joachim von Ribbentrop's place as foreign minister, as well as continue as an éminence grise molding *his* new Führer to his own advantage.

Schellenberg considered Ribbentrop a fool whose folly had been to encourage Hitler to provoke a hopeless war in the first place. He believed that in Ribbentrop's place he could set things right; he could make peace with the West, thereby restoring Germany to a respectable place in Europe. But Schellenberg was realistic enough to imagine a less pretty picture of himself dangling from a hangman's noose if he failed in his plot to reach détente with the West.

Upon learning in the British press of this "act of infamy" by Himmler, the man he trusted the most, Hitler, in a rage, ordered his execution shortly before taking his own life. Fleeing in disguise, Himmler evaded arrest by his own SS (Schutzstaffel, or Defense Corps) but was captured by chance when a British patrol encountered him walking deep within a forest. He committed suicide in a melodramatic scene during which he crunched a cyanide capsule secreted in his mouth.

The war ended, and the curtain came down on the last act of a drama that had been drowned out by the noises of war. The "thousand-year Reich" envisioned by Hitler ended far ahead of schedule. There was no Götterdämmerung—no Wagnerian finale. There was only the damage and misery in the wake of a terrible "Hot War" to be dealt with, and an emerging "Cold War" featuring the United States and its European allies arrayed against their erstwhile ally, Joseph Stalin. The Soviet dictator had long been preparing in secret for this opportunity to grab greater power and extend Russia's hegemony in a tired and vulnerable postwar Europe.

Felix Kersten, an obscure youth growing up in Estonia between World War I and World War II, had witnessed the rise of Hitler and his motley misfits. As he reached manhood he was equipped with "magic hands," as Himmler later described them, with which to make his way in a troubled world. This would prove enough to manipulate the Reichsführer, super-ogre of Nazidom and two-timing acolyte of Hitler, and guide him down the fatal path to high treason. Himmler's dependence on Kersten's massages to relieve unbearable pain would provide his masseur with the leverage needed to help convince him finally that he must atone for his evil deeds by releasing Jews still alive in his death camps and at least save them from a final spasm of the Holocaust.

1

Felix Kersten

A Man of Influence

FELIX KERSTEN, a practicing physical therapist in The Hague, had since 1928 made a good professional reputation for himself by ministering to nobles and notables, particularly the Dutch royal family. This lucrative and gratifying life might have gone on indefinitely had his skill not come to the attention of Heinrich Himmler, the powerful Reichsführer SS.

Himmler was tormented by painful attacks of colic and intestinal cramps that would temporarily immobilize him. No doctor or therapist had ever been found who could give him relief. Dr. August Diehn, a friend and patient of Kersten's in Germany, told a desperate Himmler about Kersten's extraordinary massages and recommended that the Reichsführer try them. Thus it was that on March 10, 1939, Kersten, having been summoned by Himmler, found himself face-to-face with the fearsome Nazi leader "whose part in many bloody deeds" he had often heard about "in awed whispers."[1] Kersten looked at Himmler in disbelief. He had seen pictures of him, but none had so totally captured the look of insignificance that he presented in person. He was, as Kersten remembered him, "narrow-chested, weak chinned, spectacled," strangely belying his reputation for unbridled cruelty.

In a high-pitched voice, Himmler pleaded with Kersten to help him.[2] After one of Kersten's rigorous massages, which miraculously gave him relief, Himmler insisted that he be taken on as a patient. "You can and must help me," he said. For all Himmler's plaintiveness, Kersten knew that to refuse could prove dangerous.[3]

This day would change Kersten's life. Nothing in his existence so far had prepared him for what he would experience during the next six years of war as Himmler's masseur. But before telling the tale of the extraordinary career of this little-known man, it is worth glancing at his origins.

Driven from Holland in 1400 by a flood of epic proportions, the Kersten family, bringing with them what remained of its workshops for making fine Flemish linen, resettled in the western German town of Göttingen. There, Andreas Kersten, a member of the town's municipal council, found favor with Emperor Charles V, who in 1544 granted him minor nobility status replete with a family coat of arms.

After a prosperous century and a half, the Kersten family again faced disaster when its workshops burned to the ground. Fortune then looked kindly on the Kerstens for the next two hundred years as successive generations worked a royal land grant of one hundred hectares of rich farmland. All this, however, came to a calamitous end when the family patriarch, Ferdinand Kersten, was mortally injured by a maddened bull as the nineteenth century drew to a close. Aspiring to a different kind of life, his youngest son, Frederick, took a civil service job in the Russian-controlled Baltic states. He married the postmaster's daughter, Olga, and moved to the Russian town of Yurev. Olga was highly respected in the region as a skillful masseuse whose talents would soon reappear in her son. Born at Dorpat, Estonia, in 1898, this new arrival in the family was christened Felix Kersten as his godfather, the French ambassador to the Russian court, stood in attendance. This was an auspicious beginning, but Felix proved to be only a mediocre student at school. Somewhat lackadaisical, he was better remembered for a gourmand's passion for good food.

In 1914, World War I broke out, heralding a new era of chaos in Europe. The Kerstens were one of many Baltic families distrusted by the Russians on general principles and exiled to towns deeper within Russia—in their case to a small village near the Caspian Sea. Felix, who was attending an agricultural college at Guenefeld in Schleswig-Holstein, Germany, was now completely cut off from his family by the fighting.[4]

Being left to his own devices in Germany taught young Felix the rigors of survival. The somewhat indolent youth began for the first time to see the need to work hard if he were to get ahead. Within two years he had earned a degree in agricultural engineering. Then, because he was considered a German national, he was drafted into the kaiser's army. But at heart he did not feel any affinity with the Germans, resenting particularly the stiff-necked tradition of Prussian militarism. In an effort to avoid regular German army service, he volunteered to join a special legion made up of expatriate Finns living in Germany, who were mustered in 1917 to resist Russian domination of their homeland. Because of his service in defense of Finland, Kersten was granted Finnish nationality. Serving in Estonia, he had the opportunity to visit his hometown, Yurev, and by 1919, the year after the peace treaty of Brest Litovsk had been signed, his family could return home and rejoin him.

Having recovered from a bout of severe rheumatism at a military hospital in Helsinki, Felix made a fateful decision to become a physical therapist. Fortunate in having had as his first teacher in the art of massage a well-respected practitioner, Dr. Kollander, young Kersten went on to Berlin for further training.[5]

To save expenses, Kersten boarded at the home of family friends, the widow Lüben and her daughter, Elizabeth. As his training progressed, Kersten found that he not only had a natural talent as a physical therapist, but he had a certain charm that appealed to women. Throughout his bachelorhood women seemed to find him irresistible. But he found a companion and helpmate in Elizabeth Lüben, who served him through much of his life as his housekeeper—and virtually as an "older sister." They found in each other true friendship, in which mutual regard and companionship provided the ties that bound them.

Kersten's professional training would take a new leap forward in 1922, when he met a Chinese master masseur named Dr. Ko through a well-known German surgeon, Professor Bier, who specialized in unorthodox medicine in Berlin. Ko, a wizened, wrinkled Chinese gentleman with a graying goatee, had been trained in a Lamaist monastery in northwestern Tibet by monks who were masters of the art of healing through massage. He found in Kersten a worthy apprentice to whom he could pass on his "secret" technique of "physio-neural therapy."

After long discussions—part philosophical, part therapeutic theory—and having subjected himself to a rigorous test massage by Kersten, Dr. Ko took him on as his student, explaining ". . . you are the one I have been awaiting for thirty years. According to my horoscope, fixed in Tibet when I was still a novice, I was to meet, this very year, a young man who would know nothing and to whom I would teach everything. . . ."[6] In later life

Kersten would often quote from Goethe's *Roman Elegies* to describe his art: "See with a feeling eye, feel with a seeing hand." He described the process more scientifically with somewhat enigmatic words such as these:

> The fundamental effect of this physio-neural therapy, which is often really astonishing, rests on an intensive treatment of the tissues, based on anatomy and physiology. The essential point is its ability to penetrate in a way that is quite beyond the scope of ordinary manipulation. Blood and lymphatic fluids in the vessels treated are pressed towards the heart while unwanted blood is correspondingly sucked back. In brief, the circulation in the blood and the lymphatic vessels is strengthened and accelerated. The consequence of this is a more rapid renewal of the blood and a more effective nourishment of the tissues and muscles treated. Ordinary massage cannot include this specialized procedure, as this demands a fundamental and specialized insight into the anatomy and physiology of the human body and a technical training which is no less fundamental.[7]

The rigid life discipline that Dr. Ko demanded of his student did not include a monklike existence; Kersten was delighted to discover that Dr. Ko believed that pleasure was salutary if balance was to be sustained in the nervous system. But Kersten's bliss in studying under Dr. Ko would not last. It was in the autumn of 1925 that Dr. Ko confided in his pupil that his horoscope, prepared in Tibet long ago by wise lamas, stipulated that he must return to his Tibetan monastery and prepare for a state of "apparent death," awaiting a new foreordained incarnation eight years later.

Kersten was distraught. He knew he would never see his teacher, nor benefit by his inspiration again. But taking some of the sting out of Ko's departure was the realization that he would assume control over his teacher's practice. Kersten prospered; helped by his faithful friend Elizabeth Lüben, he soon moved to a more gracious apartment and made his rounds in an elegant limousine driven by a liveried chauffeur. Launched on what began as a successful career in Germany, Kersten broadened his clientele to include patients throughout western Europe. In 1928, Queen Wilhelmina of the Netherlands was among the notables who summoned Kersten. Her consort, Prince Hendrik, who was suffering with serious heart problems, had been told by specialists that he probably would not survive for more than six months. Kersten miraculously revived the prince's health with a series of "physio-neural" massages. To assure Hendrik's complete recovery, or at least extend his reprieve from death, Queen Wilhelmina convinced Kersten to make his home in The Hague as royally appointed physician. While he kept his apartment in Berlin, which was minded by Elizabeth Lüben, he resided in The Hague, devoting most of his time to the prince, who responded to his treatments by leading a normal existence for many years thereafter.[8] Kersten felt good about his return to the Netherlands, homeland of his ancestors. But his newfound prosperity made him property-conscious and he could not resist a tempting bargain back in Germany—a three-hundred-hectare estate at Gut Hartzwalde, some fifty miles east of Berlin.

In February 1937, Kersten, the ever-eligible bachelor at age forty, met in Berlin a lovely and well-educated young woman from Silesia named Irmgard Neuschaffer. After two months of courtship, conducted mainly through correspondence, they became engaged. Soon thereafter they were married and departed on a whirlwind honeymoon to Finland. The Kerstens' first child, a son, was born on the estate at Hartzwalde, although he was then spending most of his time with the Dutch royal family. The Kersten family's idyll was, however, rudely interrupted by the dislocations of Hitler's war, which would thrust Kersten into a strange and almost unbelievable career as

Felix Kersten with his wife, Irmgard, and their three sons—Ulf, Arno, and Andreas—at their home in Hartzwalde during World War II. (Courtesy of the Kersten family)

Himmler's physical therapist—as well as a secret intriguer along the fringes of power in the heart of the Third Reich.

When Dr. Diehn, president of the German Potassium Syndicate, introduced Kersten to Heinrich Himmler in March 1939, he had an ulterior motive that went beyond bringing relief to Reichsführer's acute attack of colic. He hoped that Kersten would also "persuade him not to nationalize [privately owned] property"—particularly Diehn's potassium empire.[9] Kersten may not have single-handedly saved Diehn's potassium, but he was so successful in treating Himmler's ailment that the Reichsführer asked him to leave the Dutch royal family and tend him exclusively. Kersten refused, but he agreed to treat Himmler as often as his time and royal obligations permitted.

Suddenly Felix Kersten suffered, much as his ancestors had when they had been driven from Holland by the flood in 1400; but the flood that now engulfed him was of a different sort. It was the flood of Hitler's panzers that inundated the Lowlands in May 1940 as the first strike in Germany's campaign to conquer western Europe. The Wehrmacht's lightning seizure of the Netherlands caught Kersten in Germany, where he was making his medical rounds of patients. When his career with the Dutch royal family ended after the queen and her family escaped to London to avoid capture and exploitation by the Nazis, Kersten had little choice but to remain in Germany and succumb to Himmler's insistence that he work for him. Himmler's private aide, Rudolf Brandt, remembered that the Reichsführer had offered Kersten 100,000 reichsmarks as a carrot to sweeten the deal if his treatments proved successful.[10] But whatever monetary incentive was offered him was not as compelling as the implied threat that he had to accept Himmler's offer or suffer serious consequences. Nor could any payment compensate Kersten for the risks he would have to take as an employee in the devil's domain with its endless internecine plotting and its all-pervading aura of mutual suspicion.

Any probability of achieving job gratification by serving Himmler, much less being able to avoid guilt by association as his doctor, seemed remote to Kersten as he thought about the pitfalls ahead. Kersten seemed to have been genuinely appalled by Himmler's philosophies and beliefs—an amalgam of destructive Nazi dogma and psychic fantasy. The Reichsführer had convinced himself that he was a reincarnation of Germany's ninth-century mythic folk hero Henry the Fowler, duke of Saxony, who became King Henry I in 919, and had chosen Genghis Khan as his personal role model.

Why, then, did Kersten accept the position given him by such a neurotic man, devoted to such an evil cause? The short answer is that Kersten, as a person without a country to protect him, was trapped in a web of dangerous circumstances from which he could not easily extract himself. There was probably little or nothing he could have done to reject Himmler's "invitation" to serve him. With the Gestapo under his command, the Reichsführer was in a position to decide the fate of most everyone in Germany—certainly defenseless expatriates such as Kersten. And it could not have cheered Kersten when, after the German invasion of the Netherlands in 1940, the Gestapo told him that it would not be responsible for his or his family's safety unless he moved to Berlin. This was said more as a threat than a warning,[11] and reminded Kersten that because of his favored position with Himmler, he was an object of envy and jealousy throughout the Reichsführer's inner circle, particularly among Gestapo leaders who suspected his Dutch connection.

Kersten did, in fact, try to find a way out. He was a Finnish national and, having fought in Finland's defense against Russia, was still a reserve officer in Finland's army, but his country's ability to protect its nationals in Nazi Germany was virtually nil. Nonetheless, he paid a discreet visit to the Finnish embassy and appealed to the ambassador, T. M. Kivimäkki, for help. Kersten explained his predicament. He described how the Reichsführer was frequently beset by almost unbearable pain that only he, with his unique massage treatments, could relieve—at least, that is what Himmler firmly believed. Kersten also explained how his privileged vantage point provided a window on the war's progress, and that his insider's view of Nazi leaders in action made him a remarkably well-informed person. But this did not compensate for the personal risk to which he was exposed. He confessed his grave doubts about the wisdom of treating Himmler under the present tense circumstances—he admitted that he was frightened.

The Finnish ambassador, however, made it clear to Kersten that it was "his duty" to remain in Himmler's employ and report secretly to the Finnish embassy all intelligence he gleaned as a result of his proximity to the founts of Nazi power. Kersten was apprehensive, but he promised to do what his government wanted of him. He was flattered that he had been asked to play a role in a war that promised to be one of the greatest dramas of history, but he was worried as well. Kersten left the Finnish embassy that day with the exhortations of his ambassador and key officers to do all he could to increase the already astonishing degree of confidence shown him by Himmler and report to Helsinki on a regular basis what he was able to learn.[12]

Reichsführer SS Heinrich Himmler with his physical therapist, Felix Kersten. (Courtesy of the Kersten family)

How and when it was that Kersten came to realize what levers of influence his skillful hands represented, and how the proximity to Himmler they gave him could be exploited, is a matter of conjecture.

Himmler considered Kersten his property. While he insisted that his needs had first priority and Kersten must be on call at all times, he also felt that he had the right to loan him out to friends or political associates for whom he wished to do favors. Kersten's only defense was to perform test massages permitting him to drop a patient if they did not work. And it was his professional prerogative to make the determination whether or not his ministrations were useful.

In late January 1940, Himmler requested—that is, ordered—Kersten to accept as a patient Foreign Minister Joachim von Ribbentrop, who, according to the masseur, seemed to suffer from bad headaches, giddiness, impaired vision, and stomach pains. Aside from the fact that Ribbentrop was not a likable person, Kersten saw troubles ahead in treating such highly placed officials: if the therapy did not help the patient, or if the patient capriciously did not find Kersten's ministrations to his liking, the masseur ran the risk of falling into his bad graces. Already suspect as a foreigner, Kersten did not want to make new enemies who would undermine his protected position at Himmler's court. Ribbentrop was a particularly risky case; he and Himmler were rivals for Hitler's favor, and Ribbentrop resented the Reichsführer's interference in foreign matters through his foreign intelligence apparatus, RSHA (Reichssicherheitshauptamt—Reich Security Main Office) Amt VI. But there was nothing Kersten could do about it, particularly since he realized that Himmler expected him to produce any potentially useful morsels of information gleaned from Ribbentrop in the course of the treatments. Realizing that this could be a two-way track, Himmler warned Kersten not to divulge to Ribbentrop information about his own health. Specifically, Himmler did not want the foreign minister to know about his stomach and intestinal affliction. Kersten commented in his memoir: "Ribbentrop had to think Himmler was perfectly strong. Once he knew that Himmler was ill and unfit, he could intrigue and snipe at him even more than at present."[13]

Trouble began almost immediately. Ribbentrop questioned Kersten's loyalty. He was aghast to learn that the masseur was not a Nazi Party member and had no intention of joining it. Ribbentrop complained to Himmler, asking why his masseur had not been politically trained or been "encouraged" to apply for party membership.

For a variety of other reasons, Ribbentrop's demeanor grated on Kersten. He recalled, for example, one conversation with Ribbentrop in which the foreign minister defended a well-publicized and much-criticized incident that occurred while presenting his credentials as German ambassador to the king of England at the Court of St. James's: he had snapped to attention and given His Majesty a stiff-armed Nazi "Heil Hitler" salute. In recounting the incident for Kersten's benefit, he protested that he had been correct in abiding by Nazi protocol, rather than British. Ribbentrop argued that by simply accepting Germany's outstretched hand, England would have been spared war and survived under the "powerful protection of the Greater German Reich," but by snubbing him—in effect, snubbing Germany—England was doomed to "lose everything." Nazi Germany, particularly Ribbentrop, badly underestimated and misunderstood Britain's resolve under Churchill's leadership.[14] The German foreign minister's festering hatred for England, and his advice to Hitler on the eve of the war that the British would not fight to protect Poland despite its agreement with Warsaw to do so, have been credited by many as encouraging the Führer to attack, thus sparking the world war that erupted in 1939. Certainly, Kersten was among those who had no respect for Ribbentrop. He would soon become exasperated with his patient on many counts; by September 1943, he refused to continue his treatment and thereby made a highly placed enemy out of the foreign minister.

Among other prominent Nazi patients treated by Kersten, thanks to Himmler, was Dr. Robert Ley, leader of the Deutschearbeits, the Nazi's German Labor Union. This relationship, beginning in November 1940, contributed to Kersten's growing realization that most high-ranking Nazi officials were unstable, neurotic men, not only evil of intent but quite unfit for the duties demanded of them.

Ley had been fired from a prewar job with the I. G. Farben Chemical Works because of chronic drunkenness, dishonesty, and general trouble making. Had it not been for Himmler's insistence that Kersten treat Ley, the masseur would have had nothing to do with this badly flawed, unattractive man. Kersten would try to alleviate Ley's pain, which was caused perhaps by a malfunctioning pancreas, but rarely did he have any success. It would be easy to suspect that Kersten on purpose had not tried very hard to please his patient. When Kersten related the sordid details of Ley's chronic drunkenness to Himmler and asked him to relieve him of this hopeless case, the Reichsführer suggested that he taper off the treatments so that no scandal about Ley's excessive drinking would occur.

Ley, on one occasion, tried to pressure Kersten to donate his estate at Hartzwalde to the German Labor Union, arguing that he, Ley, needed a love nest where he could entertain girlfriends. As an incentive, Ley promised Kersten that through his labor movement he would finance a physiotherapy clinic, ostensibly to train students in the art. Kersten declined the offer and left as Ley drunkenly shouted after him: "I, Robert Ley, will make you famous! Heil Hitler."[15]

During the two years that Kersten treated Ley, he admitted to secretly jotting down items of more than usual interest concerning government plans that were carelessly mentioned by Ley while under the influence of drink. Among the nuggets of intelligence Ley mentioned was Hitler's intention to establish a comprehensive system of socialized medicine and socialized industry.[16]

While treating Ley, Kersten had the occasion to meet his wife, who was clearly embarrassed by her husband's chronic inebriation. Kersten also treated this woman, whom he described as a "beautiful, . . . tall, elegant and ice-cold blonde" for a gallbladder problem. She once confided in Kersten that she was terribly unhappy with her husband, described by her as a "wild beast," whom she feared would one day murder her. Her fears may have been justified. He once allegedly lunged at her in the presence of Kersten and began to rip her dress off, shouting drunkenly that she was beautiful and he, Kersten, "must see more of her." Only when Kersten threatened to report this unseemly tableau to Himmler did Ley calm himself and beg him not to ruin his career. Within a year, Mrs. Ley committed suicide by shooting herself.[17]

Kersten's patients were not confined to German notables. Himmler bragged about his masseur's skill on one occasion and recommended that Italian foreign minister Count Galeazzo Ciano, Mussolini's son-in-law, try him. Himmler, when introducing Kersten, said that he "is the magic Buddha who cures everything by massage." The Reichsführer was clearly impressed with Kersten's skill and found it politically useful to loan him out.[18] Count Ciano, suffering from chronic stomach trouble, had earlier been told about Kersten by Signor Cerutti, the former Italian ambassador to Germany. Upon meeting Kersten, who was traveling with Himmler in Italy during the summer of 1940, Ciano engaged the masseur's services. Kersten found the cosmopolitan Ciano a pleasant person to be with. Once again Kersten was ever alert for gossip—or better—and seemed to have learned much about Mussolini and Fascist political attitudes during his stay in Rome during November and December of 1940. Among other conclusions Kersten drew from his experience with Ciano in Italy was that the Nazi regime in Germany was not well thought of by either Italian aristocrats or the common man. Ciano, in confidence, criticized Germans as pompous and haughty. Guido Buffarini, Italy's minister of the interior and a friend of Ciano's, with whom Kersten had also become friendly, predicted correctly that there would inevitably be a separate Italian peace concluded between Italy and the Western Allies. Ciano felt the same way, but confided in Kersten that before peace could be reached, his father-in-law would have to be overthrown. This, Ciano believed, was a certainty.

A measure of the confidences exchanged by the Italian foreign minister and Kersten during their massage sessions can be noted by the fact that Kersten admitted that Himmler and Ribbentrop were fierce rivals at sword points. This apparently pleased Ciano, who had little respect for his German opposite number, blaming him for getting the Axis into a European war that could not be won.[19]

Himmler was no better disposed toward Italy than Ciano was toward Germany. But Ciano nonetheless was willing to make frank comments to Kersten that revealed his animosity and deep fear of Germany. "National Socialism," in Ciano's opinion, was "a poor imitation of Fascism." The

Italians are afraid of the Germans, Ciano told Kersten, because they never know what Hitler will do next. Kersten felt that Ciano spoke with him so frankly because he was a Finn, not a German, and because he could thus trust his discretion.[20]

Count Ciano was pleased by his new friendship with Kersten, and believed the masseur's massages had been beneficial to his health. On December 12, at a farewell banquet, Ciano bestowed on Kersten on behalf of the king of Italy the "Cross of a Commander of the Order of Maurice and Lazarus." In his speech, Ciano observed impishly, but apparently sincerely: "Most persons receive orders because they give good dinners. But I am giving this to you because of your excellent services as a physician."

In his memoirs, Kersten observed that his stay in Italy had provided him with a breath of fresh air. Germans, he complained, were essentially the same barbarians of antiquity: "They do not know how to amuse themselves." As a self-proclaimed good judge of women, he observed that German women "left him completely cold in contrast with Italian beauties." And, he added, "the pattern of the German mind was alien to the Italian soul."[21]

Kersten's many satisfied patients kept him from being overly modest, and the urgency with which Himmler often summoned him when unbearable pain struck and his unique ability to bring relief made it obvious to Kersten that he could exert considerable influence on his present master. But Kersten first awakened to the potential of his influence when he courageously intervened with Himmler to save anti-Nazi dissidents, Jews, and many others perceived as malcontents in his adopted homeland, the Netherlands, from mass deportations to Polish Galicia and the Ukraine on orders from an enraged Hitler during the winter of 1941.

2

Kersten's Dutch Connection

Hitler Hated the newly conquered Dutch, who had met their new masters with undisguised hostility. Their acts of rebellion, reaching a climax during February 1941 in riots throughout the Netherlands, maddened the Führer. Himmler was witness to Hitler's wrath when he ordered the Reichsführer to resettle millions of "irreconcilable" Dutchmen in the Ukraine, or elsewhere in the western marches of the Soviet Union, as soon as these lands were overrun and occupied by German forces in accordance with Hitler's still-secret plan to invade the USSR.

Kersten first heard of this operation early in March 1941 while lunching alone at the general staff dining hall in Berlin. He observed at a nearby table the powerful Reinhard Heydrich, Himmler's deputy in charge of all security and intelligence affairs, and Hans Rauter, Gestapo chief for the occupied Netherlands, engrossed in serious discussion. The gist of their conversation as overheard by Kersten deeply shocked him. From what he could hear, SS troops under Himmler's overall command would on April 20—Hitler's birthday—begin implementation of a plan to transplant forcibly "undesirable" Dutch citizens en masse to newly occupied Soviet territory conquered by the German army.[1]

According to his diary entry of March 1, 1941, Kersten immediately questioned Himmler's assistant, SS *Standartenführer* Rudolf Brandt, who confirmed this astonishing information: "At six o'clock this afternoon Brandt let me have a look at secret documents about resettling the Dutch. The file comprised 43 typewritten sheets in a yellow cover; they were signed by Hitler, countersigned by Bormann and marked 'secret'." Kersten summarized certain details in his diary to the effect that some 8.5 million people were to be eventually resettled in stages, some in eastern Poland. The first to be transported would be an estimated 3 million "irreconcilables,"[2] a euphemism, in large part, meant to cover Jews. Ten days later, a distraught Kersten found a favorable circumstance, when Himmler was suffering more than usual from his stomach pains, to protest this outrage.

According to Kersten's memoir, Himmler's response was to justify German plans for the Netherlands: "We occupied Holland mercifully; we tried to persuade the Dutch people to remember they belonged to the German[ic] nations." He then heaped blame upon the Dutch Jews—"the wretched Jewish traders-parasites responded with pinpricks, rebellion, and sabotage . . ."[3] Himmler confirmed to Kersten that the whole operation would begin about April 20, 1941, and take some thirteen months to complete. The first contingent to be transferred would be the Catholics of southern Holland and the Flemish people, whose destination would be somewhere in the eastern states of a Greater Germany, which would include parts of the western USSR after it was conquered by the Nazis.

The transplanted Dutch would ultimately be given cultivatable lands between the Vistula and Bug Rivers in the region east of Lemberg. Only those who had cooperated with the Nazi occupying forces—and, after the War, perhaps deserving German SS veterans as well—would inhabit the Netherlands. Kersten was shocked by the Nazis assumption that Russia, still at peace with Germany and joined by a mutual nonaggression pact, would soon be engulfed in a lightning surprise attack. He was further shocked when Himmler told him that as SS chief, he would be held personally responsible to make certain that Dutch Jews being transferred to the East "would never reach their designated destination—or any destination!"[4]

In fact, Nazi actions aimed specifically at the Jews in the Netherlands had been perpetrated since the beginning of the German occupation. There had been a series of decrees hostile to the Jews, starting with an order issued on August 30, 1940, abolishing a Jewish holiday. Then, in October, Jewish business enterprises were forced to "register"—with all the ominous implications that this bureaucratic word used in this context promised. The February 1941 uprisings, particularly in Amsterdam, were marked by violent clashes between Jews and Dutch Nazis goaded by Hans Rauter. These episodes resulted ultimately in the deportation of thousands of Jews, held first in temporary forced labor camps until they were finally sent to Auschwitz or other notorious camps for execution.[5]

Kersten had been secretly kept informed of developments in the occupied Netherlands by friends in the Dutch resistance movement and was well aware of the excesses perpetrated by the Gestapo in controlling the population, particularly the Jews, but nothing he had heard compared in horror to what Hitler and Himmler apparently now planned for his adopted homeland. He felt keenly an obligation to do something to save this unfortunate country. The strategy Kersten adopted was to convince Himmler that his health would be at serious risk if he undertook such a demanding project.

In his postwar memoirs, Kersten described how he had talked frankly to Himmler, asserting that it was beyond comprehension how he could embark on such an inhumane proceeding. Kersten added his warning that it was more than his weakened physique could stand.

Himmler's pain grew progressively worse. In despair, he pleaded with Kersten to do everything he could to alleviate his suffering. Taking full advantage of his obvious distress, Kersten warned his patient to "obey his

Felix Kersten in the garden of his home at Hartzwalde. (Courtesy of the Kersten family)

orders if he wanted to be fit for work." Above all, Kersten warned him against taking on the resettlement of the Dutch and all that would mean in terms of stress and fatigue. Kersten argued, "The end of the War would be time enough to resettle the Dutch." Referring to Himmler's fragile health, Kersten added, "If you put ten amps on a circuit made for six you are bound to blow a fuse."[6]

Throughout the first half of April 1941, Kersten continued to nag Himmler, warning him over and over again that his health would break down if he proceeded with Hitler's misbegotten project to transplant the better part of a nation's population. No matter how strenuously he massaged him, Kersten complained that he could not undo the terrible stress that had been inflicted on his system by events. Unable to stand the increasing physical as well as psychological burden that was immobilizing him, Himmler finally agreed to make an effort to convince Hitler that now, as Germany faced the awesome challenge of defeating Russia on a wide-ranging battlefield along the Eastern Front, it was no time to overtax Germany's logistical capability by mass-moving people across an entire continent. Kersten's relief was unbounded when he received a phone call from Himmler on April 17: Hitler had agreed to put off indefinitely the relocation of the Dutch.[7] Kersten could relax for the first time in weeks at Gut Hartzwalde. He put a bouquet of flowers from his own garden behind photo portraits of Queen Wilhelmina and Prince Hendrik in gratitude. After an exhaustive postwar investigation into Kersten's contributions, the Netherlands government awarded him the coveted Order of Orange-Nassau.

Always reluctant to admit his errors, Himmler sometime later in discussion with Kersten regretted that he had allowed himself to be talked into abandoning the Netherlands project. The Führer's instincts, he believed in retrospect, had been right; Kersten had been wrong. Himmler grouchily complained that the postponement or abandonment of the Dutch relocation had been "all the fault of my wretched health and [the influence of] the good Dr. Kersten."[8]

No matter what Himmler might have advised at the time, for whatever reasons, it is probable that Hitler, on his own or on strong advice from his military leaders, had come to the conclusion that such a logistical disruption would not be wise just as the Wehrmacht was about to launch Operation Barbarossa, the exceedingly risky invasion of the USSR. What is significant in this episode, however, is that the Reichsführer SS seemed unable to take on daunting challenges without succumbing to mental and physical distress that only Kersten could relieve. The masseur was beginning to realize that he could exploit Himmler's weakness despite the other side of his boss's psyche, which clung to Nordic mysticism, Nazi dogma, and near worship of Hitler.

Kersten noted in his memoir:

> His [Himmler's] severe stomach convulsions were not, as he supposed, simply due to a poor constitution or to overwork; they were rather the expression of this psychic division which extended over his whole life. I soon realized that while I could bring him momentary relief and even help over longer periods, I could never achieve a real cure. The basic cause of these convulsions was not removed, was indeed constantly being aggravated. It was inevitable that in times of psychic stress, his physical pains should also increase.[9]

A new cause of stress affecting Himmler soon became evident to Kersten, a cause traceable to a fateful command uttered by Himmler's godhead, Adolf Hitler. It was on November 11, 1941, that Himmler emerged from the Führer's presence and soon confided in Kersten that the "destruction of the Jews is being actively planned!"[10] In fact, Hitler had issued the order for the aggressive implementation of the "Final Solution" of the Jewish "problem," assigning primary action implementing this policy to Himmler and the SS, as early as the late spring of 1940; and by late summer of 1941, *Einsatzkommandos,* mass execution teams of the SS, had been assembled to hear Himmler pass on Hitler's orders and address them on their future duties. Hitler had made it clear that the "liquidation orders" were his personal responsibility, but it was the responsibility of the SS Einsatzkommandos to carry out his orders to execute Jews as a "political-ideological task."[11]

This horrifying announcement went well beyond the earlier decree of January 24, 1939, intended "to solve the Jewish question by emigration and evacuation. . . ." In a letter to one of his top officers in the SS, Himmler had specified: "The occupied Eastern territories are to become free of Jews."[12] This comment is consistent with Himmler's intention to separate the Dutch Jews from other citizens of the Netherlands marked for eventual relocation so that they could be executed in accordance with the Final Solution.

Hitler's ranting and his outbursts of temper were often interpreted by his lieutenants as policy edicts to be carried out literally. Himmler, in his awe of Hitler, was among those guided by the adage "Your wish is my command." On occasion, Hitler was known to have remarked something to the effect that "What India was for England, the lands of Russia will be for us."[13]

Kersten knew that Himmler's original solution to "the Jewish problem" had been to recommend the expulsion of Jews from Germany as undesirables, but foreign resettlement proved impractical or altogether impossible. Madagascar, which Himmler had favored as a Jewish resettlement place, would have created problems with the French, who governed it. Other suggested disposal locations were no more acceptable for any number of reasons. Himmler blamed Goebbels for originally promoting the Final Solution of killing all German Jews, but in his discussions with Kersten the Reichsführer nonetheless seemed to have embraced Hitler's genocidal decision without qualms or questions.

Kersten's claimed that his reaction was one of horror when he heard from Himmler that total destruction would be the fate of the Jews. He protested to the Reichsführer, expressing shock at such "fearful cruelty" and the sinfulness of wanting "to destroy men simply because they were Jews." He asked, "Hadn't every man a right to live?" Himmler's monologue in rebuttal—he often lapsed into lectures rather than be outscored in dialogue—sounded to Kersten as unreal as it was terrifying. Unfortunately, it was all too real. On November 16, 1941, Kersten noted in his diary that he had tried to reopen the conversation about the fate of European Jews, but Himmler, contrary to all his habits, only listened in silence. Kersten's reactions were frank: "Since I labor in vain against the atrocious principles to which Himmler is committed . . . I will undertake as many interventions as possible to rescue Jews, hoping that they will be granted by Himmler."[14]

Kersten often invoked his license to bring up most any subject with Himmler—and always got away with it. In raising a lesser-known but similarly cruel Nazi breach of human rights, the masseur discussed with Himmler the imprisonment of some eight thousand members of the Jehovah's Witness sect, known in Germany as the *Bibelförscher*, whose faith forbade their taking part in or even countenancing war. Nor could they approve joining the Nazi Party on the grounds that "man's welfare comes from God, not man." To extend the Nazi salute to a megalomaniac like Hitler would be to blaspheme the true God.

The plight of Jehovah's Witnesses was close at hand to the Kersten family. The concentration camp of Ravensbrück, where most of the Jehovah's Witnesses were kept, was only ten miles or so from Kersten's country home. In 1942, Kersten realized that because of the shortage of agricultural workers, many of the farmers in this area were permitted to draw on Ravensbrück's inmates to work their fields. It helped the farmers, and it helped the government by sustaining agricultural production when labor was short because of the military draft. But it also made life more bearable for the hapless Jehovah's Witnesses, who were thus fed and housed relatively humanely by the farms to which they were paroled.

It was when Kersten, with Himmler's permission, took on parole workers from Ravensbrück that he was able to gain firsthand knowledge of the appalling conditions that existed at the camp. Ten women prisoners were initially assigned to Hartzwalde; soon male farm workers were also assigned. Hearing their tales of mistreatment and seeing the state they were in made clear that they had barely survived the starvation-level diet on which they had been forced to exist. They told stories of filth, malnutrition, unattended illness, and abuse by the guards. Kersten was "horrified to the point of feeling sick" upon hearing details about their treatment. It was then that he recorded in his diary that as a physician, his obligation was to heal; he thus vowed to try and do something about this sort of institutional mistreatment. I was going to be obliged to act if I was to keep my peace of mind," he wrote. He launched his campaign by informing Himmler about the inmates of concentration camps and how they were systematically tortured and killed.

Himmler scoffed at Kersten, accusing him of falling for enemy propaganda. From then on Kersten claimed to have used his growing influence on Himmler to free innocent people unjustly persecuted. As a beginning, he used Hartzwalde as a haven for a "great number" of imprisoned Jehovah's Witnesses, for whom he and his wife provided food, honorable work, and the shelter of a good home. Above all, the Kerstens treated them sympathetically. Thanks to Kersten's influence on Himmler, Hartzwalde was given immunity from search and investigation by the Gestapo. But because Kersten was beyond the reach of the secret police, Gestapo chief Heinrich Müller had to satisfy himself with rumors and self-inspired fantasies. Müller convinced himself that Kersten was using Hartzwalde as a secret refuge for escaping English POWs and German resistance collaborators and Jews on the run sought by the police. "Gestapo" Müller complained to Himmler, but the Reichsführer insisted that the Gestapo must not harass the Kerstens in any way—an order honored in the breach.[15]

Understandably, Kersten's instincts and actions were more complex than performing humanitarian acts for their own sake. He was concerned with his and his family's safety during the War and conscious of the need to prosper after its conclusion. Somehow he had to counteract what he feared might be a tendency on the part of the Allies—if they were destined to win the War—to link him to Himmler as an accessory to the Reichsführer's war crimes. While the War still raged and his very existence depended on pleasing Himmler, he needed at the same time to nurture contacts in western Europe on whom he could depend after the war.

Sweden was of practical importance to him since he hoped to be granted Swedish citizenship, enabling him to settle there to carry on his profession as a physical therapist free from the still-raw, roiling sentiments that would surely be rampant in a disillusioned, defeated, and economically depressed postwar Germany. But it would be inaccurate and unfair to imply that Kersten was not genuinely appalled by Nazi atrocities. Trapped as he was in Himmler's domain, he would do his best to mitigate his master's dreadful misdeeds and, within his limitations, succor victims of Nazi terror.

Himmler had become Kersten's protector; already he could not bear the thought of being denied the all-important relief his masseur could provide him during vicious attacks of pain. But the Reichsführer's office was not a reliable refuge. Aside from Himmler's assistant, Rudolf Brandt, in whom Kersten had found a good friend, most of the other senior officers in Himmler's inner entourage viewed the privileged *Ausländer* with Finnish citizenship and Baltic ancestry with jealousy—and serious suspicion.

Early in 1941, two most unpleasant Gestapo officers paid Kersten a visit and viciously interrogated him, accusing him of having medically treated Jews in Berlin. Kersten stood up to his tormentors and made clear to them he had friends in high places. By the end of the session, the two policemen apologized and left, but Kersten had the uneasy feeling that the unexpected visitors had been sent to harass him by Reinhard Heydrich, Himmler's powerful deputy. Upon hearing of the incident, Himmler became livid with rage and immediately gave instructions that no one should bother Kersten in any way.[16]

Himmler, however, scolded Kersten, pointing out that suspicions had probably been aroused within the Gestapo because of his continuing ties with Holland—specifically, he had not yet sold his house in The Hague as he had promised to do. Himmler warned Kersten that if he did not do so quickly, even he, as Reichsführer, would have difficulty in preventing Heydrich and Ernst Kaltenbrunner, Heydrich's deputy, from plotting against him. Rudolf Brandt also warned Kersten as a friend that Heydrich was out to destroy him.[17]

Having no choice in the matter, Kersten obeyed Himmler and in March 1941 visited The Hague to straighten out his personal affairs and move his effects to Germany. Himmler had insisted that while in The Hague he report daily to the local Gestapo chief, Hans Rauter, who had made himself loathed and feared by the Dutch. On the bright side, this was an occasion for Kersten to look up old friends, including some who might be in trouble with the Gestapo. And he was especially anxious to make contact with close friends with whom he could arrange a secure communication system, enabling him to stay in secret touch after he returned to Germany. Thanks to Rudolf Brandt, he had been entrusted with one of the Reichsführer's "protected" addresses (Military Postal Sector number 355360), immune to Gestapo interception and inspection. By using this address he could maintain a correspondence without fear of compromise. Specifically, he wished to use this link as a means of maintaining secret contact with the Dutch Resistance. Kersten explained that upon returning to Germany he would in effect become "secret ambassador for Dutch patriots in distress." In fact, he noted, "appeals for help did pour in upon me."[18]

Kersten put his greatest trust in an old friend, an art dealer and antiquarian named Bignell. But, by calling on Bignell, he alerted the Gestapo's suspicions and triggered a feverish investigation that resulted in Bignell's arrest. Rauter accused Kersten of trafficking with a "traitor who was in secret contact with London." Although Kersten was able to get Bignell out of jail by pleading his case by phone with Himmler, the episode gave some substance to the Gestapo's conviction that Kersten was a spy in contact with the British-supported Dutch underground.[19]

Like a terrier with a rag doll, Heydrich continued to harass Kersten. In a long and terrifying conversation in late February 1941, Heydrich demanded that Kersten furnish him with continuing information received from his friends in Finland and Holland. Kersten realized that Heydrich's real aim was to get the names of his contacts in those two countries so that he could incarcerate them. Ernst Kaltenbrunner also hated Kersten, who, he was convinced, was an agent of the "English Secret Service." Only because Himmler would ultimately have to warn Kaltenbrunner to leave Kersten alone was the masseur spared imprisonment—or even death.[20]

Heydrich became further suspicious of Kersten because of the masseur's talks with Rudolf Hess just before Hitler's trusted deputy made his historic black flight to Scotland to meet with RAF wing commander David Douglas-Hamilton, the duke of Hamilton. Impressed with Kersten's talents as a therapist, Himmler had introduced him to Hess, who suffered from various aches and pains. The two men, doctor and patient, had become friends. In one conversation with Hess, not long before the latter's spectacular flight to the enemy's camp in Scotland, Kersten remembered that Hess described

Caught by camera at the Nuremberg War Crimes Trial is Rudolph Hess, flanked by Hermann Göring in dark glasses and Joachim von Ribbentrop, once a patient of Kersten's, as haughty poseur. Hess, also a former patient of Kersten's, hinted to him just before he secretly flew to the United Kingdom that he would soon "make history." (U.S. National Archives)

Hitler's attitude toward England, then generally assumed to be Hitler's next target. According to Kersten, Hess told him confidently, "We'll make peace with England in the same way as with France."[21] He claimed that the Führer believed that England should stand against the threat of Soviet Bolshevism, saying: I can't imagine that cool, calculating England will run her neck into a Soviet noose instead of saving it by coming to an understanding with us."[22]

In the hectic aftermath of Hess's flight on May 10, 1941, Heydrich went so far as to arrest Kersten and rigorously interrogate him about Hess's state of mind on the eve of his flight. It became obvious as he ranted that Heydrich believed that Kersten had encouraged Hess in the latter's "friendly feelings toward England." More ominously, Heydrich accused Kersten of being in the pay of the English and having helped Hess prepare for his flight.[23] Not until Himmler ordered Heydrich to stop questioning Kersten could the frightened therapist breathe a little more easily. What Kersten had not told Heydrich was that Hess had confided in him that he was getting ready for an act of "historic importance," a deed calculated to secure "the salvation of Germany."[24] Such a comment would surely have excited

Heydrich's suspicions that Kersten was privy to Hess's intended flight to the United Kingdom, something that Hitler would never have condoned even though he had probably agreed to Hess being in touch with the West through an intermediary.

If Heydrich harbored suspicions about Hess's motives, a paranoid Joseph Stalin imagined an even more ornate and grandiose plot. The Soviet dictator was convinced that Hess's flight was part of a German-British plot against him. Soviet historian A. M. Nekrich wrote: "Hess's flight made a big impression on Stalin; he was certain that Britain was inciting Germany to attack the USSR, that secret negotiations were taking place in London."[25] He was never completely disabused of London's "treachery" despite denials made to him by Winston Churchill, in person.

Kersten only knew that he was in jeopardy—a target of high-ranking officers who resented his propinquity to Himmler and the influence he had acquired over the "Chief." He could trust Himmler's assistant, Brandt, to keep him informed, and he had confidence that Himmler himself would protect him, but a powerful insider like Heydrich, a master of guile and treachery, could easily outwit Himmler.

After questioning Kersten about Hess, Heydrich said: "I'm sorry but I have to arrest you. I don't believe a word you say." Then, switching to the Netherlands, Heydrich accused Kersten of being the one who influenced Himmler in calling off the Dutch deportation plan.[26] He then insisted in his own sly way that Kersten must reveal to him his sources in The Hague. Only a timely call from Himmler saved Kersten. Heydrich released him with a parting shot over his bow, the meaning of which Kersten knew only too well: "Don't worry, we will see each other again."[27]

In fact, Kersten did not see Heydrich again. In September 1941, Heydrich became Nazi proconsul *(Reichsprotektor)* in Bohemia and Moravia, as well as chief of the RSHA, the Nazi security and intelligence apparatus. On May 27, 1942, he was wounded in Prague by a team of Czech resistance fighters trained by the British SOE (Special Operations Executive), a secret paramilitary organization, and died of his wounds on June 4. Unfortunately, Ernst Kaltenbrunner, who replaced Heydrich as head of the RSHA and Himmler's number two man, was equally eager to get rid of Kersten. Kersten still had much to worry about, even though Himmler had made it clear to Kaltenbrunner that he must not harass his therapist.

Kaltenbrunner had been a close friend of Brigadenführer Heinz Jost, so when the latter lost his position as head of Amt VI (Foreign Intelligence) he resented Schellenberg, the new head of Amt VI, whom he blamed for his friend's ouster, and vowed to take revenge. Luckily, Schellenberg was given the rare privilege by Himmler of reporting directly to him rather than having to go through Kaltenbrunner as the old chain-of-command wiring diagram indicated. Certain reforms made by Schellenberg after he took over his new position as chief of Amt VI irritated other officers now under him and whose turf he had invaded.[28]

While at first Kersten's only reliable friend among Himmler's senior officers was his adjutant, Rudolf Brandt, he soon recognized Schellenberg as a

GERMAN INTELLIGENCE COMMAND STRUCTURE
MID-1942 TO MID-1944

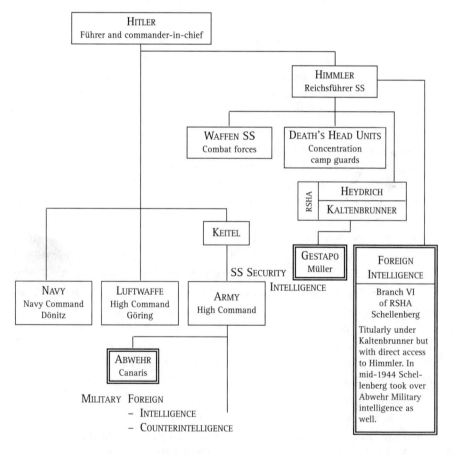

German Intelligence Command Structure, 1942–1944.

potentially useful ally, not only because he had power as one of Himmler's favorites, but because he, too, was an enemy of Kaltenbrunner. Kersten recalled that Schellenberg, instead of being suspicious as he might well have been, was on the contrary most cordial and friendly. His friendliness, Kersten believed, was a product of his hatred of Kaltenbrunner, who was consistently so very outspoken about his hateful feelings toward Kersten, as well.

A rising, ambitious officer within the RSHA and Himmler's privileged protégé, Schellenberg had lost faith in Hitler's ability to govern and was contemptuous of Foreign Minister Ribbentrop, whose bad advice he believed had caused the Führer to plunge Germany into a war for which it was not prepared. Schellenberg harbored a secret agenda in which he ambitiously dreamed of convincing Himmler to exercise his SS military power base to overthrow Hitler and negotiate peace with the Western Allies. Only in this way, Schellenberg believed, could Germany defend itself from Bolshevik Russia—even defeat Russia in a single-front war for hegemony over Europe.

Felix Kersten, with his unique access to Himmler and his astonishing ability to influence him through administering pain-relieving massages, began to interest Schellenberg as a potential ally in manipulating the Reichsführer in crucial matters of war and foreign relations. Schellenberg's career to date had been a dynamic one, catapulting him to the position he now held. Espionage, imaginative double-agent operations, and secret political action were skills he had mastered. Now he dared to take on high treason in the midst of war. What had his annealing in the dark arts consisted of? Who and what was Walter Schellenberg?

3

Walter Schellenberg

Senior Nazi Intelligence Officer

T HE NAZI GRASP OF POWER in Germany in January 1933 had brought
to the party's ranks a rush of youth. Disheartened by Germany's crippling
depression and disillusioned by the Weimar Republic's feckless performance since the end of World War I, Walter Schellenberg was one of the
many attracted to Hitler's new movement. Despite three years at the University of Bonn, where he had first studied medicine but soon changed to
law, the young man's prospects were not promising. It became obvious that
if he were to qualify for a government grant enabling him to serve the
required period of legal apprenticeship, he would have to participate in
some branch of the Nazi apparatus.

The "elite" SS corps appealed the most to Schellenberg. Compared with
the SA's (Strumabteilung, or storm troopers) street brawlers, the SS had a
"better type of people," he believed. He joined the party and was appointed
to the SS in June 1933. But it soon became apparent that there would be
more to all this than parading in a smart black SS uniform. Despite the
pomp and paraphernalia of power, Schellenberg was soon disillusioned.

As one of the SS guards sent to mount patrols in Bad Godesberg on June
20, 1934, Schellenberg caught glimpses of top Nazi leaders stealthily gathered to plot the destruction of the SA, an aggressive rabble whose ruffians
had played such an important part in bringing Hitler to power and

protecting him in the early days of his reign. Now, however, the SA's continuing existence was more of a threat than a boon for Hitler. Encouraged by rivals jealous of the SA leader, Ernst Röhm, the Führer believed that his old friend had become a traitor, making secret plans to seize power from him.

On this occasion in June 1934, Schellenberg witnessed the preparations for a mass bloodletting in which the SA leadership would soon be annihilated. Röhm's long friendship with Hitler could not save him from being murdered—a victim of intraparty rivalries among Hitler's lieutenants who constantly vied for the Führer's favor and its prize of power. Among other discredited and distrusted leaders targeted for murder were General Kurt von Schleicher, an old enemy of Hitler's, whose sin was that "he knew too much," and Gregor Strasser, leader of the Nazi Party's left wing. This was a lesson in power politics, Nazi style, that made an impression on Schellenberg as he watched a line of Mercedes limousines carrying Hitler and senior officers to the airport, knowing that their destination was Munich, where they had a rendezvous with mass murder. The great purge of the SA on June 30, 1934, which has come to be known as "the night of the long knives," set the tone for future Nazi brutality and political-military method.

More to Schellenberg's liking was the Sicherheitsdienst (SD for short), the party's security-intelligence arm to which he transferred in the spring of 1935. Here he was soon introduced to the fine art of counterespionage in the Soznovski case—the spy story of the decade preceding World War II. A Polish cavalry officer, Lieutenant Colonel Jerzy Soznovski, was a talented spy for his country and an apparently irresistible ladies' man who combined both talents to manage one of the most successful penetrations of the German General Staff. His skill and audacity were remarkable, as he preyed on well-placed, well-informed, and usually well-built women to whom he made love before recruiting them to steal the deepest secrets of the Third Reich.

The final roundup of Soznovski and his secret-agent lady friends in this melodrama almost defies imagination. Tipped off that the Gestapo was about to close in on him, the Polish colonel staged one last lavish party as cover for his planned escape from Germany. One of his agents, an exotic dancer, performed for the benefit of a prominent café-society crowd of partygoers at the colonel's place. As the champagne flowed, the lights were dimmed, the music quickened its beat, and the scantily clad dancer undulated ever more lasciviously. Then, as the party veered toward erotic wild abandon, Soznovski plunged his apartment into total darkness so that he could slip out unseen and make good his escape in a waiting auto. Waiting instead were Gestapo agents, who seized him.

Schellenberg had acquitted himself well in this operation; he had even managed to spare two of Soznovski's femmes fatales the fatal consequences of their treason so that they could be doubled back against Polish intelligence. Other women less fortunate were found guilty and beheaded in a macabre mini-guillotine execution that the Gestapo favored for its female victims. Soznovski himself beat the executioner by being traded for German agents captured and held by the Poles.[1] Whatever else Schellenberg may have learned from the Soznovski operation, he had seen at close range evidence of the bitter rivalry between the party's Gestapo/Sicherheitsdienst apparatus and the German General Staff's military intelligence, the Abwehr, that would plague the relationship between the agencies throughout much of the War. The services had together worked on the Soznovski case with something less than mutual cooperation and good grace.

Still another prewar operation, this one aimed at Stalin, gave Schellenberg experience in the techniques of international covert political action. Tipped off by an SD informant named General Nikolai Skoblin, prominent within the White Russian community of Europe, that Soviet Marshal Mikhail Tukhachevsky was plotting to overthrow Stalin, RSHA chief Heydrich seized an opportunity to sow discord between the Soviet dictator and his Red Army. Hitler was shown Skoblin's information, made even more damning by artful forgeries added by Heydrich on the basis of records stolen from Abwehr files suggesting long-standing close ties between certain officers of the German army and Soviet officers. The Führer decided in mid-May 1937 to make Stalin aware of this compromising information, using President Edvard Benes of Czechoslovakia as go-between and thereby hoping to drive a wedge between the Russian dictator and his officer corps. Stalin did not need encouragement to purge his army of elements already suspected of dubious loyalty, but was grateful for Hitler's gesture of support to him; the Führer could instead have clandestinely supported Tukhachevsky's planned putsch—in fact, he had considered that course of action.

Fascinated by this maneuver, Schellenberg saw that it had succeeded in accomplishing two objectives useful to the Nazis: it had helped to create an atmosphere of some cordiality, if not trust, preparatory to the signing of a German-Russian pact, and had provided Stalin with evidence to use against certain of his officers, made more convincing to the public because it seemed to originate with the Germans and was not just the usual falsified evidence forged by Stalin's NKVD for Soviet show trials. Stalin's great purge of the Red Army in 1937 very nearly destroyed Russia's military capability, inspiring Schellenberg to dub Heydrich "the puppet master of the Third

Reich."[2] This case illustrates Heydrich's modus operandi of playing one person off against another, a technique that he would use to harass Schellenberg in the tense days to come.

Heydrich's technique was to prove less successful in domestic intrigues such as those that flourished when he took on the German General Staff. In order to curry favor with Hitler, Himmler tried to discredit the Wehrmacht by bringing trumped-up charges of homosexuality, crafted by Heydrich, against Field Marshal Werner von Fritsch, the popular war minister. Von Fritsch strongly disagreed with Hitler and his aggressive intentions against Czechoslovakia, a stance that had made the war minister's continuing presence most unwelcome. Thanks to strong backstage support from Abwehr chief Wilhelm Canaris and Colonel General Ludwig Beck, the chief of staff, this invented charge was thrown out by the military court to the humiliation of Himmler, who had been responsible for the prosecution's weak case. In desperation, the Reichsführer had even enlisted a panel of psychics to conjure up incriminating evidence based on astrological signs. Himmler's unorthodox methods were signally unsuccessful. Heydrich's less exotic but no more honest casework, replete with false witnesses, fared no better. Von Fritsch was declared innocent. But despite this verdict, Hitler used the case and the attendant publicity to remove the war minister and take over direct control of Germany's military machine himself.

The von Fritsch trial was the spark that ignited anti-Hitler sentiment in the armed forces, and in 1938 gave rise to a military resistance movement whose leaders—including Beck and Canaris, among others—hoped to block Hitler's efforts to take over the German-populated Sudetenland as military prelude to dismembering Czechoslovakia and seizing Prague itself. The Wehrmacht feared that this adventure by Hitler would bring France and England to the defense of the Czechs and begin a war for which the army was not yet ready. Many in the military feared that defeat was inevitable.

Having heard of military plotting against Hitler, Heydrich feared for his own life. He ordered Schellenberg, an expert sharpshooter, to stand guard over him one evening when rumors of an imminent putsch by the army became intense. As Heydrich cowered in his barricaded quarters, Schellenberg could see that "the man with the heart of steel," as Hitler sometimes referred to Heydrich, was in reality a coward.

A busy schedule did not prevent Schellenberg from marrying a woman to whom he had been rashly engaged but did not love. On May 18, 1938, he took his vows of marriage to Kathe Kortekamp, much against his better judgment. He did not want to marry her; however, according to his postwar

testimony, his superior officer, a Brigadenführer Albert, head of administration in the SD, insisted that it was his duty to marry the woman on
"moral grounds"[3] because he had expressed his intention to marry her by
becoming engaged. The mental anguish caused by a virtually coerced
marriage and a heavy work schedule plunged Schellenberg into a nervous
breakdown. Making matters worse was a growing friendship between Schellenberg and Lina Heydrich, wife of Reinhard Heydrich.[4] Becoming excessively friendly with the wife of a superior officer is not usually wise, but, as
Schellenberg would discover, making Reinhard Heydrich jealous could be
fatal. Schellenberg remembered vividly that Heydrich liked to play cat-and-
mouse games with his officers. In his games of "trickery and deception, Heydrich always played the part of the cat, never resting until he had the mouse
completely in his power, to be struck down at the slightest sign of trying to
escape."[5]

Schellenberg described Lina Heydrich as a "cool Nordic beauty, not without pride and ambition, yet completely enslaved by Heydrich." Lina discovered that Schellenberg could satisfy her hunger for "the better things of
life." She longed for "more intelligent and cultivated society in the world of
literature and art." While Schellenberg denied ever having had a sexual affair
with Lina, he knew that his close friendship had become a subject of gossip.
Heydrich, "the cat," aggravated by his wife's cultural pretensions and suspicious of her relationship with Schellenberg, considered him the "mouse."
Schellenberg realized that Heydrich was trying to catch him in a trap so that
he could destroy him as a threat to his marriage—and as a rival for Himmler's favor.[6]

Heydrich often invited one or more of his subordinate officers to dine
and go pub-crawling of an evening. On one such night, when he had chosen Schellenberg as his companion for an outing on the town, there was a
tenseness between them. After they had a few drinks, Schellenberg saw
another unattractive side of Heydrich; his behavior bespoke sexual obses-
sion and perversion. As his boss drank too much, it was obvious that he
became predatory toward women. Schellenberg noted that bar girls, who
recognized Heydrich from previous encounters, recoiled in fear and
retreated out of range if they could. Rumors had spread that Heydrich was
sadistic with prostitutes and usually frightened those ladies of the night
unlucky to have been "favored" by him.

Suddenly Heydrich accused Schellenberg of having spent his afternoon at
Ploener Lake, near Lina's summer place, in amorous dalliance with her. He
threatened Schellenberg by warning him that if he did not answer this

accusation truthfully he would die within six hours because the drink he was sipping had been poisoned, and promised that he would withhold the antidote in his possession that could save him. Schellenberg sounded sincere in his explanation; moreover, everything he said tallied with what a Gestapo tail who had followed the couple reported, and by what Lina herself said. Heydrich finally let Schellenberg off with a warning while fetching the antidote from his pocket and pouring it into his drink.[7]

On another occasion Schellenberg had been startled when the sex-obsessed Heydrich ordered him to create a "honey pot"—that is, a high-class bordello—where very important customers could romp with prostitutes while their indiscreet conversations were being secretly recorded. Schellenberg suspected that Heydrich envisioned an SD-operated bordello as a place where he himself could be "entertained" under secure conditions. In time Schellenberg did create such a place of ill repute. VIPs such as foreign diplomats and high-ranking Nazis, unaware that their every word was being recorded, flocked to Salon Kitty, named for its madame, Kitty Schmidt. Kitty presided over a group of girls trained in elicitation techniques whose pillow talk with clients was recorded by 120 hidden "bugs" and preserved on 25,000 wax disks before the War ended.

Particularly interesting to spymaster Schellenberg were the indiscretions and secrets of such luminaries as Italian foreign minister Count Ciano and, of course, some careless or drunk high-ranking Nazis would often unwind at Salon Kitty and talk too much. Who could resist the charms of Kitty's girls?

Allegedly, Foreign Minister Ribbentrop, whom Schellenberg hated, Sepp Dietrich, commander of Hitler's SS bodyguard, and, to Schellenberg's special delight, Himmler himself would sometimes drop by. When Heydrich or Himmler visited Salon Kitty, Schellenberg was always careful to enforce the strict orders that no recordings be made of their pillow talk with the girls. Once, however, there was a slipup and Heydrich tattled to Himmler, blaming it all on Schellenberg.[8] Schellenberg wiggled out of this untrue allegation, but it served to remind him of the dangerous threat he faced from Heydrich.[9]

Despite the complications in his personal life, Schellenberg was doing well in his professional career. Posted to Amt IV-E, dealing with counterespionage, he made a name for himself by staging an ingenious sting operation against British Secret Intelligence (MI-6), sometimes known as the Venlo Incident. With a small team that included a psychiatrist, an opera singer, and a hit man, Schellenberg masqueraded as an Army Transport Service officer named Captain Schammel. Sporting a monocle, he played the part of a German military Resistance *(Widerstand)* officer seeking contact with British intelligence. After preliminary indirect secret negotiations, Schellenberg, in late October 1939, lured senior British Secret Service officers S. Payne Best and Richard Stevens to a rendezvous at a restaurant in the town of Venlo, on the Dutch border. Instead of sitting down to negotiate a plan in which the German army would overthrow Hitler and make peace with the Western Allies as had been promised, Schellenberg signaled to an automobile full of SS thugs, who appeared on the scene and kidnapped the two British officers. They were spirited away to a Gestapo jail in Germany, where they were ultimately forced to divulge details of British agent networks in northern Europe. Best and Stevens were kept in German concentration camps for the duration of the war, where they could brood about the disaster that had befallen them and their service as a result of the sting. Most British spy nets in western Europe were compromised, leaving England almost devoid of agents on the eve of the German invasion of France and the Lowlands.

At Hitler's insistence, the Nazis tried to derive additional propaganda benefit by publicly blaming Best and Stevens, as well as their "Dutch Government collaborators," for the plot to bomb the Führer during a Nazi Party reunion in Munich on November 8, 1939. Schellenberg privately speculated that the attempt on Hitler's life by George Elser, an unknown cabinetmaker who specialized in crafting zithers, may have been deliberately staged by elements within the SD to enhance the popularity of the Führer and justify the German invasion of the Netherlands on the eve of the German offensive against western Europe.[10] Whatever the truth, it is curious that Hitler, in an apparently shortened speech to his followers honoring an anniversary of the failed Munich putsch in 1923, left the beer hall only moments before the lethal charge went off, killing and wounding many of those in attendance.

Elser, under pressure, still maintained that he acted alone—that he was not part of a conspiracy. Himmler tried hard, but without success, to extract a confession implicating others. The Reichsführer, addicted to the occult in many forms, even enlisted the help of a psychic to determine who else might be involved, but to no avail. Felix Kersten's memory of Himmler's reaction at the time is revealing: a blaring headline in a prominent newspaper, the *Völkischer Beobachter,* blamed a "scoundrelly plot" by the British. "Only Providence saved the Führer, cried the paper in bold type. But Kersten's suspicions were aroused after Himmler clammed up when asked about the subject. And others in Himmler's office seemed afraid to talk about it.

While the official Nazi line, of course, continued to blame the plot on British agents Best and Stevens, Kersten picked up certain facts strongly suggesting that the bombing had been a fake attempt on Hitler planned by the Gestapo to create anti-British sentiment and to martyrize Hitler, but that it had been overdone. Kersten claimed that on one occasion he caught Himmler off guard; in a slip of the tongue, Himmler implied that Heydrich had been involved in the Munich affair.[11] Within the Abwehr's Resistance circles as well, there were those who believed that Heydrich was responsible for the bombing, but had used Elser as a convenient scapegoat.[12] German Resistance activist Ulrich von Hassell was also inclined to believe that ambitious or dissatisfied Nazi Party leaders were responsible for the plot.[13] Arthur Nebe, president of the Criminal Police, Branch V, RSHA—and secretly a Resistance collaborator—had the lead role in investigating the beer hall crime; he could find no evidence linking Elser with the Communist Party or any other known opposition group. Nebe instinctively believed that Heydrich had been the architect of some diabolical scheme to kill Hitler and to propel Himmler to power in a new regime in which Heydrich would be the man behind the "throne."[14]

Wilhelm Hoettl, an SD officer who would try to interest OSS Bern chief Allen Dulles in an anti-Hitler "Austrian nationalist" peace plan as war was drawing to a close, was another who concluded that Heydrich had been the perpetrator of the bomb plot. But in his version, Heidrich had arranged to save Hitler by convincing him to leave the meeting early, thereby stirring up public sympathy for Hitler and using this "close call" to enhance the Führer's popularity just before the autumn offensive against western Europe began.[15] Hoettl's analysis of Heydrich in his memoir, *The Secret Front: The Story of Nazi Political Espionage,* included a few words that probably represent an accurate assessment of Heydrich's power and ambition at the time—how he could undertake self-serving operations without concern for how his chief, Himmler, would react if he discovered them: "Heydrich carried him [Himmler] to the top, and it was he who made Himmler the man he became; his, too, was the idea of pushing this inconspicuous, diffident man of mediocre intelligence upwards until he felt the right moment had come to topple him and take his place."[16]

While Schellenberg in his interrogation by the Allies after the War suggested that the Munich bombing may well have been "deliberately staged [by the Nazis] and designed to establish Hitler's popularity beyond question,"[17] he changed his testimony in his later-published memoir, *The Labyrinth,* when he suggested the possibility that the Black Front organization of Otto Strasser, a defector from the Nazi Party, was responsible. No suggestion was made in his memoir that the whole thing could have been staged by the Nazis themselves.

Some measure of how stressful this whole incident had been at the time—particularly the pressure brought to bear by Hitler himself to exploit evidence "proving" a British connection—can be seen by the fact that Schellenberg had a heart attack. Contributing to this were problems in Schellenberg's personal life. However brilliant he may have seemed in the darkness of his operational life, Schellenberg's first marriage was not successful and soon failed. A divorce was granted in November 1939.

Schellenberg, in a lapse of good judgment and swept away by love, then entered into a second marriage that caused new problems. His new bride was Irene Grosse-Schönpauck, whose mother was Polish, a nationality never popular among SS officers but particularly objectionable after Germany invaded Poland. Nonetheless, Himmler gave Schellenberg permission to marry, and Heydrich dutifully interposed no objections in view of Himmler's acquiescence. But Heydrich could not resist a scarcely veiled jibe. He indicated his disapproval by returning to Schellenberg photos of his bride-to-be, which had been submitted per regulation as part of the clearance process, on which Himmler had scrawled comments complaining that the lady's lips and eyebrows were made up in an "exaggerated" way. Before Schellenberg could breathe easily, a copy of a "secret" report sent from the State Police in Posen to Gestapo chief Müller was passed on to him. This report included the results of a thorough investigation of his new in-laws, with an emphasized comment that his mother-in-law's sister was the "wife of a Jewish mill owner!" Schellenberg knew that Heydrich now had a hold on him. No one knew better than Heydrich what it meant to be tainted by Jewish connections in Nazi Germany, being one-quarter Jewish himself. He had always tried to suppress this "blemish" on his Aryan image although he was aware that both Himmler and Hitler knew about his Jewish lineage. Just as Heydrich held over Schellenberg the fact that his new Polish wife had a Jew in her family, Heydrich could assume that Himmler held over him the secret of his grandmother's Jewish bloodline. As Himmler once simplistically confided to Kersten, Heydrich was zealous in implementing "the final solution" to prove the dominance of his Aryan side.

Having made a name for himself in the service by pulling off the Venlo sting, crippling British intelligence in Europe, Schellenberg was assigned another daring operation targeted against the British. It had been Foreign Minister Ribbentrop who conceived this wild idea, code-named Operation Willi, to suborn or, failing that, to kidnap the Duke and Duchess of Windsor! Ribbentrop warned Schellenberg not to tell anyone about the operation—including Heydrich, Schellenberg's immediate superior officer.

Rather than worsen his already strained relationship with Heydrich, Schellenberg, in strict confidence, nonetheless told him about it. Heydrich's reaction was predictably unenthusiastic: "Ribbentrop always wants to use our people when he gets ideas like this; you are really too valuable to be wasted on this affair," he told Schellenberg.[18] Schellenberg also considered the plan impractical, but there was nothing he could do about it; Hitler himself seemed enthusiastic. The Führer even gave Schellenberg the benefit of his wisdom on the subject: "Bear in mind the importance of the Duchess's attitude and try as hard as possible to get her support. She has great influence over the Duke.[19]

Toward the end of July 1940, Schellenberg left for Madrid, where the Duke and Duchess of Windsor had fled by way of southern France when Paris fell to invading German troops. Ribbentrop's ill-considered scheme called for Schellenberg to recruit the duke and exploit him as an alleged pro-German advocate residing in Madrid under Francisco Franco's protection. From this relatively safe place of exile, Ribbentrop hoped the duke could become a rallying point for appeasement-minded British notables who despaired of their country's survival if it did not capitulate to the Germans as France had done. If the duke could not be enticed into the German camp with offers of a restored throne in England, Schellenberg should kidnap him and force him to acquiesce with propaganda drafted by the Nazis aimed at beleaguered Britain.

Operation Willi, during which clumsy overtures were made to but rejected by the Duke of Windsor before he sailed from Lisbon to the Bahamas to assume his new duties as governor-general of the British island colony, soured Schellenberg. He had never liked the plan, which he knew could not succeed. The whole affair depressed him as a reminder that Ribbentrop was a fool.[20]

In mid-November, Schellenberg again fell ill. This time his illness was diagnosed as "poisoning of the liver and gall bladder." He claimed to have suspected the British of having poisoned him in Lisbon while he was working on Operation Willi. He reasoned that British intelligence wanted him dead by way of punishing him for both the Venlo sting and Operation Willi. Schellenberg's doctor did not rule out the possibility of purposeful poisoning by the enemy, but was inclined to feel that the ailment had been of many months standing, predating Operation Willi.[21] Whatever the cause, Schellenberg's illness was chronic and would continue to plague him throughout his short life, leading to an unsuccessful surgical operation in 1952 from which he died.

After the Willi affair, Schellenberg brooded about the inadequacy of German foreign policy as handled by Ribbentrop and Hitler. And he did not believe that German intelligence, in whatever form, was providing adequate situation analyses to support sound policy making. In his opinion, Admiral Canaris's Abwehr, primarily responsible for foreign intelligence, was too involved in military affairs to do justice to political intelligence. Moreover, Schellenberg knew, or at least strongly suspected, that elements of the Abwehr, including Admiral Canaris himself, were rabidly opposed to Hitler's whole war policy and were less than eager to provide any foreign intelligence that might justify the Führer's aggression abroad. Canaris was secretly encouraging the dissemination of essentially defeatist information with particular focus on the War on the Eastern Front—which was, in fact, going badly.

In order to have more leverage on matters of foreign policy, Schellenberg was able to wangle a transfer from RSHA Amt IV-E, the department of counterespionage and security, to Amt VI, charged with the collection of foreign intelligence. He began making plans for a more sophisticated center for strategic political and economic foreign analysis that would expose Hitler's fantasies.

Taking advantage of Himmler's power and his own brains, he felt he could forge an effective foreign policy—one that could be used to discredit Hitler and drive him from power.[22] Schellenberg was secretly convinced that Hitler's military adventures would cause Germany to lose the War and perhaps its sovereignty as well.

There were other reasons why Schellenberg had sought a transfer to Amt VI. The head of Amt VI, Brigadenführer Jost, was in Schellenberg's opinion grossly deficient as a manager. Put bluntly, he was tired and lazy.[23] Moreover, Schellenberg could not get along with Gestapo chief Heinrich Müller and was constantly ill at ease with Heydrich himself. By moving to Amt VI, he hoped he would not be as squarely in the sights of these two men, whose interests were security and secret police matters, not foreign affairs—and were resentful of Himmler's patronage of him. Schellenberg's stewardship of

Amt VI provided a breath of fresh air for this important department, but his new power position alarmed Gestapo chief Müller, threatening an already fragile relationship between the two men. Müller no longer had chain-of-command power over Schellenberg, but despite the latter's new independence from the Gestapo and Himmler's protection, he was still vulnerable to Müller's backstairs intrigue. Making matters worse, Müller would ally himself with Martin Bormann, Himmler's archrival, at the expense of Schellenberg's piece of mind.

The ambitious Schellenberg was, however, a tough infighter in the intramural, bureaucratic warfare that raged among Hitler's lieutenants. He knew what he wanted; thus, after Heydrich's assassination in Prague during the late spring of 1942, Schellenberg replaced him as Himmler's closest adviser. Schellenberg's agenda called for systematic manipulation of the Reichsführer with the objective of overthrowing Hitler with the combined power of SS and Wehrmacht forces, then negotiating a peace with the Western Allies, permitting a reconstituted Germany under Himmler's leadership to turn its military power eastward and defeat the Soviet Union in a one-front war.

In August 1942, Schellenberg found an opportunity to meet alone with Himmler and discuss with him Germany's prospects for the future, particularly in view of the U.S. entry into the War and Russia's stubborn defense on the Eastern Front. Himmler had summoned him to his field office at Zhitomir, southwest of Kiev, in Ukraine. Recognizing his obligation to stay near to Hitler's headquarters at Vinnitsa and the German General Staff headquarters at Berdichev, Himmler had found suitable quarters in Zhitomir from which he ran his security and intelligence empire. Schellenberg, who was suffering from his mysterious stomach ailment, looked forward to finding a few days of rest from the stressful atmosphere in Berlin; he also hoped to find Himmler in a mood to talk about the importance of finding a way to withdraw from a two-front war that could not be won. Moreover, he wanted to get to know Kersten better in an effort to enlist his help as a friend in Himmler's court.

4

Rendezvous at Zhitomir

Genesis of High Treason

T HERE WOULD BE MUCH to talk about at Zhitomir. The so-called Nazi Peace Offensive was in motion. Various Nazi leaders and German diplomats, generally with Hitler's approval, were sending discreet feelers to the British during early stages of the War. Walter Schellenberg, acting for Himmler, was actively engaged in this game, the rationale for which was based on Hitler's hope that the British could be induced to negotiate a peace with Germany much as France had done after its defeat. While France had capitulated and negotiated under duress following the French army's surrender, Hitler believed that the British, faced with German control of western Europe, would welcome peace rather than risk German occupation. Hitler's terms would prevail under these conditions, of course, but the Führer could hope that the British would be relieved and enjoy the prospect of Russia's total defeat. Certainly, he believed, the British would prefer German victory on the Continent to a Soviet victory resulting in Russian hegemony over all of Europe and much of Asia and the imposition of Russian-style Bolshevism, hated as much in Britain as in the Third Reich.

During Prime Minister Neville Chamberlain's administration, the Nazis had seen a convincing expression of England's fear of war. In the 1938 Czechoslovakia crisis, the Chamberlain government and France embraced "Peace in our time," the well-remembered statement that the British prime minister uttered as he disembarked in London from his aircraft following his Munich meeting with Hitler, waving the agreement selling out Czechoslovakia. Shortly before the German invasion of Poland, Hermann Göring's initiative through his Swedish go-between, Birger Dahlerus, revealed Chamberlain's willingness to talk about peace once again for all his disillusionment with Hitler in the wake of Germany's seizure of Czechoslovakia. And on June 24, 1940, Rudolf Hess told his physical therapist, Felix Kersten—on loan from Himmler—that the British Empire must survive so that England could resist Bolshevism. He also said that it would be hard to believe that the pragmatic English would "rather put their heads in the Soviet's noose than come to an agreement with us."[1] In June 1940, Hitler announced in a radio speech that he would offer Britain "generous terms" for peace. This caused the British War Cabinet to call a special meeting. Understandably, the cabinet rejected this enticement as fraught with trickery. Then, in an address before the Reichstag, the Führer stated, "A great world empire will be destroyed should the war continue—an empire that I never intended to destroy.[2] He added, "I can see no reason why this war should go on."[3]

Hitler's abandonment of Operation Sea Lion, the German plan to invade England, came as a surprise to Mussolini. After talking with Hitler, Italian foreign minister Galeazzo Ciano noted in his diary that he believed Hitler's desire for peace was sincere; he "would like an understanding with Great Britain. He knows that war with the British will be hard and bloody."[4]

Even after Winston Churchill became prime minister and made clear that Great Britain would stand firm against Germany, there were those among the British who saw merit in reexamining this policy after the German eastern offensive stalled at Stalingrad. In January 1943, William Cavendish Bentinck, the influential chairman of the British Joint Intelligence Committee, would write a report suggesting that a postwar Soviet threat to Britain was a real enough possibility that "it would be in British interests to encourage the Germans and Russians to tear each other to shreds." He suggested that the opening of an Allied second front in France should, therefore, be put off.[5] And, of course, Ribbentrop's Operation Willi, managed by Schellenberg, had been based on the premise that the Duke of Windsor, if controlled by the Germans, could be induced to rally still-active British peace advocates to seek a negotiated peace with Germany.

Himmler, however, had a secret agenda: Germany should make peace with the Western Allies, but *only if Hitler were removed from power* and he, Himmler, became Führer in his stead. Schellenberg had a hunch that

Himmler shared his own view that Hitler had been misguided by Ribbentrop in starting the war in the first place and, if allowed to continue, would drag the Third Reich to certain destruction. This scenario of high treason was what Schellenberg wanted to try out on Himmler at Zhitomir, as risky as such a discussion would be.

Schellenberg was by now well schooled in secret dealings with the enemy. He had already made several British contacts, but in his conversations he had stayed within the bounds of Hitler's "peace initiative," carefully skirting any treasonous implications. Reflecting Hitler's views, Himmler himself extolled the concept of a Greater German Reich, protected by the mighty British fleet. Germany, he believed, was destined to become Europe's unchallenged European land power, helping if necessary to guard England and its far-flung empire from predators.

Never attuned to the subtler features of international politics, Himmler misjudged the resolution of the British people, however many might waver and retreat into defeatism. As history has shown, Great Britain had been dedicated to preserving its power in Europe for centuries, and in World War II would never have willingly forsworn this policy. In February 1942, Himmler seemed puzzled and disillusioned, telling Kersten that the English, who had not reached for the olive branch extended by Hitler, were following a very shortsighted policy.[6]

Schellenberg thought it was time to work on Himmler, to convince him that Hitler's presence as Führer was a serious stumbling block to reaching a peace agreement with the Western Allies, arguing that he would never be acceptable to the West under any circumstances. For that matter, Hitler's fitness to rule was doubtful even by the most objective of judgments. Since becoming head of Amt VI, Schellenberg had been flexing his operational muscles in pursuit of the Nazi peace offensive, although, in fact, he had been using this as cover to explore possibilities for interesting the Western Allies in an anti-Hitler putsch.

After Reinhard Heydrich's death in Prague in June 1942 at the hands of British-trained Czech underground assassins, Himmler temporarily took personal charge of the RSHA, but permitted Schellenberg considerable autonomy in running Amt VI. Knowing that Hitler was committed to an eastern strategy of defeating the USSR, thus acquiring the *Lebensraum*— living space—allegedly needed by Germany, Schellenberg was actively seeking out western contacts by July. He knew that Hitler hoped he could neutralize Britain by negotiating from strength to reach a peace agreement favorable to the Third Reich without risking a cross-channel invasion or assuming the daunting burden of occupying the British Isles in the face of widespread and hostile popular opposition. Hitler also relied on Britain's ally, the United States, to refrain from attempting landings in continental Europe so long as a neutralized Britain, relegated to the sidelines, could not offer a convenient staging area. And Hitler assumed the United States would be so engaged in the Pacific War against the Japanese that it would not want to play an active role in the European War in defense of the Russian Bolsheviks. But Schellenberg's own secret addendum to Hitler's strategy eliminated the Führer as a player, and would call upon Himmler, using mainly SS forces, to overthrow him. Then, as a power behind the throne and a manipulator of Himmler, Schellenberg foresaw himself exercising great power in Germany.

Schellenberg's attention was first focused on Sir Samuel Hoare, British ambassador to Spain, who was believed to be relatively open-minded with regard to reaching some kind of peace with Germany. If anyone of rank within the British government would be receptive to a peace feeler, Schellenberg thought Hoare would be. The next problem facing Schellenberg was how best to reach Hoare. Schellenberg had already established contact with Prince Maximilian Eugen zu Hohenlohe-Langenburg, a member of the German nobility, who seemed equally at home among several Western Allied representatives as he did with the powerful in his own government.[7] Allen Dulles, the OSS station chief in Bern, Switzerland, who had long known Max Hohenlohe, responded to warnings about him sent by OSS headquarters more than a year later: "Agree Max is a tough man and it will be necessary to use an unusual degree of caution in dealing with him. There is a high degree of possibility that Himmler might use Max for feelers of major importance. On the opposite side of the picture, he can be of use to us. . . . His property interests will be his main concern."[8] Certainly Schellenberg, in the summer of 1942, without benefit of OSS opinions, thought Max would be of use to him.

Hohenlohe, who secretly belonged to the anti-Nazi resistance, the Widerstand, had made discreet contact with Sir David Kelly, British ambassador to Switzerland, as early as July 1940. Kelly had earlier received German peace feelers through the papal nuncio in Switzerland and had been in touch with Dr. Carl Burckhardt, former president of the International Red Cross, who brought secret peace overtures from Berlin. Hohenlohe quoted Hitler in his talk with Kelly, saying that the Führer was "prepared to accept an agreement with the British Empire, but time was very short and England must choose."[9]

Schellenberg also thought of Lindemann, president of the Nord Deutscher Lloyd steamship line, who believed as he did that Germany should make peace with the Western Allies, and probably would have agreed if asked that neither the United States nor Britain would ever make a deal with Adolf Hitler. Lindemann and Hohenlohe both figured prominently in Schellenberg's plans to establish contact with the West. Allied interrogators of Schellenberg after the War summarized his testimony on these matters:

> Schellenberg now arranged to bring Hohenlohe and Lindemann together in order that they might discuss the subject of a compromise peace with the Allies and at the same time inform Schellenberg as to their position. After speaking to each of them separately he arranged an informal meeting, but on the day that this was to take place he was called away by Himmler and therefore delegated to Dr. Paeffgen, who was partly informed on the matter, to take his place. The object of the conversation was to see if Hohenlohe should attempt to obtain an interview with Sir Samuel Hoare with whom he was already in social contact, but after discussions they came to the conclusion that the internal political situation was not at the moment propitious and that the matter should be left in abeyance for the time being. It was not until the end of 1942 or the beginning of 1943 that the question was once again reopened."[10]

En route to Zhitomir in August 1942, Schellenberg doubtless rehearsed what he would say to Himmler. The Reichsführer was well aware of his power position. He did not get along well with Bormann, whose star was rising in Hitler's entourage at his expense. He also counted Ribbentrop as a rival and enemy. But as commander of SS forces and head of the RSHA intelligence/security complex, Himmler had more physical power under his command than either of them. While Göring had the Luftwaffe, he was losing ground in Hitler's estimation. Hitler had been disappointed in the German air force's performance during the Battle of Britain. The German army, some of whose leaders Schellenberg knew were in the resistance, would of course be a factor to contend with, but passive acceptance of an SS play for power, if not cooperation, might be possible. Yet whatever the power equation, Himmler considered himself unswervingly loyal to Hitler, and would need much convincing before he could rationalize high treason against his Führer.

To propose a putsch against Hitler would be dangerous, but Schellenberg was gambling on Himmler's sense of self-preservation—his fear of being hanged as a war criminal at War's end. Schellenberg sensed that Himmler now saw the defeat of Germany as inevitable and had seriously begun to worry about his postwar future.

The German military offensive in Western Europe had gone well—much better than the German high command had believed possible. Norway had been quickly occupied, France had collapsed, and the Lowlands had been easily overrun. The Battle of Britain, however, had been an air war in which the Royal Air Force (RAF) performed extremely well while the German air force had been unable to gain air superiority. And while the Battle of the Atlantic had wreaked havoc with Allied shipping, German U-boats were being sunk at a progressively greater rate, thanks to the effectiveness of Ultra intelligence against German naval targets. This spectacular product of the British ability to intercept and break Germany's "unbreakable" ciphers on land, in the air, and at sea would be kept secret until long after the War. A not-so-secret weapon was Winston Churchill's charisma and strong leadership, by which the British people were inspired to stand firm against the enemy. Contrary to Hitler's hopes, there was little danger of defeatism infecting the British will to win.

Great Britain, for ethical reasons as well as self-interest, would not be disloyal to its trilateral unconditional surrender agreements with the Soviet Union and the United States. As the German campaign in Russia bogged down, beginning perhaps with the Wehrmacht's failure to take Moscow but definitively recognized after German reverses at Stalingrad during the summer of 1942, and because of the rapid assemblage of American armies and armaments, England had no valid reason to be tempted by negotiated peace offers from the Axis.

Because Schellenberg believed that Himmler must be having pangs of defeatism, he reasoned that the Reichsführer was nourishing hopes that he could strike a deal with the United States and Britain. In fact, Himmler's friend and lawyer Carl Langbehn, whom Schellenberg knew to be in the German Resistance, had discussed with him the hopelessness of Germany's position on more than one occasion in late 1941.

Both Himmler and Schellenberg, at first cautious in their conversations together, would each cling to the possibility that the Western Allies might find merit in making "an honorable peace" with Germany—even if it were on Allied terms—based on the assumption that a Himmler-led Germany, unencumbered by Hitler, would continue its war with the Soviet Union, weakening both Germany and Russia to the point that neither would pose a threat to British and American strategic and economic interests after the War. In previous conversations, Schellenberg had made his views known to Himmler as objective analyses, but had stopped short of making any specific operational proposals. Himmler, however, had listened to him with interest. Schellenberg had become more than a talented intelligence operator in Himmler's eyes; he had ingratiated himself to the point where his judgments were solicited by Himmler and his advice taken—except, perhaps, on matters about which Hitler himself held strong views that were inviolable.

As Schellenberg set out to meet Himmler in Zhitomir in early August 1942, he could look back on a critical year of the War. Britain had not been invaded by the Germans, but was not yet in a position to launch any major offensive against the German-held European continent. The British awaited badly needed munitions and supplies of all kind from an American industry that had been quickly mobilized for war. Schellenberg believed that now was the time for extracting Britain from the War through negotiations, leaving Germany to concentrate its resources against Russia along the Eastern Front.

The nimble-minded Schellenberg did not rule out reversing the equation: secretly negotiating a peace with the Soviet Union, then dividing continental Europe between them as had been discussed prior to the German invasion. But this, he realized, was unlikely now that the German offensive in Russia was running out of steam and the USSR had proved itself capable of defending itself—even of putting Germany on the defensive. Moreover, Germany would find it difficult to bargain with Russia in view of the Axis pact between Germany and Japan, not to mention the long-standing friendship between the United States and Great Britain and the U.S. commitment to achieve unconditional surrender on the part of both Axis powers. Yet, Schellenberg thought, it might not be beyond possibility to sow discord within the Grand Alliance by exacerbating Stalin's deep-seated, somewhat paranoid suspicions against Britain and the United States. Even if there was no chance of secretly enticing the Western Allies into concluding a separate peace with Germany, it may have occurred to Schellenberg that his very act of making clandestine contact with the West would add substance to Stalin's already existing suspicion that Britain and the United States would make a deal with the Germans, with or without Hitler, and turn on him before the War's end.[11]

In August 1942, Schellenberg, as first order of business at Zhitomir, intended to brace Himmler with the reality of Germany's position and, appealing to his fears and vanity, convince him that Hitler had to go and that he, armed with a powerful SS force and the Gestapo, was the only logical successor to the Führer. In his book *Hitler's Secret Service*, Schellenberg wrote, "For these reasons I determined at the first opportunity to exploit the possibilities of my position with him and make an attempt to launch plans for negotiations [with the Western Alliance]."[12]

It had been Himmler's assistant, Rudolf Brandt, who put through Himmler's call asking Schellenberg to report to Zhitomir. Brandt was trusted implicitly by Himmler, who relied on him for a wide variety of chores and depended on his encyclopedic grasp of useful details on almost any subject of interest to the Reichsführer. The tireless aide put Himmler on the line to give Schellenberg a long list of documents he wanted brought to their meeting.

At dinner on the evening of his arrival in Zhitomir, Himmler's conversational approach was to leave to the end matters of great import while he loosened up his guest with less important talk—sometimes even trivia. Himmler's favorite subject, one he took seriously, dealt with Nordic philosophy and Germany's Aryan roots, which he believed were in India and Tibet. Himmler had, in fact, sent an expedition to Tibet for ethnic research as well as intelligence purposes.[13] Even as they spoke, Major Ernst Schaefer, head of the Reich Institute of Central Asian Research and a noted Tibetan explorer, as well as a member of Himmler's staff, was preparing for an expedition to another destination, but one more relevant to the war—the Caucasus.

While being interrogated by an American intelligence officer just after the War's end, Schaefer explained Himmler's odd attraction to Tibet. The Reichsführer SS had fallen for an occult version of the "glacial theory of cosmogony" in which the Nordic race was considered to have come from "heaven."[14] While Schaefer was not interested in the occult, he played along with Himmler's hobby, as it provided him with opportunities to visit and explore Tibet as a center of "syncretic science." He believed that the remote kingdom of Tibet had served as "the cradle of mankind." He had even received a contribution of $1,000 for his Tibet expedition in 1938 from fellow mountain climber and Tibetologist Brooke Dolan II,[15] who would later accompany Major Ilya Tolstoy on an OSS mission in 1942–1943 to explore the feasibility of using Tibet as an alternative overland route to China.[16] When the Japanese overran the Burma Road between India and China, it had become necessary to ship supplies to the Chinese leader, Chiang Kai-shek,[17] by air over the Himalayas; the "hump" route, as it was known, was proving to be very dangerous.

In 1938, Schaefer had been warmly received by the Tibetan government, much to the distress of the British rulers of India. For his achievement he was awarded an SS death's-head ring, an honorary sword, and applause from a proud Himmler.[18] Hoping for a timely defeat of the Russians on the Eastern Front, Himmler was currently preparing Schaefer for a secret mission to the Caucasus for the purposes of enlisting the peoples there in the German cause—in effect, preparing a pro-German fifth column.[19] This was one of the subjects Himmler discussed with Schellenberg soon after his arrival in Zhitomir, since the latter would be headquarters manager of the endeavor in Berlin.

At their meeting, Himmler, having expressed concern for Schellenberg's chronic intestinal pain, urged him to take physical therapy massages from Kersten during his stay at Zhitomir. Schellenberg, however, instinctively felt that there may have been another reason behind Himmler's suggestion that he take treatment from Kersten. Schellenberg knew that Kersten enjoyed the Reichsführer's confidence and was used for various sensitive matters, personal as well as official. Himmler had told Schellenberg that he trusted his masseur, even if he did sometimes "talk too much." Himmler added that Kersten, while "very inquisitive, was good natured and extremely helpful."[20] It immediately occurred to Schellenberg that this kind of endorsement bespoke something beyond simply having a massage.

Kersten was known to Schellenberg as a man who frequently used his influence over Himmler to extract favors. He had heard that the masseur was "manipulative," a quality he recognized would be useful to him in guiding Himmler toward high treason.[21] After the War, Schellenberg would comment on Kersten: "During all the years of the War he was Himmler's shadow ... for Himmler believed that without Kersten's treatment he would die.... In the end Himmler became completely dependent upon him." This, of course, gave the doctor considerable influence over his patient.

Schellenberg, having in mind his own introduction to Kersten, added: "So great was Himmler's faith in Kersten's ability that he submitted everyone in the Third Reich, whom he regarded as important, to a sort of test which consisted of a physical examination by Kersten, for Kersten claimed that through his massage manipulations he could feel the nature of the nervous reactions and the nervous energy of an individual and therefore judge his mental and intellectual capacities."[22]

Schellenberg's physical word description of Kersten portrayed a man who was "fat, jovial, weighing almost two hundred and fifty pounds."

Schellenberg pointed out "one disturbing feature—an unusual black ring round the iris of his light blue eyes, which at times gave them a strangely piercing look." Kersten had many enemies, added Schellenberg. Most of the enmity derived from envy—or worry—because of his close relationship with Himmler. Perhaps a talent "for backstairs intrigue" also gained him enemies. Some even suspected him of being a British agent.[23] When Schellenberg asked Himmler about Kersten and pointed out that there were those who believed he had a British connection, the Reichsführer replied: "Good God, that fat fellow? He's much too good-natured; he would never want to harm me. We must let him have his bit of egotism. . . . If you want to investigate, why, that's your business, but avoid upsetting him if you can."[24]

Schellenberg knew for a fact that Heinrich Müller kept a secret dossier on Kersten. On one occasion, the Gestapo chief had bragged, "One day I shall uncover this spy." Most of Himmler's office staff was antagonistic toward the masseur, resenting his tendency to poke his nose in things that were none of his business. Schellenberg was also aware that *Polizeiadjutant Oberstleutnant* Suchannek, a confidant of Müller's,[25] reported Kersten's every movement to the Gestapo chief. More serious in Schellenberg's mind, perhaps, had been Heydrich's attitude toward Kersten. He had been heard to say that Kersten was an enemy agent, "or at least an active sympathizer with foreign powers."[26]

Recognizing Himmler's suggestion that he be massaged by Kersten as an order, Schellenberg soon subjected himself to the masseur's punching and pummeling. While enduring a rigorous massage from Kersten's "magic hands," the two men had a most interesting dialogue on political matters. According to Schellenberg's recollection of their conversation, he had become convinced that Kersten not only agreed with his own ideas regarding a compromise peace, but "was enthusiastic about them." Before they were through, Kersten had agreed "to use all his influence with Himmler to prepare the way" for Schellenberg. "Here, at last was the first active support of my plans," Schellenberg commented ecstatically in his memoir.

Taking advantage of his session with Schellenberg, Kersten told of his problems with certain of Himmler's lieutenants and "courtiers." Expressing himself bluntly, Kersten said that he particularly needed protection from Gestapo chief Müller and RSHA chief Ernst Kaltenbrunner. As quid pro quo for Kersten's "insider" influence with Himmler, Schellenberg promised to do all he could to shelter him from officials such as Müller who had the will and the ways to intrigue against him behind Himmler's back.

The next day Himmler greeted a refreshed Schellenberg, exclaiming that he was glad that Kersten's massage had been helpful and that they had hit it off so well. Himmler also took the occasion to tell Schellenberg that he wanted him to get to know better his friend and lawyer Carl Langbehn. This line of talk hinted at more than casual social banter. Himmler had something serious in mind, and Schellenberg thought that he knew what it was. Emboldened by this, he decided this was the time to bare his own plans, hoping they coincided with Himmler's secret ruminations.

Pointing to Himmler's desk drawers, Schellenberg asked the Reichsführer which one contained his plan for a postwar future in which, as events were going, Germany would find itself beaten and destroyed. Himmler's initial reaction was one of alarm and disapproval: "Have you gone mad?" he asked. "You have been working too hard, shall I give you a few weeks leave?" Then, overcome by Schellenberg's presumption, Himmler shouted at him: "How dare you talk to me in this way?"[27]

Schellenberg responded by appealing to Himmler's reason. Recognizing that Germany had been blessed with battle successes and was perhaps at the zenith of its power, it should bargain from strength with its Western enemies toward making a negotiated peace, he suggested. As Schellenberg continued his estimate of the situation, he could see that Himmler was beginning to calm down, but he argued that Hitler could never accept such a course of action "so long as that idiot, Ribbentrop, advises [him]." [28]

Some idea of how bitter Himmler felt about Ribbentrop can be seen in comments he made to Kersten in January 1941: "Since basically he [Ribbentrop] does not understand a thing about diplomacy, he has to let the old school have its way, with the result that everything goes wrong. On the other hand, *we* have both the personnel and the experience in intelligence matters; what couldn't we do, if only Ribbentrop had a little more sense!"[29]

Schellenberg had the same contempt for Ribbentrop as Himmler did and felt strongly that the foreign minister had to be removed from office. They were fierce rivals. But Schellenberg realized that Himmler would need more persuasion before he would bring himself to take any such dynamic action. In the meantime, Schellenberg would be treading on dangerous ground even to talk with Himmler about a putsch against the Führer. Hitler was still Himmler's godhead, to whom he had sworn undying loyalty, while Hitler considered Himmler his most loyal supporter. Contact with the Western Allies as part of Hitler's peace initiative did, however, find favor with the Reichsführer, who gave Schellenberg license to proceed. Schellenberg, confident that he could soon convince Himmler to face the specific issue of overthrowing Hitler, insisted that he hold the whole matter very closely within his Amt VI.

Chewing on his fingernails and fiddling with his SS death's-head ring, Himmler asked how Schellenberg proposed to begin. Schellenberg claimed in his memoirs that he replied to Himmler by saying: "If you are ready to appoint me to run the plan, and . . . promise to get rid of Ribbentrop by Christmas 1942, then I would take up contact with the Western Powers." Schellenberg then explained: "Ribbentrop's removal would prove to them that a new wind was blowing and that our plan had powerful backing." He added that "rumors of a new Foreign Minister, representing a more concil-iatory policy, would strengthen my position even more."[30]

This line of argument struck a responsive chord in Himmler; because he had contempt for Ribbentrop's handling of foreign affairs. Getting down to specifics, Schellenberg gave as his opinion that the British would insist on the Germans evacuating at least the northern part of France; Holland and Belgium would probably have to be restored to full independence, although pro-Nazi collaborators in those countries would be resettled within German-held territory and given necessary protection.

Schellenberg, who was already developing close contacts with the Swiss military, insisted that in any settlement Switzerland must be allowed to remain neutral and independent—a useful bridge to the West and an entre-pôt for trade and currency matters. Italy, too, despite its feckless perfor-mance in the war, should be left to its own devices but be deprived of its colonial holdings. Austria would remain an integral part of Germany, as would Sudetenland. The Czechs and Slovaks should be allowed to enjoy autonomy, but Schellenberg believed that they should be economically inte-grated with the Reich. Schellenberg added that the same formula should be applied to the southeastern European peoples: the Croatians, the Serbians, the Bulgarians, the Greeks, and the Romanians.[31]

Himmler seemed dubious about the feasibility of all this; such grand designing was beyond him. Polish territory, in Himmler's opinion, should not be given up to Germany. As for the Baltic states, Himmler allegedly expressed his wishes by saying: "Here an area of expansion must be created for Finland." Summing up Schellenberg's territorial formula for a compro-mise peace with the West, as he understood it, Himmler saw it as essentially "the preservation of the Greater German Reich in its approximate territorial extent on September 1, 1939."[32]

By mid-afternoon of their first day of substantive discussion, Himmler had accepted Schellenberg's blueprint and had granted him complete and full authority to work toward these ends. Realistically, however, Schellenberg knew that there were many obstacles to overcome, not least of which would be Himmler's predilection to change his mind without notice and succumb to influences beyond Schellenberg's control. But, at least, he took heart that the Reichsführer had given his word of honor that by Christmas Ribbentrop would no longer be foreign minister. Words of honor were not very reliable among Nazi leaders, and Schellenberg's dream would not be realized for a variety of reasons, but the long night of discussions was cause for rejoicing. He was on a new basis of working with Himmler. Also he had forged a mutually useful partnership with Kersten—although each realized that the other had his own separate agenda of special objectives, not all of which had been revealed to the other.

Kersten's massages had worked wonders for Schellenberg. During his postwar interrogation, Schellenberg recalled that he had felt himself a new man by Kersten's fifth massage. And, not unlike Himmler's response to his "Magic Buddha's" therapy, Schellenberg soon found himself "dependent" upon Kersten's treatments. He added euphorically that he was grateful for what Kersten had done for him medically, but he felt from their first meeting that they liked each other and had established "terms of confidence." Kersten, for his part, felt relieved that he had found a protector in Schellenberg—no small advantage in Himmler's treacherous domain.[33]

The meetings at Zhitomir provided Schellenberg a more comprehensive view of Kersten's reliability, as well as his motives. There is little evidence that he knew the details of Kersten's foreign relationships, which included acting as an informant, but he certainly was aware of Gestapo files on the subject that, among other things, linked Kersten with the British; and he must have assumed that Kersten's insider knowledge had been accessed by the Swedish government, whose favor he courted in his efforts to find a future safe haven. Since Kersten was a Finnish citizen, Schellenberg had to assume that he would keep the Finnish government posted on matters important to it. And, for the most part, Kersten would share with Schellenberg his contact with the American OSS in Stockholm, with the object of realizing Himmler's secret peace proposals.

A paragraph in Schellenberg's postwar interrogation report summarized some of Kersten's views and motives:

> Kersten shared Schellenberg's views as regards the necessity of Germany ending the war at the earliest possible moment, and also believed that this could be best accomplished by Himmler taking power forcibly into his own hands and deposing Hitler. Kersten's main consideration in this was more material than political as he feared that the outcome of the War would be disastrous for Germany and he would be deprived

of his German estate. But whatever the reasons, he would use his influence to support Schellenberg in his policy of an early termination of the War."[34]

As a virtually stateless man whose survival forced him to live by his wits, material gain was doubtless one of Kersten's motives; but in light of other evidence, particularly evidence revealed by his future actions, Schellenberg's assessment seems simplistic. For one thing, Kersten had had no choice but to accept Himmler's original "offer of employment," which had been, in fact, forced upon him. Then, when he secretly made contract with the Finnish embassy in Berlin, asking to be rescued from Himmler, he was urged to remain in place and provide the Finnish government with a lever of influence and a source of valuable intelligence available to him at this fount of Nazi power. Kersten would also render assistance whenever possible to old friends in the Netherlands now in the Dutch Resistance. Kersten would help the Swedish government by arranging the release of certain Swedish nationals jailed by the Nazis and providing critically important information. While his motive in this case was probably influenced by his hope of finding safety in a new home in Sweden, it would be unfair to deny that he had humanitarian instincts as well.

Schellenberg, who knew well the hostile attitude toward Kersten on the part of the Gestapo, admitted after the War that the masseur had been constantly at risk.[35] And as Himmler himself once admitted while making a macabre joke, "Every time Kersten treats me, he massages a life out of me," meaning that Kersten used his influence as a reliever of pain to talk Himmler into releasing friends or worthy cases brought to his attention from Nazi death camps. This did not endear Kersten to the Gestapo.

Trying to keep Kersten out of trouble, Himmler had made it plain to Schellenberg that he did not want Kersten involved in foreign espionage operations in behalf of Amt VI, but this did not keep Nazi intelligence practitioners from hoping that Kersten would pass on to them useful information gleaned from his many contacts abroad.[36] Allied interrogators of Schellenberg after the war concluded that Kersten "was the recipient of information obtained from numerous contacts outside Germany and in Germany made through his medical practice which he sometimes passed on when it suited him to Himmler and later also to Schellenberg." Schellenberg, however, was explicit when he testified: "It could not be said that Kersten took part in [German] intelligence activities in the accepted meaning of the term. He had no official or, for that matter, even unofficial, standing in any [German] intelligence service." Because of information on military or other matters dropped into his lap "on account of his peculiarly close association with Himmler . . . Kersten was enabled and actually did pass information on to higher Nazi authorities."[37] Under interrogation, Schellenberg provided specific examples of this.

One of Kersten's most interesting contacts was a beautiful Chinese woman named Mrs. Kou. During one of their early conversations at Zhitomir, Kersten confided in Schellenberg that he had once been in love with this woman and had wanted to marry her. Even after she married someone else, Kersten claimed to have been on cordial terms with her, most recently during a trip with Himmler to Rome. While allowances should perhaps be made for exaggeration, Kersten seemed to be sure of himself when he related that Mrs. Kou claimed that she was "on particularly close terms with the Chinese Military Attaché in Moscow" and even "had direct access to Stalin."

Schellenberg was at first dubious about Kersten's story when he attributed to Mrs. Kou a further report, dating from late 1942, that the Soviets were planning an imminent major offensive in the center and along the northern part of the Eastern Front. Kersten had also passed this extremely important intelligence to Himmler, who asked Schellenberg to check it out. This information seemed particularly important to Himmler as it bolstered his own instinct that Germany was facing serious trouble in the East.

The German General Staff, with whom Schellenberg discussed the matter, expressed interest because it seemed to confirm other reports in their possession.[38] In fact, on July 12, 1942, Stalin appointed Marshal Semyon Timoshenko to take command of a new sector of the front with orders to defend Stalingrad. German radio signals, intercepted and broken by British Enigma/Ultra operations, and made available to their Russian allies on July 13, 1942, further indicated that the Germans would try to hold the Voronezh area with three armies in the face of Russian pressure.[39] This lent some credence to Mrs. Kou's information and may have been what the German General Staff had in mind when they claimed to have "confirmation" of her report.

However interesting such nuggets as Mrs. Kou provided Kersten on rare occasions may have been, Schellenberg was more interested in learning from his newly solidified friendship with the masseur what Himmler was up to in the foreign policy arena. But the Zhitomir meetings were particularly significant because they launched a collaboration between Kersten and Schellenberg in a campaign to manipulate Himmler. Each man saw in the other usefulness. Schellenberg ran an intelligence apparatus that had considerable access and power within the world of Nazi overlords, while Kersten had a unique influence because of Himmler's dependence on his physical therapy ministrations, and because of his propinquity had the Reichsführer's ear. He could defend and talk up Schellenberg in discussions with Himmler.

The following personal "memorandum of meeting," written by Kersten during the Zhitomir conference and retained by his family through the present, provides a first-hand flavor to the genesis of their secret cooperation—the genesis of their high treason against Hitler.

> Schellenberg has again been summoned to headquarters for a couple of days. I use the opportunity to treat him. I do not feel quite well today; I am seriously worried about Finland. Schellenberg asks whether he could come over to my room to see me tonight. I like the idea, since we could talk without being disturbed. He hasn't turned up by 8 o'clock, so I go to bed. Schellenberg arrives at 9 o'clock. I ask him to excuse my remaining lying down. He gladly agrees. Now he is sitting next to me and we converse, having a heart-to-heart talk together. There was so much to speak about that he left me only at 3 o'clock in the morning. He is a very reputable man. He also promised to forward mail to Holland. This is of great importance to me wishing to remain in contact with my dear old friends there. Schellenberg is in a very difficult position. The old party bosses distrust and hate him. They consider him an outsider. The only one to stand by him is Himmler, but even in Himmler's circle they are already working against Schellenberg, as Brandt told me yesterday. I will support Schellenberg by influencing Himmler in his favor. It is necessary for him to keep Himmler's confidence. Only then can Schellenberg help me in my fight for human rights. [Author had document translated.]

Just before the Zhitomir meetings, Himmler had taken Kersten with him on an official visit to Finland, a pivotal country on the Soviet Union's doorstep which, after Hitler went to war with the Soviet Union, had come under German influence and now played an important role in Scandinavian matters. Kersten's version of the matters discussed, recounted in postwar memoirs and personal memorandums of meetings, reveals a new dimension in his ability to influence and manipulate his master.

5

Helsinki

SHORTLY BEFORE KERSTEN joined forces with Schellenberg in their ambitious plotting at Zhitomir to manipulate Himmler in the interests of ridding Germany of Hitler and reaching a negotiated peace with the Western Allies, he had experienced a preview of backstairs political action at Himmler's elbow in Helsinki. In July 1942, to Kersten's astonishment, Himmler asked him to accompany him on an official—albeit discreet—visit to Finland. He was flattered to realize that he would be privy to confidential discussions with top Finnish officials concerning Scandinavian problems and German policy issues affecting both Sweden and Finland. Himmler was, of course, not aware of Kersten's secret role as a Finnish informant. But he knew that his masseur, as a Baltic German with Finnish citizenship, still had useful contacts there.

The most sensitive subject discussed in Helsinki was Swedish-Finnish relations—present and future. During an informal talk with Finnish foreign minister Rolf Johan Witting in late July with Kersten in attendance, Himmler revealed most frankly Germany's plans for the postwar handling of Finland's neighbor, Sweden. This meeting occurred about a month after Hitler himself had made a state visit to Finland on June 4, ostensibly to pay his respects to Carl Gustaf Mannerheim on the occasion of the venerable Finnish field marshal's seventy-fifth birthday. In fact, Hitler wanted to

Gathered at the Kaiserhof Hotel in Berlin on November 27, 1941, to sign the Anti-Comintern pact are (left to right) Walther Funk, president of the Reichsbank; Count Galeazzo Ciano, Italian foreign minister and at one time a patient of Felix Kersten's; Serano Suner, Spanish foreign minister; German foreign minister Ribbentrop, another of Kersten's patients; Rolf Johan Witting, Finnish foreign minister, with whom Kersten and Himmler discussed Scandinavian problems in July 1942; and Joseph Goebbels. (Courtesy of Angus Thuermer)

explain Operation Barbarossa and why this ambitious invasion of the Soviet Union had encountered unexpected difficulties. Visits abroad were rare for Hitler, and it is significant that he had thought this trip to Finland necessary. A record of Hitler's talks with Field Marshal Mannerheim provides insights to the Führer's thinking, and is an important backdrop to German-Finnish relations in general and Himmler's follow-on discussions in particular. Hitler had taken advantage of the occasion, not only to reassure the Finns that German setbacks on the Russian front were not serious, but to put to rest fears the Finnish government may have that Germany was still considering plans to invade Sweden.

Unknown to Hitler or Himmler, the Danish military intelligence chief, Hans Lunding, had come into possession of plans for an invasion of Sweden, having been given them secretly by Admiral Wilhelm Canaris, head of Abwehr (German military intelligence). The plans called for a German invasion in February or March of 1942. A collaborator of the German Resistance, Canaris was opposed to further military adventures by Hitler, so he had asked Lunding, his friend and sometimes accomplice in anti-Hitler actions, to warn top Swedish authorities. Lunding immediately did as Canaris requested, "which resulted in Sweden's rapid mobilization, and caused Hitler to call off the operation [invasion]."[1]

In light of Hitler's discussions with Field Marshal Mannerheim, it is strange that Himmler so soon afterward raised the sensitive issue again during his July trip with Kersten. In his talks with Foreign Minister Witting in late July, the Reichsführer gave his opinion that Germany and Finland should now reach an agreement on the fate of Sweden after Germany won the War. Himmler stated that Sweden must be divided—Finland being awarded the Finnish-populated northern part of the country, while Germany incorporated the southern and central part of Sweden within a Greater Third Reich.

Kersten could sense that Himmler's proposition was annoying Witting. The Finnish foreign minister was clearly uneasy; he protested that such a plan would be rejected by the Finnish people, who felt indebted to the Swedes for help given them during the Russian invasion of Finland. Finally realizing that he had probed a hornet's nest of opposition, and because he secretly hoped to reach a negotiated peace with the Western Allies in which Finland's friendship would be important, Himmler backed off, saying that these were only his thoughts, not necessarily representing official policy.[2]

Finland was a cobelligerent, not an ally, of Germany in its war against the USSR, and was feeling vulnerable after Germany's Leningrad offensive failed. The ensuing Soviet counterattack made an ultimate German victory less likely. This failure on the part of the Wehrmacht was important in forming Finland's posture toward Germany. Himmler's comments to Witting were not helpful in reassuring the Finns.

In his discussions with Finnish president Risto Ryti and Field Marshal Mannerheim, Hitler had admitted his misjudgment in launching Barbarossa; he had underestimated Red Army strength, particularly Soviet tank strength. Bad weather had slowed the German blitz in France so that the attacks on the East could not be launched before June, in consequence of which inadequately prepared German forces had been stalled by a formidable Russian winter that followed the initial attacks. Hitler also blamed Italian weakness, referring to the fact that the Germans had to divert resources badly needed on the Eastern Front to bolster Mussolini's inadequate forces in North Africa, Albania, and Greece.

The Führer claimed to have feared the prospect of a Russian attack on Romania in the fall of 1940 when Germany was in no position to defend that country, thus losing access to oil supplies badly needed by the Wehrmacht and the Luftwaffe. Had the Red Army occupied the Romanian oil fields at Ploesti at that time, the German war machine would have been helpless by 1941. Hitler admitted that without the addition of 4 to 5 million tons of Romanian petroleum, Germany could not have fought the War. Moscow's unreasonable demands while negotiating with Germany, as articulated by Soviet foreign minister Vyacheslav Molotov in 1940, included license for Russia to protect itself from the "Finnish threat." Hitler told Mannerheim that he had found this laughable. This "exaggerated, if not invented" fear was, in his opinion, brought up only to justify Russia's aggressive plans regarding Bessarabia as the forerunner for an attack on the Romanian oil fields. Thus, Hitler had wanted to drag out his negotiations with Russia until Germany "would be strong enough to counter such extortionist demands."[3]

Stalin's fear was perhaps understandable if one recalls the events of the winter of 1939, when Soviet forces invaded Finland. France's premier, Edouard Daladier, found himself pressed by public opinion to support a French-British expeditionary force to relieve the beleaguered Finns in their brave but hopeless defense against the Russian invasion, and block further threats to Scandinavia. More cautious minds in London were unenthusiastic about any such sideshow distracting the British from their critical war preparations against Germany. Soviet operations within Finland were ended by negotiation in Moscow on March 13, 1940, before the French and British could get very far in marshaling troops for action against Russia in Finland. But Stalin was deeply perturbed by such anti-Soviet attitudes within the top echelons of the French and British government. Britain's consideration of hostile acts against Russia at the same time as Britain was at war with Germany enraged and perplexed Stalin because he had assumed they would be too consumed with the Western Front to pay heed to Finland. Winston Churchill, who was waiting in the wings to replace the faltering Neville Chamberlain, shared his frustration.[4]

The Nazis had followed these developments with great interest, as they did a related plan cooked up by the French calling for the Allies to "relieve Finland" by an air attack against the strategically vital Soviet oil installations in Baku on the west coast of the Caspian Sea. As the result of intelligence from the German embassy in Turkey, sent to German chief of staff Franz Halder on February 26, 1940,[5] Hitler must have been puzzled—and most likely worried—by the implications of increased British military involvement in Iran and the Caspian region of the Caucasus. Such operations would deprive Germany of its hoped-for prize of Baku oil once its forces fought its way into the Caucasus. Iranian and Iraqi oil would also be at stake.

Soviet intelligence penetrations of the British government certainly kept Stalin well informed of this curious but alarming threat to Russia. But had he harbored any doubts about the authenticity of such reports, they must have been dispelled when British reconnaissance aircraft from the Middle East did, in fact, overfly Soviet oil installations in Baku and Batumi, provoking spirited Soviet antiaircraft fire.[6]

It is difficult to understand the attitude of the British chargé in Moscow, who had reported to the British foreign secretary in January 1940, while the battle of Britain loomed ominously: "The effective and continuous bombardment of Baku should . . . present no great difficulty to us, and it alone should be sufficient to bring Russia to its knees within a very short time."[7]

During Himmler's mission to Finland, Kersten, secretly serving the interests of the Finnish government, found an occasion to give Foreign Minister Witting advance warning of another important subject on Himmler's agenda: the Jewish issue in Finland. In a behind-the-scenes session, Kersten and Witting agreed that the latter should parry any suggestion by Himmler that Finland round up its Jewish population and ship them off to Nazi death camps.[8] Kersten thought the best tactic for Finland to follow in resisting Germany's demands would be to stall, claiming that Finnish legal problems and widespread popular anger by resentful citizens tired of having Germans push them around would seriously harm German-Finnish relations. Kersten promised to persuade Himmler not to raise the issue, thus avoiding a troublesome confrontation. True to his word, Kersten convinced the Reichsführer that nothing would be gained by provoking the Finns.

Upon returning to Germany, Himmler, well briefed by Kersten, discussed the Jewish matter with Hitler. Rather than create a breach with the Finns, both of them agreed that it would be better to postpone discussions with the Finnish government on this touchy subject. Later, Witting expressed his gratitude to Kersten,[9] giving him credit for defusing the Jewish issue and thus helping Finland avoid aggravating its already fragile relationship with Hitler.

In a U.S. Foreign Service dispatch from Stockholm entitled "Activities of

Dr. Felix Kersten," just after the War in Europe ended, U.S. mission chief Herschel V. Johnson reported that the result of Heinrich Himmler's employment of Felix Kersten as physical therapist was that Himmler soon found himself dependent on Kersten's medical skill, which enabled the therapist to induce him to release a considerable number of people from concentration camps, to spare the lives of several persons and to save 2,500 Finnish Jews from deportation to Germany in August 1942.[10] The Finnish News Bureau in Helsinki, however, was authorized officially to comment that the Finnish government in 1942 had not been aware of any such German designs regarding Finnish Jews as have been reported in the Swedish press and that Finland in no circumstances would have yielded to demands of that nature. This would seem to confirm Kersten's account of Himmler's visit in which the Reichsführer, on Kersten's advice, did not raise the issue, knowing that the Finns would refuse. And Kersten's account is more accurate than the account in Lucy S. Dawidowicz's *The War Against the Jews, 1933–1945:* "Himmler attempted to induce the Finns to deport the Jews, but Finnish Foreign Minister Rolf Witting refused to give the matter any consideration."[11]

Another problem that would exacerbate Germany's relations with Finland concerned indications that the United States might involve itself in arranging a détente between Finland and the Soviet Union at the expense of German interests and influence. In September 1942, the Japanese informed the Vatican that rumors were abroad that Finland was considering initiating a peace process with Russia that would call for the United States, through the good offices of the Vatican, to mediate an agreement guaranteeing Finland's territorial integrity. Substantiating this information were reports from the Finnish embassy in Berlin describing contacts with the Soviet minister to Sweden, Aleksandra Kolantai, in Stockholm, and stating that Stalin "was considering a Finnish-Soviet peace formula calling for a return to the 1939 pre-war borders."[12] This was perhaps related to possible overall Soviet-German peace talks being considered.[13] The United States and Great Britain would have certainly looked upon any Soviet-German détente as a most serious violation of their agreements with the USSR—a defection from the Grand Alliance having grave consequences for the Western Allies. But the United States had been very interested in the possibilities of extracting Finland from the War, hoping that this would relieve German pressure on its Russian ally and lessen Germany's influence in Scandinavia. Cordell Hull, in mid-March 1943, instructed U.S. envoy Robert McClintock in Helsinki to query the Finnish government as to its interest in having the United States act as mediator with the USSR in making peace. Unfortunately, from the U.S. point of view, the Finnish government secretly informed the Germans about this American initiative, having reason to believe that the Germans had already found out about it through their capability to break and read American diplomatic ciphers.[14]

This episode did not help U.S.-Finnish relations. In a closely held memorandum dated April 19, 1943, ending on a most pessimistic note, the U.S. secretary of state informed President Roosevelt of developments concerning Finland. The following excerpts from Hull's memo provide an interesting summing up of the deteriorating U.S.-Finnish relations at that time:

> As you will recall, in recent discussions with Finnish Government with a view to arranging contact between Finns and Soviets, we had unmistakable evidence that Germans, learning of our approaches, brought increased pressure on Finns not to enter into any discussions with us with a view to any contact with Soviet Government. We also gathered impressions that the Finns were greatly influenced by such German pressure. These impressions led us to believe there was no further advantage in continuing relations with Finns because of the impossibility of accomplishing two principal objectives we had in mind in continuing such relations, (a) the hope that we might bring about cessation of hostilities between Finns and Soviets, and (b) that presence of our diplomatic representation in Helsinki would be a deterrent to Finnish acceptance of German pressure for cooperation with Germany.
>
> In order to avoid losing any advantages which might result from continuing relations, if there were any advantages in such continuation, which in the opinion of the Soviet Government might affect their military situation, we had Standley [U.S. ambassador to the USSR] ask the Soviet their opinion in that respect. Standley now reports Molotov stated Soviet Government considers rupture of Finnish-American diplomatic relations would be advantageous to both Soviets and United States. Molotov raised the question of whether Procope [Finnish ambassador to the United States in Washington] should not be sent home and whether he had communicated information to the Japanese.
>
> We see no course now to pursue other than to proceed to the discontinuance of our diplomatic relations with Finland, based upon increased German pressure and lessening of Finnish freedom of action, but before proceeding, I shall await final word from you.[15]

The president replied to the secretary of state, expressing his concurrence: "Your suggestion regarding Finland is fully approved by me. The Finns for the last two years have been playing both ends against the middle despite our previous sympathy when they were under attack by Russia and in spite of our continuing sympathy for their independence. The Nazis are employing Finland to help them wage war against the Soviet Union and they have in effect been greatly helped by the Finnish Government."[16]

Despite the exchange between Secretary Hull and President Roosevelt, which seemed to write finis to U.S. efforts to rescue Finland from German domination, there would be further U.S. diplomatic action regarding that unfortunate country trapped between the Third Reich and the Allies. Kersten, moreover, would play a role as a contact of the U.S. Office of Strategic Services working the Finnish problem. But, before that, the OSS would make its presence felt in Stockholm, and Himmler, through certain of his own friends and through contacts of Schellenberg and Kersten, would attempt to build bridges to the Western Allies, secretly exploring ways to arrive at some negotiated peace formula.

6

Searching for Contacts with the West

At ZHITOMIR, Kersten had offered to be helpful to Schellenberg by enlisting the assistance of others whom he knew had considerable influence on Himmler and whose contacts with the Western Allies could be valuable. One such person was Himmler's friend and lawyer Carl Langbehn, whom he introduced to Schellenberg.

Carl Langbehn was one of Himmler's oldest friends, dating from well before World War II. The friendship was forged after Langbehn's daughter asked her father's permission to accept an invitation to visit the home of a schoolmate. Langbehn was startled to discover that his daughter's friend was the daughter of Heinrich Himmler, described by the girl only as someone who had "something to do with the SS." The two school chums became close friends and their respective fathers, thrown together by this liaison, became friends as well. Himmler seemed to find satisfaction in his political chats with Langbehn, a brilliant lawyer, who provided a frank and refreshing voice of objective wisdom. The two men had the kind of candid exchanges of opinion that Himmler could not have with most of his Nazi colleagues.

As early as 1938, Langbehn, in his heart, had rejected Nazism. He had been enraged when his former law professor, Fritz Pringsheim, was sent off to a concentration camp because he had Jewish blood. Langbehn sought help for Pringsheim from Himmler, who obligingly had him released from camp and given permission to leave Germany. This episode was significant not only because Pringsheim's arrest and detention on racial and religious grounds soured Langbehn on Nazism, but because he saw that Himmler, whom he would serve as personal attorney, also seemed to have within him the seeds of opposition—not on ideological grounds but in his own self-interest.

Himmler had on occasion, while talking with Langbehn, Schellenberg, and Kersten, betrayed doubts about Hitler's grandiose dreams of conquest. For all his power, Himmler had enemies who, he believed, threatened him and one day might do him in. The intramural struggle for power among Hitler's inner circle of top lieutenants was at times frightening. Himmler believed that the most insidious influence was that of Martin Bormann, particularly after he took over as Hitler's assistant following Hess's one-way flight to Scotland. And, of course, another "rotten apple" in the Nazi barrel, in Himmler's opinion, was Foreign Minister Ribbentrop, whose foreign policy advice to Hitler, he believed, was almost always bad—if not catastrophic. Despite omens of pending defeat that revealed themselves after the Wehrmacht's failure to take Moscow, Ribbentrop persisted in goading Hitler to fight on against hopeless odds. The only thing that Ribbentrop and Himmler had in common was their devotion to gaining influence in the rarefied hierarchy of the Third Reich. As a former chicken farmer, it was perhaps small wonder that Himmler was preoccupied with gaining ground in the "pecking order" of power. But so was Ribbentrop, a former champagne salesman, who resorted to such self-inflating tricks as buying a "von" to add to his family name.

During his discussions with Himmler at Zhitomir, Schellenberg emphasized "the importance of getting Germany out of the War, for now that America had entered hostilities there was no longer any hope . . . of eventual success."[1] Himmler seemed to agree with Schellenberg, although it would soon be seen that the Reichsführer SS was of two minds on this score. It would take the best efforts of Kersten and Schellenberg to keep Himmler on track. He would vacillate between his deep-seated devotion to Hitler as well as his fear of fatal opposition by infighters such as Bormann and Ribbentrop—even RSHA chief Ernst Kaltenbrunner and Gestapo chief Heinrich Müller of his own staff—on one hand, and on the other hand his conviction that his Führer could not win the War and must be relieved of power.

Schellenberg's remarks on this subject, given under Allied questioning after the European War had ended, were summarized by his interrogator:

Kersten shared Schellenberg's views as regards the necessity of Germany ending the war at the earliest possible moment and also believed that this could be best accomplished by Himmler taking power forcibly into his own hands and deposing Hitler. . . . he used his influence to support Schellenberg in his policy of an early termination of the War. In this connection can be quoted the case of . . . Carl Langbehn whom Kersten introduced and who was [already] implicated in subversion activities against the ruling Nazi regime" [within the secret ranks of the Resistance].

According to Schellenberg's interrogation testimony, "This case was [later] used by 'Gestapo' Mueller, albeit unsuccessfully, to involve Schellenberg and possibly Kersten in an espionage charge."[2]

The Resistance activities of Langbehn, referred to by Schellenberg, concerned an underground relationship with Johannes Popitz, Prussian finance minister in the early days of the Third Reich, and Ulrich von Hassell, for a while the German ambassador to Italy. Both men had been involved in the abortive putsch hatched by military dissidents led by Colonel General Ludwig Beck, chief of the army General Staff, who in 1938 did not want to risk war with Britain and France over the Sudetenland and Czechoslovakia. Strongly opposed to Hitler's military management, Beck had resigned from the army in the summer of 1938, but continued to serve as a leader in the continuing underground Resistance movement against Hitler.

Carl-Friedrich Goerdeler, once mayor of Leipzig, and Admiral Wilhelm Canaris, head of military intelligence (Abwehr), had worked with Beck in organizing this first serious plan to defy Hitler and avoid a European war. The plan, while well advanced, was abandoned when England's prime minister Neville Chamberlain signed the Munich agreement—the pact that he promised would provide "peace in our time." Chamberlain's misbegotten deal appeasing Hitler only encouraged the Führer to pursue further aggression, rather than deter him. And, for the time being, it cut the ground out from under the anti-Hitler military plotters.

Langbehn's friendship with Himmler and his soon-to-be role as Schellenberg's go-between with the U.S. Office of Strategic Services in neutral Stockholm and Bern complicated his simultaneous secret relationship with Canaris and other Resistance conspirators, and would ultimately cost him his life. Langbehn's Widerstand world involved him in a close relationship with Popitz and some fourteen other intellectual Resistance activists who called themselves the "Wednesday Society" because of the day on which they met secretly in Berlin. This made such military Resistance members such as

Beck and Canaris most uneasy because of Langbehn's close relationship with Himmler, a rival and a man whom they abhorred. Further complicating this situation was Langbehn's connection with Popitz and his friend Albrecht Haushofer, son of Professor Karl Haushofer, author of the concept of *Lebensraum,* or living space, a Nazi ideological centerpiece justifying Hitler's invasion of the Soviet Union.

Albrecht Haushofer, however, had distanced himself from many of his father's views and did not consider himself a Nazi. Not only was he opposed to Hitler, he did not like or respect Himmler, either. But he was an agreeable soul and kept his more disparaging views of Nazis to himself. He had seen advantages to being close with Hess, but once his good friend was no longer on the scene, be felt exposed and unprotected from his enemies, particularly as suspicions of his intertwined Resistance activities for two rival masters, Canaris and Himmler, began to leak out to the ever-watchful Gestapo. More specifically, there were those within the Gestapo and the Sicherheitsdienst, the Nazi Party's foreign intelligence arm, who suspected that Haushofer had been the instigator of Hess's black flight to Scotland seeking peace with England—much as Heydrich had suspected Kersten of encouraging Hess in his ill-starred venture. Lord David Douglas-Hamilton, the Scottish nobleman known by his title as the duke of Hamilton, had been described by his friend Albrecht Haushofer as a man of influence in Great Britain, one who was on excellent terms with the British royal family and someone to whom Hess could usefully appeal in his quest for peace and common cause with Germany against Russian Bolshevism.[3]

Himmler, in moments of despair, still dreamed of a brighter future for himself if he could shed his role as loyal acolyte of Hitler before Germany was defeated. But desperate fears about his postwar survival tugged at his psyche, gaining strength with every German setback. At the same time, he feared that his involvement with treason would be discovered. Himmler, in his secret dealing with the West, thought of his go-betweens, Schellenberg and Kersten, as potential scapegoats who could be sacrificed if Hitler learned of his perfidy.

With Schellenberg's encouragement, Himmler considered Langbehn a useful secret envoy to the Western Allies, and hopefully a link with the Resistance—including military Resistance leaders—whose support, or at least tolerance, would be necessary when and if he made his move against Hitler with SS forces.

Schellenberg's postwar interrogation by the Western Allies provides insight as to how his contact with Langbehn developed in September 1942 after returning from the meeting with Himmler and Kersten at Zhitomir. Kersten introduced Langbehn to Schellenberg in Stockholm at a dinner meeting he had arranged. Schellenberg and Langbehn got on well, satisfying Schellenberg that they both saw Germany's fate and future through the same lens. Thereafter they saw each other frequently. Langbehn proved useful in expediting visas and other frontier formalities, making Schellenberg's trips to neutral Sweden and Switzerland easier.

Deeply involved already with military and Abwehr Resistance plotting, Langbehn began confiding in Schellenberg. Eventually he disclosed a wealth of details about plans that would culminate in Claus Schenk von Stauffenberg's abortive bombing of Hitler in July 1944. Schellenberg's postwar Allied interrogation officer summed it up in a paragraph based on Schellenberg's testimony:

> Himmler was to effect an agreement with the *Wehrmacht* to enable Hitler either to be forcibly overthrown or abducted by force to some place in the neighborhood of Obersalzberg near Berchtesgaden. Popitz, a secretary of state in the Prussian Ministry of Finance, was to be set up as a leader of a new party. Simultaneously peace feelers were to be put out to the Allies through the intermediary of Langbehn and the Swedish banker, Jacob Wallenberg.[4] Under the plan Schellenberg was expected to exert his influence with Himmler in such a manner as to harden the *Reichsführer's* wavering resolve to take effective measures to deal with Hitler.[5]

Schellenberg, however, did not immediately pass this fascinating information on to Himmler, presumably because of its sensitivity and because the reference to Himmler himself might cause the Reichsführer, already jittery, to back off from further involvement. But in March 1943, Schellenberg screwed up his courage to give Himmler certain details of this plot, as well as another about which he had become aware.

This latter plot focused on Fraülein Erna Hanfstaengl, sister of Ernst (Putzi) Hanfstaengl. Hans, a Harvard graduate whose mother was an American from the socially prominent East Coast Sedgwick family, returned in the early 1920s to Germany from New York, where he had managed his family's art publishing business. He first met Adolf Hitler in the summer of 1922. After serving as Hitler's press relations officer during the first part of the War, Hanfstaengl became disenchanted with the Nazis and, believing that his life was in danger from certain other high-ranking officials who were jealous of his closeness to Hitler, fled Germany to find a haven in the United States as secret consultant on the Third Reich at the behest of his old friend from Harvard University days, Franklin Roosevelt.

Himmler had become interested in Fraülein Hanfstaengl's activities because of her friendship with his wife. He urged Schellenberg to look into this lead as it might point to useful contacts within the Western Allies. To cite one possibility, she claimed to have been on familiar terms with Prime Minister Churchill's son, Randolph. Schellenberg went so far as to advance her the sum of 500,000 French francs so that she could provide herself with a cover—an art store in Paris, where she would cultivate French underground members. Her treasonous plans were original, if nothing else; she envisioned Himmler having the Waffen SS (military units of SS) abduct Hitler, but propping him up as a front through whom the Reichsführer would, in fact, rule Germany and make peace with the Western Allies. By early 1944, the fraülein had become an embarrassment and a potential problem for Himmler, so she was dropped.

Schellenberg testified under interrogation after the War that "under other circumstances [I] would probably not have employed this woman for she was somewhat temperamental, but since her employment was virtually at Himmler's instigation, the chance was too good to be missed."[6]

If Schellenberg's objective to make a useful contact with the Western Allies through Fraülein Hanfstaengl was not achieved, he could perhaps blame Himmler for encouraging him to waste time and jeopardize security on a friend of his wife. Would Himmler's own good friend, Langbehn, recommended by Kersten, prove to be any more useful? And was Schellenberg, eager to set his plot in motion, operating too recklessly, particularly since the next objective, the OSS in Stockholm, was new and inexperienced in these kinds of matters, and had no license from Washington to involve itself in such politically charged operations?

The OSS's first agent in Stockholm, Bruce Hopper—initially with OSS's predecessor, the office of the Coordinator of Information (COI)—had arrived there in March 1942. This Harvard University political science professor, new to the ways of espionage and political action, had not been wanted or welcomed by the American minister, Herschel V. Johnson. Johnson disapproved of spying and warned Hopper that he would be sent home if caught engaging in such activities. The local British Secret Intelligence Service (MI-6) man in Stockholm was probably no more enthusiastic than

Johnson, fearing that an American novice dabbling in these dangerous and delicate affairs might hurt his own operations.[7]

It was in December 1942 that Hopper found himself in a secret talk with Langbehn, who described how Himmler was seeking some way to oust Hitler and find a formula for ending the futile war. From his conversation, Langbehn seemed to have assumed that the United States would prefer an early return to peace in Europe so that it could concentrate on its Japanese enemy in the Far East. Langbehn also believed that Great Britain and the United States favored peace with a Germany free of Hitler, and would welcome having the German army fighting on only one front, the Russian front, with the hope of saving Europe from Communism and Russian domination.

He miscalculated when he concluded that the Western Allies might consider a deal involving Himmler, a Nazi war criminal by almost anyone's definition, or countenance any such action behind Stalin's back that would surely reinforce the Soviet leaders' obsessive conviction that the United States and Britain would in the end turn on him.

Hopper, in fact, showed no interest in Langbehn's approach.[8] Some indication of Hopper's attitude is suggested by comments made in the World War II diary of Robert Bruce Lockhart, remembered as a famous British agent in Moscow during the Bolshevik Revolution in 1917, and head of the Political Warfare Executive (PWE) in Churchill's World War II government. In his March 24, 1943, diary entry, Lockhart wrote that Hopper held in low esteem his own service, the OSS, believing that "cloak and dagger" operations did more damage than good. Hopper disapproved of any collaboration with German opposition groups and felt that the Allies should make a "clear distinction between German people as a whole and the Nazi's regime [certainly including Himmler], and design propaganda targeted at Germany accordingly."[9] Apparently disillusioned with his work, Hopper left Sweden soon afterward and returned to Washington.

Schellenberg had struck out again, but he persevered and turned to other possibilities.

7

Saving Switzerland

BY MID-1942, SCHELLENBERG had been convinced that Germany was losing the War—witness his goading of Himmler to unseat Hitler in a putsch during their fateful August 1942 meeting at Zhitomir, and his insistence that as first step Joachim von Ribbentrop be removed from office by Christmas 1942. Only by getting rid of Ribbentrop could Schellenberg and Himmler hope to make a secret deal for a negotiated peace with the Western Allies in exchange for license to continue Germany's war with the Soviet Union unhindered.

Schellenberg's autobiographical summary of his career, sometimes known as the "Troza Memorandum," written in the town of Troza in Sweden, is revealing of Schellenberg's thinking. This long-classified, unpublished treatment of his role during the War, written at War's end in anticipation of putting his best case forward if apprehended by the Western Allies, is in many ways more interesting than *The Labyrinth*, his published memoir. While biased and obviously self-serving, it has the merit of not being the typical apologia offered up by Nazi captives. Schellenberg's comments, as written for Allied interrogators, describe the disgust he felt toward the many "tin gods, large and small, of the [Nazi] regime." But he avoided referring to having served in SS field units, early in his career, that had committed atrocities against Jews, concentrating instead on matters that revealed his German nationalist orientation and anti-Nazi activities. This is understandable since he faced a legal proceeding, the outcome of which could determine his fate—perhaps his very life.

In the "Troza Memorandum," Schellenberg describes setting for himself the daunting task of "protecting Germany from the yawning abyss" he claims to have seen coming "since the end of 1940 onwards."[1] Schellenberg saw this task as having had two main objectives:

> First to put the task as such into effect, at the same time to use the results to provide Germany with an antidote to the obstructive Führer-Ribbentrop policy. The Reichsführer [Himmler] was the only real counter that one could use at all for this purpose. It was up to me to work to this end and to inform him as completely as possible of the true disposition and distribution of world potential and I considered him to be sensible and clever enough to be able still to reach a compromise with the outside world.
>
> It was a long and tiring road that I had to travel, a road presumably predestined, and in the end without result. It was not lack of will and industry, but stupidity, vanity and brutality on the one hand (my enemies inside the RSHA) and the indecision of the *Reichsführer*, himself, on the other, which ruined all these plans. This refers to the practical application of the results, i.e., the formation of a sensible and progressive foreign policy. The main task itself, with its manifold difficulties, was obstructed by the very nature of the German character, either because it was not understood, or worse still, because it was believed unnecessary—thus Ribbentrop.
>
> The *Führer* would have nothing to do with me and my work. The only person who more or less understood me was Himmler, although he too, with his National-Socialist prejudices and policeman's way of looking at political events made things difficult for me. With him, in the course of time, things took a turn for the better and he gradually began to understand me better. Unfortunately the results were never such as were absolutely necessary, since his hesitancy always spoilt everything. For me personally it was often a struggle in which I had to play Don Quixote, while "Rosinante" was the weak humanity, and the "windmill sails" were the above mentioned prejudices of the Regime and the German character itself. That I did not give up this struggle, one must understand, was because I love my country, and was determined to guide things into the right path. I believed that the easiest way

to achieve my plan, was through the only man [Himmler] who was capable of offsetting Hitler.

Already in 1940 I counselled peace with France, in 1941 I warned against a war on two fronts, and at the beginning of 1943 my report on Russia lead to Hitler, and later Himmler, wanting, at the instigation of *Obergruppenführer* Dr. Kaltenbrunner, to imprison me and my associates in a concentration camp for defeatism. In 1943, I managed to save Switzerland from being invaded by Germany, thanks to my adept dealing with [Swiss] General Guisan. . . .[2]

Schellenberg's extravagant-sounding claim to have saved Switzerland leaps out of his memorandum and is worth exploring further in the context of the situation existing in that neutral island entirely surrounded by Nazi forces. By the spring of 1943, Germany's relations with Switzerland were definitely strained. Schellenberg blamed this on his nemesis, Ribbentrop, as well as others within the German Foreign Ministry and the Wehrmacht High Command, who saw Switzerland only through the prism of military planning. Certainly, Switzerland was a strategically valuable area. Himmler hinted to Schellenberg that based on Foreign Ministry and military apprehension, there were certain top party members who were trying to convince Hitler that he should order a "preventive" occupation of the country. Conscious of this threat, Schellenberg believed that Switzerland might feel compelled to abandon its policy of strict neutrality and "throw in her lot with the Western Powers."[3] To make sure that the Swiss were aware of the full gravity of the situation, Schellenberg revealed his "insider" knowledge to Colonel-Brigadier Roger Masson, head of the Swiss Secret Police. After discussing this matter with Himmler, he was given the Reichsführer's authorization to find a formula by which to meet this "emergency" by inducing some responsible Swiss authority—meaning the Swiss army's commander in chief, General Henri Guisan—to issue a reassuring statement of Switzerland's intention to defend its neutrality from aggressive acts by *either* the Western or Axis powers. In this way, Schellenberg believed, the Swiss could make it clear that the Swiss army would strongly resist invasion, but by addressing this threat to both sides, it would be preserving its neutral posture. In fact, Schellenberg recognized that such a statement would be applicable only to the Germans, since there was very little likelihood that the Allies would ever violate Swiss neutrality.

Schellenberg aggressively lobbied Himmler from January to June 1943 to use his influence in preventing a German invasion of Switzerland that was being seriously considered in Berlin. Himmler did, in fact, try to influence Hitler, but, as Schellenberg recalled with bitterness after the War, "Ribbentrop was working in opposition to [the] plan for prevention of an invasion of Switzerland." He believed that Germany should take over this neutral enclave used so actively for intelligence purposes by the Western Allies.[4]

Toward the end of March 1943, Schellenberg had spent considerable effort in Switzerland meeting with Colonel-Brigadier Masson and General Guisan, trying to impress upon them how important it was for Switzerland to make clear that any invader would pay dearly in combat against a mobilized Swiss army deployed in hard-to-subdue mountain defenses.

In addition to more conventional considerations of diplomatic imperatives, Schellenberg saw Switzerland, as he did Sweden, as an important operating base for his secret peace initiative on behalf of Himmler. He also saw Switzerland as a potential haven for himself if needed at the time of Germany's inevitable defeat—or before. With an eye on the future, it was now necessary to ingratiate himself with the Swiss.

In September 1942, soon after his talks with Himmler and Kersten at Zhitomir, Schellenberg held his first meeting with Masson at the Swiss border town of Waldshut. This meeting had been made at the initiative of Masson, who was already distressed at the steady deterioration of German-Swiss relations, caused in part by German intelligence activities on Swiss soil that threatened to tarnish Switzerland's neutral image. The press of both countries was also to blame for fanning the flames with angry diatribes. But Masson believed the worse offender was Dr. Paul Schmidt, press and public relations officer of Ribbentrop's Foreign Ministry. Schmidt's "fiery utterances" hostile to Switzerland had to be restrained if relations between the two countries were ever to be improved.[5]

This first encounter between Schellenberg and Masson went well. Masson reported their conversation to Guisan and his somewhat skeptical adjutant, Bernard Barbey. Masson told Barbey that Schellenberg was a young SS general of refinement who was strongly opposed to Ribbentrop and had strong influence on Himmler. Masson told Guisan that he was puzzled by a comment dropped by Schellenberg that he was worried about Hitler's security. Perhaps Masson thought that by sharing such delicate matters, Schellenberg was signaling his intent to be frank with him. Indicative of the need for secrecy in their relationship, subsequent meetings between the two men were circuitously arranged by SS Stormtroop Leader Hans Wilhelm Eggen, from Schellenberg's staff, through two Swiss intelligence officers on Masson's staff, a Swiss lawyer named Meyer and Captain Paul Holzach.

The next meeting between Schellenberg and Masson took place at the Schloss Wolfsberg on the Swiss shore of Lake Constance in mid-December 1942. Schellenberg later claimed that he had taken the occasion to discuss with Masson with considerable frankness the possibility of making contact with representatives of the Western powers through him with the object of extending peace feelers. Masson responded positively, agreeing to help him in arranging secret meetings—an activity clearly outside the scope of their formal liaison relationship. As quid pro quo, Schellenberg promised to do everything in his power to protect Switzerland's neutrality and block any German plans under consideration to violate Swiss territory.[6]

At still another meeting, this one in February 1943, Schellenberg was emboldened to ask if he could meet privately with General Guisan himself. Despite qualms about taking the risks involved—the Swiss government was still in the dark about the Schellenberg contact—a meeting was arranged with Guisan and took place on March 3, 1943, in the village of Biglen, near Bern. Schellenberg stated that Hitler wanted to be assured that the Swiss would effectively defend themselves against any effort by the Allies— Britain, the United States, and Russia—to compromise their strictly neutral stance. This struck Guisan as an odd request, considering the fact that Switzerland was surrounded by German forces. Guisan surely realized that Switzerland had no reason to fear aggression from the Western Allies. And he was all-too-well aware that Germany had posed a real threat in 1940. First, when Germany invaded Denmark, he must have reasoned that if Hitler was willing to invade that small neutral country, he could have easily rationalized that Switzerland's neutrality was no more sacrosanct. And when planning to invade France and the Lowlands, Hitler must at least have considered the advantages of crossing Swiss territory to avoid France's Maginot Line defenses, even though he finally decided to invade France through the Ardennes Forest. Now, in 1943, as the Allied Mediterranean strategy unfolded and it became clear that Germany was in trouble on the Eastern Front, Hitler surely realized the need to have uncontested access to Italy, which would pose an obvious threat to Switzerland.

General Guisan must have shrewdly guessed that Schellenberg's comments were often diplomatic double-talk intended to convey the possibility of a German violation of Swiss territory without specifically naming Germany. Guisan's response, exactly what Schellenberg hoped to hear, made it clear that Switzerland would fight to its limit to protect itself, whoever the enemy might be. Guisan even put this conviction in writing. Guisan gave Schellenberg an unequivocal "signed, secret declaration setting out [that] the purpose of the Swiss army was to preserve the neutrality of Switzerland wherever this should entail fighting, either in the North, South, East or West."[7]

Schellenberg had good reason to anticipate Hitler's intention to invade Switzerland: Germany was secretly considering a military invasion of the neutral country so as to include the Swiss Alps within the Wehrmacht's defense framework—a foresighted consideration in the event German forces would have to fall back through the Alps in the face of a strong Allied offensive through Italy. On March 14, 1943, Hitler presided over an important meeting of his field commanders in which he played his favorite role of "military strategist," reasoning that once Tunisia was lost to the Allies, Sicily would be invaded (as it would be on July 10, 1943). The Swiss Alps would then be important as a German redoubt area in defending itself against powerful Allied forces that inevitably would advance up the boot of Italy. In fact, by March 18, German plans to invade Switzerland—"Case Switzerland"—were sent on to Hitler's HQ.

Complicating matters for Schellenberg was the fact that Swiss intelligence almost immediately learned of Hitler's plan from a highly placed agent— part of a Swiss spy network known in-house as the "Viking Line." But the episode proved most helpful to Schellenberg when Masson inadvertently revealed the contents of the Swiss spy's report to him, thus tipping him off that the Germans at the highest level of their government had been penetrated by the Swiss.[8]

Having in hand General Guisan's written statement that the Swiss would staunchly defend itself in the event of invasion "from any quarter," Schellenberg convinced Himmler that the Swiss were resolute in their determination to keep out the Nazis. Both Schellenberg and Himmler agreed that Ribbentrop should be made to reciprocate with a written guarantee protecting Swiss neutrality—an ingenious gambit that checkmated Germany, making it more difficult for its army to invade. While Ribbentrop promised to prepare such a written guarantee, he simmered with resentment at Himmler for interfering in foreign affairs and procrastinated for three months before drafting a response. Even then he used language so offensive that Himmler, without telling him, had it redrafted. Realizing that the Swiss had well-positioned, albeit unidentified, spies in the German government (the Viking Line network) who could discover the backroom maneuvering among the Nazi leaders, Schellenberg made the best of this muddle by sending his man, Eggen, back to Switzerland in person to reassure Masson that Schellenberg had, in fact, been successful in convincing the German high command not to entertain plans for violating Swiss neutrality, much less launch a full-scale invasion.[9]

To his dismay, Schellenberg discovered that the German minister in Switzerland, Otto Carl Koecher, had lied to Guisan by claiming it had been Schellenberg who had recommended that Germany take "precautionary action" against the Swiss. This lie may have been perpetrated by Himmler to keep his and the government's skirts clean by making Schellenberg the scapegoat. More likely, Ribbentrop, infuriated because of Schellenberg's dabbling in foreign affairs, may have been responsible in an effort to discredit him. Whatever the case, Schellenberg was irate. It became obvious to him that something had gone wrong when Masson sent an emissary to him requesting clarification.[10]

Masson was relieved when Schellenberg reiterated the "true facts" of the case. He was willing to believe that Schellenberg had saved Switzerland from German invasion. Not everyone, however, was convinced. Some in Guisan's office suspected that Schellenberg had been playing a double game, exploiting Masson as an agent of influence so as to peddle misinformation within Swiss intelligence. Guisan, himself, was not convinced that the danger of a German attack on Switzerland no longer existed despite Schellenberg's assurances. The threat posed by Germany, Guisan believed, increased as Germany's Eastern Front contracted, lending credence to the "Fortress Europe" fallback strategy that required the Wehrmacht to control the Swiss Alps. Guisan would not lower his guard; his fears, confidentially elucidated to the Swiss Federal Cabinet on January 6, 1943, well before even meeting with Schellenberg, were still valid in his considered opinion. In reporting to the cabinet, Guisan had dramatized his case, saying that the Nazis would tunnel into the Alps, if necessary, to make their defensive positions impregnable.

After the war, when Guisan described to the Swiss Federal Assembly what had occurred, he explained his motive in meeting with Schellenberg: "I did not want to neglect an occasion to affirm for our northern neighbor's [Germany's] mind the sentiment, which was evidently not strong at all, that our Army would fulfill its mission under all circumstances and would fight against anybody attacking our neutrality."[11]

While Schellenberg was involved with secret backdoor diplomacy in Switzerland, the newly arrived OSS officer in Bern, Allen Dulles, began to operate aggressively against Germany.[12] In secret he established contact with two of Schellenberg's men. He also established liaison with a Swiss intelligence officer, Max Waibel, who worked for Masson. Dulles was well aware of the Nazi contingency plans to invade Switzerland formulated early in 1943, when reverses in Russia as well as in Italy made it evident that a German redoubt would require occupying the Swiss Alps. But as Dulles explained in his postwar book *The Secret Surrender:* "At the peak of its mobilization Switzerland had 850,000 men under arms, a fifth of its total population. . . . The cost to Germany of an invasion of Switzerland would certainly have been very high." As chief of OSS in Switzerland—but referring to himself as "President Roosevelt's Special Representative"—he made certain that the Swiss understood "the stronger they were in their preparations against a German attack, the better we [the United States] liked it."[13]

Guisan surely had his own reasons for defending Switzerland without being unduly influenced by either Schellenberg's or Dulles's lobbying. Guisan genuinely feared renewed German designs on Switzerland, despite Schellenberg's assurances that Germany had abandoned any thought of invading his country. He knew the Swiss government was reluctant to bear the high cost of preparing itself with a well-entrenched and well-armed force, despite his urging. Guisan's fear that the possible loss of Italy to the Western Allies would require Germans troops in Italy to retreat through the Alpine passes into Switzerland haunted him. Masson's more optimistic estimate, influenced by Schellenberg's assurances, did not change Guisan's opinion. The Swiss army commander was convinced that the summer of 1943 would be a dangerous time for Switzerland. Guisan's predictions were prescient: Mussolini would be toppled in a coup d'état and the successor Badoglio government would defect to the Western Allies, putting increasing pressure on German forces stranded in northern Italy. Moreover, the Soviet Union, during the latter part of 1943, would achieve significant victories over the Wehrmacht on the Eastern Front. At home, Guisan was discouraged by the fact that Pilet Golaz's Swiss government refused his request for more troops to be raised through wider mobilization in July 1943.

A more optimistic Schellenberg was nonetheless pleased with his relationship with Swiss intelligence chief Masson. Schellenberg was achieving an important part of his objective in Switzerland; Masson provided him with a certain freedom of movement in his attempts to establish contact with Western intelligence in pursuit of peace in fulfillment of the Zhitomir plan agreed to by Himmler. Prince Maximilian zu Hohenlohe-Langenburg, used by the Nazi foreign intelligence—the Sicherheitsdienst's Amt VI—in Spain and elsewhere, was asked by Schellenberg during the early spring of 1943 to renew his long acquaintanceship with Allen Dulles in Switzerland. On April 7, Hohenlohe and Dulles, who had known each other since World War I, had an amiable reunion in Bern. Dulles's telegram to Washington describing their meeting did not specifically indicate that he knew of Hohenlohe's role as one of Schellenberg's agents, but the Bern OSS chief described him as having "access to Nazi leaders including Heinrich Himmler . . ." Dulles reported that Hohenlohe had looked him up "partly because of the large holdings his wife has in Mexico; and also, because he hopes to render aid in eventually reconciling the Western Powers and Germany, he wishes to maintain [this] contact." Dulles added significantly that Hohenlohe was apprehensive "lest certain elements [of the German Resistance] will turn to the Russians in order to obtain the best terms possible."[14] Later, Hohenlohe went further: on the basis of talks with persons in high places, he claimed that the Nazi government, itself, was considering concluding a separate peace with Russia. He stated: "Germany will, in a final desperate effort, try to come to terms with the USSR and will give the latter virtually anything asked."[15]

This line, originating with Schellenberg, is interesting for its implied threat—the stick instead of the carrot: if the Western Allies will not negotiate a peace because of their unconditional surrender agreement and other commitments to Russia, Germany will reach peace with Russia at the West's expense.[16] But, contrary to what Dulles may have thought, there was some substance to this scenario; the USSR, despite its commitment to the unconditional surrender agreement, had by then made certain overtures to the Germans very much in violation of the agreement and at variance with the spirit of the Grand Alliance.

As so often is the case, once-secret matters in time of war come to the surface in the peace that follows. While there are advantages to taking a longer view of events, the cool dawn of peace sometimes obscures the heat of wartime events, but it is important to factor in the context of the times and giving it due weight in history. Masson's relationship with Schellenberg, for example, became a point of contention in Switzerland after the War when the case came to light. Less than a year after Germany's defeat, a long report was issued by the Swiss Federal Council describing the findings of its investigation. The official Swiss interpretation of the Masson-Schellenberg liaison, released to the public on March 8, 1946, traced the connection back to September 8, 1942, when Schellenberg's agent, Hans Wilhelm Eggen, first introduced Schellenberg to Masson, accurately recalling that the Swiss had railed against the government-controlled German press's hostile stance toward Switzerland.

Finding it useful to talk things out with Schellenberg, Masson—with General Guisan's approval—met three more times with him: on October 16, 1942; March 3, 1943; and October 16, 1943. The report noted that their discussions, while covering various specific points of contention between the two countries, was, however, mainly significant as a political exchange whose primary aim was to counteract the German mistrust of Switzerland's professed neutral attitude. According to the Swiss account, "the steps on the part of Masson far exceeded the field of endeavor prescribed for the Chief of the Army Intelligence Service."

Then the report discussed General Guisan's subsequent meeting with Schellenberg, finding his actions and further contacts between Schellenberg and Masson, undertaken with Guisan's permission, "intolerable." As for the written declaration signed by Guisan and given to Schellenberg, stating that Switzerland would strongly resist any infringement of its borders, the Swiss Federal Council recognized that the general's intentions were good—faint praise for a document that Schellenberg claimed was responsible for dissuading Germany from invading Switzerland. The council's report to the contrary minimized Schellenberg's role, claiming that "the contents of [Guisan's] written declaration [given secretly to Schellenberg] coincided with the repeated public declarations of the Federal Council." Guisan's act was described as inappropriate, posing "dangers" that might have arisen "from the fact that the Commander-in-Chief of the Swiss Army had been in contact with high official personalities of a belligerent country."[17] The Federal Council report aired a complaint against Masson that seemed to have had merit:

> Although Masson's contacts were originally intended to obtain information, in fact, they served far less as a source of military intelligence than as an opportunity to discuss political matters. In this connection it should be mentioned that the news of the danger which threatened Switzerland in March 1943 was not obtained through Schellenberg but through channels of our intelligence service entirely independent of Schellenberg. Our intelligence officers, who had set up this valuable "line" [the Viking Line] into Hitler's headquarters, were accordingly extremely upset when they learned that Masson had inquired of Schellenberg whether the alarming news from Hitler's headquarters corresponded to the facts, fearing that their own "contacts" might be unmasked and this source of information cut off.[18]

The Swiss report then addressed the role of Schellenberg in this "questionable" liaison, its comments being based mainly on a protocol signed by Schellenberg while in custody in England after the War and made available to the Federal Military Department in September 1945. While similar to Schellenberg's own account, it is interesting to see the detail and nuances given by Swiss investigators and their unvarnished opinion of Schellenberg at the end of the War as they reconstructed events with the benefit of hindsight but from their naturally biased point of view: "From the protocol signed by Schellenberg in England, it was clear that Schellenberg was in no respect the trustworthy person which Masson considered him to be. Schellenberg had taken advantage of Masson, maintaining his relationship with the Swiss intelligence officer in order to use the latter as a tool for his own political ends."[19]

In conclusion, however, Masson was exonerated of any serious charge: "Colonel Masson established and maintained his contact with Schellenberg in agreement with the approval of his military superiors. . . . Of this connection, it must be recognized that Masson acted in the good intention of serving his country. On the basis of the investigation it is further clear that he made no statements to foreign agents which were harmful to Switzerland, but endeavored to mitigate difficulties in relations between the two countries. It is also clear that he neither sought nor obtained personal advantage. His honor remains unimpaired."[20]

From Schellenberg's point of view, his secret relationships with Masson and other Swiss intelligence officers during the War were useful to him; he had, more or less, freedom of action to make, or direct other agents to initiate contacts with the West. And Schellenberg's weight behind Guisan's written statement that Switzerland would strenuously resist any foreign attacks must have helped deter Hitler from unprovoked aggression against that country. At least the opinions of Schellenberg in this instance constituted a counterbalance against the kind of foreign policy recklessness espoused by Ribbentrop.

Schellenberg was tireless in his covert political efforts. After Switzerland, his arena for action in 1943 was neutral Turkey, a hotbed of international intrigue. Then he would focus his talents on the ever-disturbed Balkans.

8

Turkey and the Balkans

SEPTEMBER 1943 saw Kersten making plans to move with his family to
Stockholm, permission for which was given by Himmler as the result of a
ruse cooked up by T. M. Kivimäkki, the Finnish ambassador to Germany,
who arranged that Kersten, as a reserve officer in the Finnish army, be
assigned to treat Finnish soldiers convalescing in Sweden. In this way he
would be available to respond quickly to Himmler's summons and continue to serve him as a commuting therapist. Otherwise, there was an
implied threat that the Finns would draft him into their army, where he
would be unavailable to Himmler. For political reasons, Himmler predictably did not want to annoy the Finnish government by rejecting this
arrangement.

Assuming that Germany would lose the war, Sweden impressed Kersten
as being his best haven from the dangers of a defeated Reich overrun with
Russians and the forces of the Western Allies. His home in Germany,
Hartzwalde, would certainly be in the path of the Red Army advancing
from the east; he could not expect mercy from them. But would any of the
victorious nations be without initial suspicions in the case of persons like
himself who had worked closely with Himmler? Guilt by association would
be the order of the day.

Since the spring of 1943, Kersten had believed that it was none too soon to move his family to neutral Sweden. He could only hope that this neutral oasis would accept them. From the early part of the war he had shown himself willing to be cooperative with the Swedish government and had responded positively when the Swedish ambassador to Germany, Arvid Richert, had discreetly approached him during the summer of 1942.

Richert appealed to Kersten to use his influence with Himmler to have released seven Swedish businessmen working in Poland, the so-called Warsaw Swedes, who had been charged by the Gestapo with espionage and jailed in Germany. The Swedish corporate officers seized by the Nazis in July 1942 were Carl Herslow and Tore Widen, directors of the Swedish Match Company; Einar Gerge, Stig Gronberg, and Stig Lagerberg, engineers of the same company; as well as two directors of the L. M. Ericsson Company named Berglind and Haggberg. Alvar Moeller, president of the Swedish Match Trust's German branch, became a good friend of Kersten's by virtue of their working together on this delicate matter. Schellenberg, as head of the Sicherheitsdienst, was well wired into counterespionage matters and was also able to be helpful in this matter by working with Kersten, who had Himmler's ear.

By being in Stockholm much of the time, Kersten was able to cement his relationship with Swedish foreign minister Christian Günther, with whom he began serious discussions about freeing Scandinavian nationals held in Nazi prison camps. Kersten also revived his relationship with the U.S. Office of Strategic Services in order to begin secret peace discussions with Abram Hewitt, a newly arrived OSS operative working under a business cover who was known to be well connected with President Roosevelt. But before examining Kersten's American and Swedish relationships, it is worth returning to Walter Schellenberg as he sought contacts in neutral Turkey and the Balkans through which he might have been able to extend peace feelers to the Western Allies.

The peripatetic Schellenberg set out for Turkey on July 25, 1943, following Mussolini's fall from power. Il Duce's opponents had vainly hoped that in his absence the Western Allies would be willing to negotiate a separate armistice. Britain and the United States, they reasoned would have been spared much trouble and would have saved lives had it not been for the rigid unconditional surrender policy binding them. The Grand Alliance, with the Soviets as a partner, saw this in a different light: nothing less than total, nonnegotiated victory over the Axis coalition would suffice. Hitler and Nazism had become metaphors for evil; Britain and the United States were in no mood to make pacts with the Devil—or any of his acolytes. And there was still Japan to worry about; it would do the Western Allies no good to alienate Stalin, whose position in the Far East would be important. Anyway, Allied victory in Europe was in sight; no compromise with the Devil was necessary.

The defeat of the Fascist leadership in Italy had not brought peace to that war-ravaged country. The German army was forced to fall back toward the north as the pursuing Western Allies steadily made their way up the Italian peninsula. Italy continued to be a bloody battlefield—and it only became bloodier during Marshal Pietro Badoglio's time as leader following Mussolini's fall, during which he joined the Allies and declared war against Germany on October 13, 1943.

As early as 1942, Mussolini had realized that the Axis could not hope for victory. During the early summer of that year he had made secret efforts to talk peace and surrender to the British. He had long been uncomfortable as Hitler's ally. In July 1941, Foreign Minister Count Ciano had been conspiring with like-minded members of the Grand Council of Fascist leaders to overthrow his father-in-law, Mussolini, believing that without him there would be a greater chance to make peace. Ciano quoted Mussolini in his diary entry of July 6, 1941: "I foresee an unavoidable conflict arising between Italy and Germany." Mussolini on more than one occasion had complained that his German allies "both in military and political fields always acted without his knowledge."[1]

Schellenberg was proud that his Amt VI (Foreign Intelligence) had forecast the imminent collapse of Italy. Yet the German high command seemed to have been taken by surprise.[2] It is interesting that Schellenberg's rival, Admiral Wilhelm Canaris, head of Abwehr, had advance information of Mussolini's overthrow, thanks to his secret contact with Italian intelligence chief Cesare Amé, an important participant in the anti-Mussolini Resistance movement. Canaris had purposely not shared this vital information with Germany's General Staff. Canaris was not only well informed of developments in Italy, but he had encouraged Amé to advise his government that it should resist German efforts to bind Italy ever closer to its hopeless war effort. "Take my advice," he told Amé, "and allow as few German troops in Italy as possible."[3]

Foreign Minister Ribbentrop had not passed Schellenberg's Amt VI information predicting Mussolini's fall to the military because he "had contemptuously disregarded these reports," preferring "to rely on the more reassuring estimates of the situation that the German ambassador to Italy had supplied."[4]

Italian intelligence records seized by Himmler's Sicherheitsdienst contained information incriminating Canaris by linking him in conspiracy with his Italian friend and counterpart, Cesare Amé. This material, held tightly by Himmler, was not passed on to Hitler, or otherwise used to score points against his rival. This was one of several indications that Canaris, secretly affiliated with the anti-Hitler military Resistance, knew too much about Himmler's own adventure in high treason and, implicitly at least, held this compromising information over him; they both found it useful and wise to maintain a mutual standoff for the time being.[5]

Schellenberg had several reasons to travel to Turkey after Italy's collapse. Protocol required that he return a visit that Turkish police president Pepyii had made in January 1943. But, more important, Schellenberg wanted to discuss with Turkish intelligence chief Perkel common information objectives targeting Russia, with particular regard to the Caucasus.[6] Also on the agenda was the chronic political turmoil in the Balkans. Turkey wanted to be assured that Germany "would not permit Bulgaria to indulge its national ambitions likely to prove harmful to Turkish Thrace"—a constant source of worry to the Turks.[7]

Schellenberg planned to reassure Turkey that despite the prestige lost because of the collapse of Italy, Germany's strength was not impaired. Even though Italy was lost, he would do his best to encourage Turkey to "swing in Germany's favor" and thus augment Germany's bargaining position with the West. In February 1943, Prime Minister Churchill had visited Turkish president Ismet Inönü in the town of Adana, on Turkey's southern coast, and done his best to lure that country to the side of the Allies with shipments of war matériel and other favors. But relations between Turkey and the members of the Grand Alliance had in general sagged, mainly because of the Turks' historic fear of Russia, which coveted political and territorial concessions from Turkey. Britain had been slow to make good on certain promises made to Turkey in a bilateral agreement reached in 1939, stating that the two countries would aid each other in the event of a war in the Mediterranean. And the United States had revealed itself less eager than Great Britain for a "soft underbelly" attack on Germany through the Balkans.

Upon arriving in Turkey, Schellenberg made a point of meeting with German ambassador Franz von Papen at his summer residence near Istanbul to describe his mission—at least as much of it as he felt would be prudent. Von Papen, known for a political "flexibility" that had enabled

Walter Schellenberg (far right), a witness at the Nuremberg war crimes trials, sits with former subordinates in the Sicherheitsdienst–foreign intelligence–including Wilhelm Hoettl (on his right), who handled Balkan intelligence for Schellenberg. (U.S. National Archives)

him to survive, even prosper, since World War I, had recently shown himself at least friendly with the Resistance, including Canaris. The Abwehr chief had secretly used Resistance activist Adam von Trott zu Solz of the Foreign Ministry, while the latter was on an official trip to Turkey in May 1943, to persuade von Papen to cooperate with the Resistance. Von Papen had reacted cautiously at the time but kept von Trott's confidence and did not report his treasonous overtures. In October 1943, von Papen went so far as to receive secretly an OSS agent, Theodore Morde, correspondent of *Reader's Digest.* With an eye to the future, the ambassador even professed to be anti-Hitler and willing to associate himself with a plot to overthrow the Führer if President Roosevelt would make promises appealing enough to "his friends in the German Resistance."[8]

Responding to Schellenberg's meeting, von Papen had his own agenda. Schellenberg's postwar Allied interrogators summarized his testimony dealing with the diplomatic matters discussed with von Papen: the ambassador showed no apparent objection to Schellenberg's visit and even asked him on his return to Germany to inform the Foreign Office and Himmler that he proposed to use "as a bargaining lever with Turkey the promise that, on the event of a favorable outcome of the War, Turkey might be offered greater influence over and better treatment for her minorities in the Crimea, Tartary and the Ukraine. At the same time, von Papen announced his intention of offering the Dodecanese Islands to Turkey at the end of the War, with the intention of offsetting the collapse of Italy."[9]

Von Papen's purpose in asking Schellenberg to convey this information was revealing: "If it were routed through Himmler, any objection of Ribbentrop might be circumvented."[10] Of course, this blatant end run of his antagonist, Ribbentrop, appealed to Schellenberg, who was more than willing to accommodate the ambassador.

Turkey played a role in the Hungarian situation in the autumn of 1943, when secret overtures were made to the Western Allies by dissident elements of Admiral Miklós Horthy's government. The secret movement for peace with the West was endorsed by the prime minister, Miklós Kállay, although Horthy, as regent of Hungary, kept close and sympathetic relations with the participants in the movement. For security reasons and convenience, contacts with the West were made initially through the Hungarian legations in Ankara and other neutral capitals: Lisbon, Bern, and Stockholm.

It was assumed by the conspirators that their plans were known to Admiral Horthy, although he was not informed by them. They realized that as the leader of his country, he had to be in a position to deny any knowledge of such treachery if asked by the Nazis. The German SD, including Schellenberg, knew about it. And certainly Canaris, a good friend of Horthy's, was well aware of what was going on. But both Schellenberg and Canaris, for different reasons, would not reveal it to their respective superiors.[11] And the Nazis, for tactical political reasons pending counteractions, did not let on to Horthy that they knew where he stood. An American colonel in the OSS secretly made it known to anti-Nazi Hungarian dissidents that he would be willing to visit Hungary in person to discuss these matters with Major General István de Ujszászy, chief of the Hungarian Security Service, who was a member of the movement. Unfortunately, a pro-Nazi informant within the Hungarian service secretly notified the Germans of this development. The OSS contact with Ujszászy in this way became known to Wilhelm Hoettl, Schellenberg's Amt VI Balkan expert, who followed closely the hostile developments in Hungary and reported them to Berlin.

Dissident Hungarian forces were buoyed by Allied successes, particularly the events in Italy and Russia, which gave them greater strength and hope of success. In March 1943, the British Special Operations Executive (SOE) made contact with the Kállay government in Hungary, but antagonized some Hungarian anti-Nazi dissidents by wanting to carry out sabotage and other violent activities which would only provoke a German occupation. In the latter part of 1943, an effort was made by the anti-Nazi members of the Hungarian government to establish contact with the Soviets to find terms for peace upon which they could agree.

Still maintaining the facade that Horthy was not involved in anti-Nazi plots, Hitler summoned him to meet with him to "receive orders." Their conversation was tense, at times degenerating into downright hostility. Horthy made it clear that the Hungarians were sick of war. He went so far as to describe the hatred felt by his countrymen toward restrictions imposed upon them by the Germans. But in the face of threats made by Hitler, Admiral Horthy had no choice but to agree to German terms: (a) a change in the Hungarian government; (b) occupation of Hungary by German troops; (c) mobilization of all Hungarian men to prepare for the forthcoming fight against Russia; and (d) unconditional application of anti-Jewish legislation. Moreover, Hitler imposed on Hungary a prime minister of his choice, the Hungarian minister in Berlin, Sztolay. Cowed by Hitler, Horthy was returned to Hungary in a locked and sealed boxcar, accompanied by RSHA chief Ernst Kaltenbrunner. Thereafter, Horthy was Hitler's prisoner and Hungary ceased to be a sovereign nation.[12]

It would have been a serious blow to Hitler had Hungary succeeded in following Italy's path by concluding a separate peace with the Allies; hence his actions in bringing that country under his control. By March 19, 1944, the facade of good relations between Germany and Hungary had disappeared altogether, provoking Germany to invade Hungary.

Kaltenbrunner's role in the Hungarian affair indicates that Schellenberg, his personal enemy and rival for Himmler's favor, was neither a party to Hitler's coup in Hungary nor in agreement with Horthy's treatment. Ribbentrop, also Schellenberg's bête noir, doubtless supported Hitler's action; Himmler had not been consulted on the grounds that it was strictly a matter of foreign affairs, despite dynamic elements of covert support that very much concerned him and Schellenberg.[13]

Had Churchill succeeded in talking Roosevelt and the U.S. Joint Chiefs of Staff into an invasion of the Balkans toward the end of 1943, the War might have ended by the spring of 1944—or so Schellenberg believed. The German southeast flank would have been decimated. But not mentioned by Schellenberg in his memoirs was the inevitable fury that would have been aroused in Stalin had the Western Allies moved their major continental invasion force into the Balkans rather than France.

There had been numerable examples of Stalin's proprietary attitude toward the Balkans. One such manifested itself in the triangular relationship between Stalin, Marshal Tito, and the Western Allies who had extended aid and on-spot liaison with Tito's partisans in Yugoslavia. A serious worsening of Tito's relationship with his U.S.-British benefactors and their missions attached to Tito's headquarters was first noticed in the spring of 1943 by German code breakers who intercepted messages from the Yugoslav partisans. Tito issued an order that all personal contact between members of the partisan army and British and American liaison officers must stop under penalty of severe punishment. Then, according to Wilhelm Hoettl, SD Bal Kan expert, decipherment of partisan radio transmissions revealed a major and imminent Anglo-American landing on the Adriatic coast of Yugoslavia.[14]

A reconstruction of events revealed also that Tito had sent a secret emissary to General Glaise von Horstenau to negotiate an exchange of prisoners. Tito's emissary, calling himself Dr. Petrovic, revealed his true identity to von Horstenau as General Ljubo Velebit, Tito's very close friend and foreign policy adviser. A personal message entrusted to Velebit by Tito stated that the latter would be willing to conclude an armistice agreement with the German army. Conditions stipulated that Tito would refrain from extending his partisan operations to other areas of Croatia if the Germans promised not to attack him inside a certain agreed-upon "reserve" territory. Von Horstenau doubted if any such proposition would be accepted by either the Wehrmacht Supreme Headquarters or the German Foreign Ministry. He had, therefore, approached Amt VI, hoping that Schellenberg could raise it first with Himmler for direct presentation to Hitler. Coincidentally, Schellenberg's secret service obtained related intelligence from another source, a member of Section II of the Hungarian general staff's military espionage organization, who reported that a secret courier sent by Stalin to Tito was carrying a startling order for the partisan leader. According to Hoettl, the message stated that the Kremlin was in possession of information indicating "Churchill had persuaded Roosevelt to undertake a landing on the Adriatic coast, contrary to their agreement with Moscow." If this proved to be accurate, Stalin "authorized Tito to join with the German Army to resist the Anglo-American invasion forces." In preparation for this contingency, Stalin approved of Tito's making contact and reaching agreement with the German high command to this effect. In a meeting with von Horstenau and a representative of the German Foreign Ministry, Velebit delivered a related conciliatory message that in the event of a landing by the United States and Great Britain, Tito was prepared to cooperate with German forces in Croatia in defense against the invaders.[15]

Recognizing the importance of this matter, von Horstenau reconsidered entrusting this information to Schellenberg and Himmler for transmittal to Hitler, believing that its importance required proper channels be observed. He therefore believed that he must approach Hitler through Ribbentrop rather than through Himmler. Hitler's reply left no doubt as to what his policy was in this matter by sending word to von Horstenau: "I don't parley with rebels [such as Tito], I shoot them!"[16]

It was clear that a joint defense of the Balkans by Germany and Tito was out of the picture. It was also evident, however, that Stalin would not hesitate to turn on his Western Allies if he thought it was in his interest to do so; but judging from Hitler's response, the Führer seemed not yet ready in 1943 to encourage a split between the Soviets and the Western Allies, which surely could have occurred if Tito, on Stalin's instruction, had found common cause with the Germans.

Ever since the understanding with Himmler forged at Zhitomir in August 1942, Schellenberg had not only sought out secret contacts with the Western Allies in an effort to gain backing for a putsch against Hitler and to find a formula for a negotiated peace that would exclude and isolate the Soviet Union—he had also devoted himself to finding means to insinuate intelligence analyses to Hitler and other top Nazis that would convince them that Germany could not possibly win the War. This was a risky business since "defeatism" in any form was an anathema to Hitler and punishable by death.

Schellenberg looked for German weaknesses that he could indirectly bring to the surface, hoping that they would come to the attention of Hitler and other unrealistic optimists such as Ribbentrop. Schellenberg also sought to present intelligence, not necessarily doctored or faked, in a way that heavy-pedaled, rather than soft-pedaled, Soviet victories on the Eastern Front so as to convey realistically the hopelessness of the War for Germany.

To this end Schellenberg employed his trusted friend Dr. Giselber Wirsing, an accomplished writer, to prepare intelligence analyses and estimates that would be disseminated only to the top six officials in the Nazi government. While maintaining an impression of complete objectivity, Wirsing's reports would be cleverly presented so as to convince the readers that

Germany had no choice but to negotiate peace with the Western Allies if the fatherland was to survive and be spared Soviet hegemony of Germany, the rest of central Europe, and eastern Europe.[17]

Wirsing was able to draw on a bonanza of authentic information whose import was such as to document the points that Schellenberg wanted to convey without having to run the risk of adulterating the reports. This intelligence treasure trove was the personal safe of the British ambassador to Turkey, Sir Hughe Knatchbull-Hugessen, which was nightly burgled by the ambassador's valet who was secretly an SD spy in the employ of Schellenberg's chief-of-station in Turkey, Ludwig Moyzisch. The spy, known by the code designation "Cicero," was a wily Albanian whose real name was Elyesa Bazna, and who may have been feeding information to Turkish intelligence as well as German. Bazna was ultimately uncovered by a penetration, run by Allen Dulles from Bern, of the German Foreign Ministry, and by a lucky break when an American OSS officer in Istanbul rekindled an old friendship with Moyzisch's secretary, which dated from their high school days in Cleveland, Ohio, where the girl's father had served as the German consul general. The OSS officer secretly recruited the secretary and debriefed her thoroughly on the Cicero matter, as well as every other operation run by Moyzisch, and arranged for her to be spirited out of Turkey to political internment.[18]

In his shrouded campaign to influence the higher circles of Nazi policy makers by emphasizing intelligence revealing Soviet successes, Schellenberg's Amt VI put out a particularly demoralizing report on Russia. This "definitive" piece was produced in conjunction with data obtained from Fremde Heere Ost, the Abwehr military intelligence unit on the Eastern Front; material from researchers at the Wannsee Institute (the Nazi ideological "think tank"); and carefully studied interrogation reports of Russian POWs. Schellenberg meant this particular report to be an accurate assessment—its findings were telling enough in their portrayal of serious German setbacks on the Eastern Front not to need any doctoring by Wirsing to make the picture look bleaker. Schellenberg felt that this and similar reports would bolster Himmler in his often flagging resolve to remove Hitler from power.

Unfortunately for Schellenberg, his arch-antagonist—but titular superior officer—Ernst Kaltenbrunner disparaged the report in discussions with Himmler, calling it "defeatist" in intent as well as wrong in its conclusions. Himmler, influenced by Kaltenbrunner's tirade, returned the report to Schellenberg in high dudgeon. Scrawled across the title page were harsh, dangerous words in which Himmler threatened to throw all those responsible for writing it and otherwise contributing to it into concentration camps.[19]

Mainly because of counterinfluence exerted on the weak-willed Himmler by Kersten and the Reichsführer's trusted adjutant, Rudolf Brandt, Schellenberg was able to gain a hearing in which to plead his own case. But Kaltenbrunner continued his dangerous campaign to denigrate Schellenberg. He picked on Schellenberg's performance in Turkey as another case in point, accusing him of passing himself off with Turkish authorities as the top man in Germany's intelligence complex.

Ribbentrop, who used Kaltenbrunner as a lever against Schellenberg, was resentful that his nemesis, while in Turkey, stepped over the line dividing his intelligence writ from Foreign Ministry responsibilities, particularly in his discussions with Turkish officials pertaining to the sensitive issues of the Caucasus. Ribbentrop went directly to Hitler to complain about Schellenberg's "meddling."

According to Schellenberg's comments as reported by his postwar Allied interrogator, "Hitler flew into a violent rage and issued an order to the effect that henceforward there was to be a complete prohibition on the initiation of any political contacts or talks with neutral countries by the intelligence services lest they should be interpreted by foreign countries as an indication of German weaknesses." Ribbentrop and Kaltenbrunner specifically felt that Schellenberg had overstepped when he made an agreement with Turkish intelligence chief Perkel to collaborate—in fact, "combine"—in joint German-Turkish intelligence operations against Russia.

Schellenberg, during his interrogation following the War, had his own views as to why in August 1943 Himmler had cooled toward him. These are reflected in his interrogator's summation: "Kaltenbrunner was sufficiently in the saddle . . . to influence Himmler against Schellenberg, who was not able through the media of Kersten and Himmler's adjutant, Brandt, to discover the specific grounds upon which Kaltenbrunner's accusations were based."[20] Prominent in the catalog of Kaltenbrunner's grievances were Schellenberg's Turkey visit and the exceedingly pessimistic, defeatist report on Russia prepared by Schellenberg's office.

Schellenberg's position was becoming precarious. Later, in October 1943, he would see another opportunity to begin conversations with the British when David McEwan, Churchill's special envoy for economic matters, arrived in Stockholm. But not wanting to get into any more trouble by being accused of freewheeling, Schellenberg discussed the matter with

Kaltenbrunner. This simply made matters worse. Kaltenbrunner squashed any hopes of proceeding along this path when he reported negatively on it to Hitler, saying that the British could be suggesting such discussions as a means of acquiring leverage against the Soviets at the upcoming Allied Foreign Ministers Conference in Moscow.[21] Hitler accordingly issued an order on October 19, 1943, forbidding anyone from pursuing British peace feelers—not that the Allied agreement on unconditional surrender would have permitted it, nor would Churchill inflame an already suspicious Stalin or upset Roosevelt by playing this card at the forthcoming meeting of the Big Three.

Events in August, however, were bad enough. That Schellenberg was in Himmler's bad graces by then did not augur well for the future of the secret Zhitomir plan. But Kersten, whose relationship with Himmler survived mostly because of the Reichsführer's compelling need for his physical therapy services, would come to Schellenberg's rescue. Kersten knew the Reichsführer better than most and for this reason as well was able to influence him. The motive behind Himmler's willingness to conspire against Hitler, his idol, was discovered one day in late 1942 by Kersten: Himmler had become convinced that the Führer, physically ill and consumed by severe neuroses, was unfit to rule Germany.

9

Hitler

Unfit to Rule

FINDING HIMMLER in a nervous state on December 12, 1942, a day that would prove memorable, Kersten asked him what was bothering him. Himmler's enigmatic reply was to ask Kersten if he could treat a person who suffered from insomnia, dizziness, and severe headaches. Cautiously, Kersten explained that he would first have to know more about such a patient and would thus have to give him a thorough examination. Solemnly, swearing Kersten to utmost secrecy, Himmler produced a black portfolio from his personal safe and withdrew from it a blue file. Handing it to Kersten, he bid him to read it carefully.

The secret document was a twenty-six-page report chronicling Hitler's history of illnesses since his army service in World War I. Beginning with his military medical record, dating from his convalescence at the Pasewalk hospital where, as a victim of poison gas at the front, he had been treated for temporary blindness, and including symptoms appearing in 1937 that were diagnosed as syphilis, the report had been brought up to date with mention of various ailments that Himmler had just described that currently afflicted the Führer. Kersten remembered hearing that in 1942 Hitler had begun to suffer from progressive paralysis.

Himmler implored Kersten to try and help Hitler. On a note of desperation, Himmler declared that every possible medical means must be used "to save the Führer." Kersten was doubtless dismayed to hear such emotions coming from the man who at Zhitomir had agreed with him and Schellenberg that Hitler must be removed. Now suddenly the Reichsführer described Hitler as "the Führer of the Greater German Reich, which is occupied in a struggle for life and death that can only be won by the Führer, for he is the only person whose powers are equal to the task; he must not fail us."[1]

Himmler's file on Hitler presumably contained the product of Gestapo investigations. But not trusting the diagnoses given, Himmler wanted to have his trusted therapist, Kersten, a physician according to Finnish medical standards, thoroughly examine the Führer. Hitler's own physician at that time, Theodor Morell, was clearly unqualified—essentially a quack—who relied on dubious nostrums. His object was to give Hitler comfort, not a cure. Kersten, however, wanted no part in the matter. At least for the moment Himmler seemed fervent in his belief that "the world regards Adolf Hitler as a strong man; and that's how he must go down in history."

Kersten wished neither to lend himself to a lie nor to risk involving himself in a potentially politically dangerous affair that he would not be able to control. Politics in Himmler's office were bad enough, but the jealousies and suspicions permeating Hitler's office could be lethal.

A week later Kersten brought up again with Himmler the question of Hitler's competence. He advised Himmler not to pretend that things could go on as they were. He told the Reichsführer bluntly: "Only a man of entirely sound mind could occupy the post of führer." Kersten added, "You still have the SS, Herr Reichsführer, and Göring has his Luftwaffe. If you lay the facts of the case before a number of important generals, explaining to them that the Führer is a sick man and that he has got to abdicate in the interests of the nation as a whole, they'll gratefully recognize it as a most statesmanlike act on your part. . . . It is up to you to make the first move."[2]

Kersten had made an impression on Himmler, but his vacillating was maddening. The Reichsführer could rationalize his high treason—Hitler was not fit to govern; that had become clear. Moreover, Himmler realized that he must somehow distance himself from Hitler if he were to survive Germany's inevitable defeat. But his loyalty to Hitler and his fundamental devotion to both the man and the ideology he represented would from time to time tug at his psyche. Yet, lurking within him was ambition. Perhaps he could best survive if he ousted Hitler and led Germany to peace with the Western Allies.

• • •

The report on Hitler's health shown secretly to Kersten by Himmler dealt more with symptoms than diagnoses. The Führer, it seemed, was clearly suffering from bad headaches, insomnia, and dizziness. Superficial diagnoses by unqualified persons attributed these symptoms to gas attacks in World War I combat and to syphilis, but more a scientifically sound post–World War II analysis points to Parkinson's disease as the principal cause of Hitler's infirmities, while in-depth psychiatric reviews of Hitler's behavior would reveal a man badly flawed by neuroses unconnected with World War I.

Meanwhile, the U.S. government was making a Herculean effort to fathom its enemy. In March 1943, the Intelligence Division of the Office of Chief of U.S. Naval Operations came into possession of a psychological profile drawn up by Dr. Karl Kronor, a refugee from Nazi Germany, who as a nerve specialist in Vienna had been part of the group examining Hitler's temporary blindness following World War I. Beginning with a tentative diagnosis that soldier Hitler had gone blind as the result of a World War I gas attack, Kronor and some of his colleagues speculated that unless Hitler was faking blindness—a highly unlikely situation—he was a victim of "hysteria or psychopathy." As Hitler threw himself into the turmoil of German politics in the early 1930s, a diagnosis of hysteria would be a black mark on his record. According to Kronor, in an effort to hide this disability, Private Hitler's former company sergeant major, Max Amann, was bribed to keep his mouth shut by being appointed by Hitler to be business manager of the entire German press, a job that made him the happy possessor of ill-gotten millions.

However, another survivor of World War I who had been privy to the diagnosis of Hitler, Professor Edmund Forster, head of the medical faculty at Greifswald University, would not be so lucky. Shortly after Hitler came to power, Forster suddenly died, the cause of death being given as suicide. According to Kronor, there could be no doubt that he had been murdered, most likely at the order of Adolf Hitler.[3]

A psychiatrist who had been retained by the OSS in World War II to study Hitler, Walter C. Langer, found documents in the 1950s that revealed that Hitler had been a draft dodger during World War I, but finally enlisted in the army before the conflict ended. In 1938, Hitler tried desperately to locate documents attesting to this fact so they could be destroyed, but he was unsuccessful. Still-extant documents also showed that several of Hitler's World War I contemporaries had been aware that he was subject to bouts of depression, severe enough to suggest serious mental illness.[4]

A later witness to Hitler's disturbed state of mind was Hermann Göring's friend Birger Dahlerus, a Swedish businessman. On the eve of Hitler's invasion of Poland in September 1939, Göring used Dahlerus as a secret peace emissary to the British government. Dahlerus had an occasion to speak directly with Hitler in an effort to dissuade him from invading Poland, an act that almost certainly would provoke war with Britain and France. He described the Führer as acting very strangely on this occasion. He would stop "in the middle of the room and stand there staring; his voice became blurred as his behavior became that of a completely abnormal person. . . ." His mental equilibrium was "patently unstable."[5] In his memoir, Dahlerus referred to Hitler as "a crazy individual," and alleged that the German ambassador to Italy, Ulrich von Hassell, and Göring, in strictest confidence, both agreed that Hitler was mentally ill and "should be removed from office."[6] Von Hassell based his conclusion in part on remarks made by the prominent German surgeon at that time, Dr. Ferdinand Sauerbruch, who after visiting the Führer in late 1942 was convinced that Hitler was out of his mind.[7]

Von Hassell recorded the following in his diary on January 22, 1943: "There are more and more reports to show Hitler's dangerous mental condition."[8] On March 28, 1943, von Hassell wrote in his diary that Resistance leader Carl-Friedrich Goerdeler "claimed that Goebbels, as well as [Wilhelm] Frick and [Martin] Bormann, had jointly concluded that Hitler is insane and must be put on the shelf."[9]

The U.S. Library of Congress in 1995 made public an official memorandum from Himmler to Bormann, dated January 23, 1944, covering two sealed envelopes that described four cousins of Hitler on his father's side who were mentally unstable. The progeny of paternal cousin Joseph Viet included a twenty-one-year-old disturbed son who committed suicide in 1920, and three severely retarded daughters, one of whom had been put in an asylum. Himmler, it appeared, had ordered the Gestapo to look into proliferating stories concerning a hereditary tendency toward mental illness or mental deficiency among Hitler's relatives, and this is what had been turned up.[10] Moreover, two of Hitler's own sisters, it was believed by some, were mentally deficient to some degree and caused the Führer embarrassment.[11] It is unclear whether Himmler ordered this investigation on his own initiative, or on behalf of Bormann. If the latter is the case, one wonders if Bormann wanted it for his own questionable purposes or because Hitler asked him to look into the embarrassing rumors going around.

While Himmler attributed Hitler's unbalanced state to progressive syphilis when discussing it with Kersten, the Gestapo investigation of the Viet family connection, presumably not known by the masseur, certainly pointed to congenital mental or emotional problems as the cause for Hitler's degeneration. Whatever the basis for Hitler's neuroses, Himmler had cause for doubting Hitler's fitness to rule. This gave him a rationalization for plotting behind the back of his beloved master. He could rationalize that he was doing it for Hitler's good as well as Germany's. As things were going the Third Reich would be ruined, destroying Hitler in the process. Something had to be done, as Kersten, Schellenberg, and even Kersten's "friend," the astrologer Wilhelm Wulff—who had the stars as his authority—kept telling Himmler. Yet Himmler's conscience kept asking him if he was doing the right thing.

If Hitler was unsound of mind at this point, he was clearly a mentally disturbed person after he survived Count Claus Schenk von Stauffenberg's assassination attempt on July 20, 1944. A witness to the bomb explosion intended for Hitler was briefly knocked out by the blast but recovered in time to attend a scheduled reception for Mussolini later that day. He was struck by how the slightly wounded Hitler behaved at the party. Hitler's right arm was visibly afflicted with worse than usual tremors and his demeanor verged on the hysterical. Everyone noticed a strangeness about him not evident before. He gulped his pills and shouted hysterically about an "eye for an eye for everyone who dared set himself against Divine Providence."[12] John Weitz, a biographer of Ribbentrop's, was moved to write, "The Hitler of old would never be again." After the July 20, 1944, episode Hitler "was a sick man, unsure of his step, slower of speech and reaction, and more deeply in thrall to the treatments of [his doctor], Theo Morell."[13]

Himmler had another interest in the attempt on Hitler's life by the Widerstand. He had known months in advance that the effort would be made, and had, in fact, known who was behind it. He even told Resistance leader Canaris, who was not part of the Stauffenberg plot but was kept informed by his colleagues who were, that General Ludwig Beck and Goerdeler were the suspected ringleaders. Then, on July 17, only three days before the bomb attack, Arthur Nebe, head of the criminal branch of the Gestapo and a Resistance activist, warned Goerdeler to go into hiding because the Gestapo knew all about the assassination plan and his involvement in it.[14]

Himmler was willing to turn a blind eye toward the impending von Stauffenberg bombing, hoping that if it failed, he could emerge as the hero for tracking down the Widerstand and still be in a position to proceed with his own plotting against Hitler. If von Stauffenberg succeeded, he could use the

SS to place him effectively in power after reaching a deal with the Wehrmacht in which peace would be made with the Western Allies preparatory to the combined forces of the SS and the army engaging the Red Army. Fighting on only one front, the Germans would be in position to defeat the Russians while, he hoped, the Americans and British cheered them on. This startling but naive analysis had been given to Allen Dulles, the OSS chief in Bern, by his Abwehr Resistance contact, Edward von Waetjen. Unrealistic as it may seem, Himmler was convinced he could secure Western support to lead a post-Hitler Japanese-German attack on Russia as part of a compromise peace settlement with the Western Allies.[15]

What concerned Kersten was that the secret of Hitler's illness would become widely known, triggering a chaotic struggle for power. Göring and Bormann were already aware of the "secret" medical report. In December 1942, Kersten also discussed the matter with Himmler's assistant, Brandt, who was horrified that the masseur, too, was in on this darkest of secrets. Brandt agreed with Kersten's fears, but despaired of doing anything about it. Bormann had ingratiated himself with Hitler to such a degree that it was difficult for Himmler to gain ready access to Hitler, much less influence him. The fact that Hitler's health was deteriorating was leaking out. According to Kersten, SS General Gottlob Berger, in command of the SS head office, had reported spreading rumors that Hitler suffered from a "progressive paralysis."

Albert Speer, Hitler's architect, was now talking about the Führer's infirmities of mind and spirit. As early as January 1938, according to Speer, Hitler urged him to build quickly the projected new chancellery, meant to be a monument to the Führer rivaling Versailles's grandeur. Hitler, who talked with Speer about a stomach ailment that had caused him distress since 1935, feared that "he did not have much longer to live." And, in a conversation with Speer, Hitler's mistress, Eva Braun, quoted the Führer as once telling her: "I'll soon have to give you your freedom. Why should you be tied to an old man?"

Hitler rejected suggestions that he seek help in a clinic, since, for political reasons, he could not be thought to be "sick." While pills and injections administered by Dr. Morell had at first provided Hitler with relief, by 1937 Speer quoted the Führer as saying: "I don't known how long I am going to live. Perhaps most of these buildings [that Speer was planning on Hitler's instructions] will be finished only after I am no longer here." And on May

2,1938, Hitler made a personal will that also suggested that he was having intimations of mortality."[16]

Himmler was not the only one to keep a secret dossier on the state of Hitler's health; the U.S. Office of Strategic Services had for quite different reasons devoted considerable effort analyzing the Führer's psyche. Faced with certain defeat, what would Hitler do? What kind of morale operations should be conducted to counteract the public's acceptance of their Führer? Following a defeat of Germany, what should be done with Hitler to prevent him from becoming a martyr under whose banner another generation might rise to repeat the obscenities and folly of the Third Reich? To answer these kinds of questions, the OSS sought to psychoanalyze Hitler from afar with the evidence available.

It was in the spring of 1943 that OSS chief William Donovan asked Walter Langer, a prominent psychoanalyst and head of OSS's "psychoanalytical field unit," to research and write an assessment of Adolf Hitler. With some success, Langer produced a secret analysis of the Führer. Not having access to the "patient," of course, Langer had to rely mostly on the statements of those who had known Hitler, as well as Hitler's own speeches and public acts prior to 1943. But it is worth noting that Langer predicted with remarkable accuracy that Hitler would probably commit suicide once he admitted to himself that all hope of victory was gone.[17] He would want to die quickly and surely by his own hand rather than meet his end ignominiously, as Mussolini had, at the end of a rope in the midst of a rabble that gloried in his death. Nor did Hitler want to be captured alive by the Russians to be "exhibited . . . like a freak."

But it was in life, not death, that Hitler's neuroses were dangerous, for they contributed to the atrocities he committed in World War II. Langer believed that a deep-seated fear of death was one of the "powerful unconscious streams" that drove Hitler during his mad career.[18] "The great danger is that if he feels that he cannot achieve immortality as the Great Redeemer, he may seek it as the Great Destroyer," Langer wrote.

Langer believed that Hitler's sexual aberrations, rooted in hatred of his father and excessive attachment to his mother, bred sadomasochistic obsessions that deprived him of a normal family life as well as normal sexual experiences. And when, with the crutch of power, he was able to lure women to his bed and attempt to have them cooperate in his acts of self-degradation, they usually felt only overpowering disgust. Langer's research revealed that several women seemed to have committed suicide after being intimate with Hitler. One poor soul, Rene Mueller, had apparently been forced by Hitler to kick him mercilessly as he groveled before her on the ground. Soon after this harrowing episode, Mueller appeared to have shot herself.

Geli Raubal, Hitler's half sister's daughter, whom he deeply loved in his own way, similarly committed suicide, although some investigators believed that Hitler may have shot her as they broke up, presumably in the fear that she might tell her friends about Hitler's strange aberrations and that the word would get out to the general public. The Führer's later constant companion, Eva Braun, had twice attempted to take her own life before their marriage and joint suicide in Hitler's bunker on April 30, 1945, as Berlin was about to be invested by the Red Army. Their relationship had not always been smooth. On August 11, 1932, Eva Braun tried to kill herself in much the same way as Geli Raubal had. And in May 1935 she unsuccessfully tried again by taking an overdose of sleeping pills.

Langer had the benefit of views on Hitler's psychopathology from no less a psychoanalyst than Sigmund Freud, who was convinced that Hitler was insane. Langer had known Freud well in 1939, and had been responsible for persuading him to flee Austria before anti-Jewish pogroms could destroy

Adolf Hitler, holding his German shepherd, Blondi, by a leash, poses for a photograph with his mistress, Eva Braun, and her two scotty dogs at the Führer's Berchtesgaden retreat. Eva would twice attempt suicide before she died with Hitler in a suicide pact as Germany fell. (U.S. National Archives)

him.[19] The famous psychoanalyst Carl Jung also thought that Hitler was not sane; at times, Hitler seemed to "act like a robot."

One of Langer's most helpful witnesses to Hitler's neuroses was Ernst ("Putzi") Hanfstaengl, who befriended—even kept at his home—Adolf Hitler before he became Germany's leader. Son of a German father and an American mother, Hanfstaengl had known Franklin Roosevelt at Harvard well before World War II. He had also run a New York branch of his family's fine art gallery. Returning to Germany as the Nazis began their march to power, he renewed his friendship with Hitler, who found Putzi's piano playing a relaxing diversion, particularly when he played Wagner. It has been reported that on one occasion Putzi claimed to have come upon a weird scene at his home in which Hitler was groveling before Putzi's wife, crying that he wished he had someone to take care of him. As he played the role of a little boy searching for a new mother, rather than a would-be lover or suitor, Hitler was asked by the startled woman why he didn't get married. His response: "Germany is my bride."[20]

Hanfstaengl had reason to fear a plot against him by certain members of Hitler's court who were jealous of his propinquity with the Führer. He also knew that Hitler had tired of him—and he had become disillusioned with the Führer. Knowing as much as he did about Hitler, he reasoned that he was no longer safe in Germany; the Führer himself might prefer to have him killed because he knew too much.

Putzi escaped from Germany in 1937, having had a close call with death when the pilot of a small aircraft, allegedly carrying him on a secret mission to Spain, confessed to him that he was to be dropped from the plane without a functional parachute. Instead, the friendly pilot landed in a farmer's field near Berlin and let Putzi flee across the border to Switzerland. He made his way to England, where he was interned as an enemy alien by the British. Hearing of his predicament, President Roosevelt had him returned to Washington. He was billeted in a country house in nearby Virginia, where he served the OSS and other U.S. intelligence units as a walking encyclopedia on Hitler and Nazi Germany. Langer found him an invaluable source on the health of the Führer, particularly his mental health. Himmler may have had the resources of the Gestapo, enabling him to assemble a dossier on Hitler's physical and mental condition, but Langer and the OSS had an infinitely better source in Hanfstaengl.[21] The conclusions reached by Himmler and the United States, however, were similar: Hitler was not wholly rational, and he certainly was not fit to govern Germany.

The U.S. Office of Strategic Services in October 1943 produced another monumental analysis of Hitler's psyche that essentially agreed with the Langer conclusions. This project, highly classified at the time, was conducted by the OSS's Henry A. Murray, M.D., working with the OSS's Morale Operations (MO) unit and titled "Analysis of the Personality of Adolph Hitler." (The report was not declassified and made available by the U.S. National Archives until the year 2000.)[22]

Murray's project was intended not only to analyze Hitler's personality and how it was formed, but what it portended as Allied military successes confronted Hitler with the likelihood of imminent German defeat, and how the U.S. government might influence his mental state. It also dealt with what should be done with him upon his capture after Germany surrendered. Murray also took on the daunting objective of analyzing the psychology of the German people, not only as it affected Hitler's psychology but as a guide to "converting Germany into a peace-loving nation that is willing to take its proper place in world society."[23]

Murray believed that Hitler's traits "were so intense and the counterbalancing forces (affection, conscience, self-criticism, humor) are so weak that we are justified in speaking of 'megalomania,'" that is, "delusions of omnipotence."[24] Hitler's personality was one that valued "brute strength, purity of blood and fertility, while being contemptuous of weakness, indecision, lack of energy and fear of conscience." Sexually, he was a "full fledged passive masochist" and had "an erotic pattern that called for infinite self-abasement...."[25]

As one of the causes of the Führer's obsessive anticommunism, Murray speculated that "Hitler instinctively retreated from too close association with the workers of Vienna," a trait based on his father's image as "an upward mobile individual" who, beginning as a peasant, worked his way into the lower middle class, establishing a boundary between himself and those below him.[26] Yet, ironically, history tells us that much of Hitler's public support came from Germany's working classes; this must have been obvious to him.

In this connection, observations of Hitler made by Birger Dahlerus, Göring's Swedish go-between with the British in his effort to prevent war between Germany and England on the eve of the invasion of Poland, are interesting. Trying to distract Hitler from continuing his ranting about Britain's failure to cooperate with Germany (on German terms) in the interest of European peace, Dahlerus told the Führer that he could not agree with his criticism of Britain. Having once been a common laborer himself in England, Dahlerus mentioned he had developed a high respect for the

British workingman. This, apparently, struck a responsive chord in Hitler, who proceeded to spend half an hour asking questions about the English.[27]

In one of his many discussions with Kersten about the Führer, Himmler asserted that Hitler was regarded by the world as a strong man and "that is how he must be remembered in history!" Himmler recoiled at the very thought of the Führer seeking medical assistance in any way that could make public his problems: "You only have to consider what an effect that would have on the German people," he added. Rudolf Brandt later described to Kersten how sensitive the Hitler dossier was and warned him that his very knowledge of its existence was dangerous to him. He told Kersten that he should not even discuss this matter with Himmler any further.[28]

Kersten, nonetheless, was audacious enough to beard his boss, impressing upon him the provocative point that only someone with sound mind should occupy the job of leading the German nation.[29]

This episode, illuminating Himmler's grave concern about Hitler's health, was based on the probable damage that would accrue if the public learned of it and reacted violently, rather than on any compassionate feelings he might have toward the Führer. This is interesting in the context of Dr. Murray's 1943 psychological assessment of Hitler, in which he expressed his belief that Hitler's success to date had depended to a large extent upon his ability to gain the sympathy and protectiveness of the people. Murray believed that power would quickly slip from Hitler's grasp should he lose this ability, which he surely would if his ever-worsening physical and mental incompetence became known. Public sympathy would turn to scorn and probably inspire increased underground resistance activity, such as that in which Himmler himself was dabbling.[30]

Murray's insightful speculation about Hitler's behavior states: "Whatever else happens, it can be confidently predicted that Hitler's neurotic spells will increase in frequency and duration, and his effectiveness as a leader will diminish. . . . indeed there is some evidence that his mental powers have been deteriorating since last November, 1942."[31]

Dr. Murray predicted wrongly the possibility of a military coup as it turned out, but not without some prescience, considering that the abortive July 20, 1944, bomb plot almost succeeded. Another prediction of Murray's was that "Hitler would commit suicide if his plans miscarried." This was the same as Langer's assessment, and it actually came to pass. Murray felt that Hitler would wait until the last minute, but would cheat captors by taking his own life "in the most dramatic possible manner"—at least the most dramatic way available to him as he and his eleventh-hour bride, Eva Braun, awaited the end, huddling in the Führer's underground bunker as the Russians swarmed into Berlin.

The impact on Kersten upon seeing Himmler's dossier on Hitler inspired two reactions in him. First, he now recognized how the deterioration of Hitler had provided the Reichsführer with a needed rationalization for his plotting against the leader whom he had followed blindly for so long and whose maniacal ideology he still embraced. This was a help in Kersten's and Schellenberg's efforts to manipulate Himmler toward overthrowing Hitler and making peace with the Western Allies. Second, Kersten was dismayed to discover just how dangerous as well as absurd the Nazi "theater of the absurd" had become. The man on whom so many relied in Germany was a badly warped and progressively incompetent psychotic. This made more urgent the steps he was taking to prepare a haven for himself and his family in neutral Sweden before they could be swamped by the chaos of defeat and the rage of his Nazi enemies, as well as the inevitable retribution of the victors against all those who had been associated with Himmler.

10

The Astrologer

AUGUST 1943 had been a difficult month for Schellenberg. Kaltenbrunner continued to stir the cauldron of rumor, accusing him of having inflated his own importance. Himmler went so far as to announce that he was considering replacing Schellenberg with Otto Skorzeny, the swashbuckling SD agent who had achieved glory by rescuing Mussolini after the Fascist leader had been thrown out of power in Italy.[1]

Kersten was doing all he could to convince Himmler that Schellenberg did not deserve the poison-tongue whispering traceable to Kaltenbrunner, and that they should patch up their differences. Himmler's adjutant, Rudolf Brandt, was also helpful in this, but this was not enough.

Kersten had an idea where he might locate someone whom he believed could help influence the Reichsführer. His name was Wilhelm Theodor Heinrich Wulff; his vocation, astrologer. Knowing Himmler's addiction to astrology, Kersten saw himself and Schellenberg behind the scenes, telling Wulff what kind of horoscope and predictions to craft for the purpose of manipulating the Reichsführer.

On June 9, 1941, the Gestapo had rounded up and jailed virtually all psychics in Germany while mounting an all-out effort to discover who may have given Hitler's deputy, Rudolf Hess, the inspiration to fly secretly to England in hopes of negotiating peace with the British on the eve of

Germany's planned invasion of Russia. Kersten believed that Wulff, one of the many psychics briefly incarcerated, would be only too pleased to cooperate with him and Schellenberg, thereby ensuring his continuing release from prison.

Wulff, born in Hamburg, began his adult life as an artist but, intrigued by the lives of Leonardo da Vinci, Johannes Kepler, Tycho Brahe, and Goethe, found himself drawn to the occult in 1920. He established a reputation as one of Germany's leading astrologists; his study of the stars allegedly enabled him to predict a number of important events, such as the July 1944 attempt on Hitler's life. And by astrological analysis, he claimed to have predicted that Hitler would die just before May 7, 1945.

Kersten introduced Wulff to Himmler, hoping the astrologer would be a counterweight to Kaltenbrunner's influence. The British World War II chronicler H. R. Trevor-Roper wrote that Himmler "seldom took any steps without first consulting his horoscope."[2] While Kersten put Wulff in touch with several other Nazi leaders besides Himmler who had taken an interest in astrology, Wulff was less than admiring of his benefactor in his memoirs. While having no choice but to accept the guidance of Kersten and Schellenberg, which was calculated to influence Himmler, Wulff perhaps resented having to prostitute his talents for a political purpose. Throughout his memoirs he insisted that his astrological analyses were truly what the stars indicated, never admitting that he had slanted them on demand.

In his description of Kersten, Wulff referred to him as "a great giant of a man who posed as a harmless masseur from Finland" but "had wormed his way into the highest aristocratic circles abroad and into the top strata of the Nazis." While "a realist" and "an extremely shrewd thinker," Kersten could not be fairly described as an "intellectual." Attempting to survive amid the confusion of Nazi Germany where he had found himself trapped, according to Wulff, Kersten had eked out a living as a dishwasher and then as a film extra before becoming a skilled masseur.[3]

Wulff skeptically referred to Kersten as having been a "doctor of manipulative therapy" from 1930 onward, but seemed more impressed that Kersten had been on Christian-name terms with the prince consort of Holland, Heinrich von Mechlenburg, and had "risen" to become "Himmler's personal physician."

Wulff had been released from a harsh incarceration in the prison at Fuhlsbuttel in the late summer of 1941 through the efforts of a man named Zimmerman, a former client, who operated a scientific research group experimenting with a cure for rickets using a process of irradiating milk.

Paroled to Zimmerman by the Gestapo, Wulff had his friend to thank for a wage-paying job, even though it provided the Gestapo with a controlled surveillance opportunity while he was being vetted for an assignment as research assistant in a newly classified navy laboratory in Berlin concerned with psychic phenomena. Astrologer that he was, Wulff found it nonetheless curious that the Nazis were attempting to exploit supernatural forces as part of their war effort.

Specifically, the navy institute was intent on targeting enemy ocean convoys through the use of "pendulum diviners" and other "supernatural devices."[4] It should be noted that there were theories bruited about in the German navy to the effect that the increasingly deadly assaults on German submarines at sea could be attributed to British "pendulum practitioners" using psychic methods. This was doubtless helpful to the British, since it tended to cloak the real cause of German U-boat casualties: Ultra decryptions that provided the British with the precise coordinates of German submarine locations at sea by breaking German naval ciphers.

Introduced by Zimmerman, Wulff first met Kersten during the winter of 1942 at the latter's apartment in Berlin-Wilmersdorf. He described Himmler's masseur as a "thyroid case" who probably "had fatty degeneration of the heart." Summarizing his first impressions of Kersten, Wulff wrote in his memoirs that "he was very passionate and sensuous, extremely vain and ambitious."[5]

Kersten asked Wulff what he thought about Hitler's horoscope. Quoting the constellations, Wulff pessimistically predicted that Hitler could not last much longer. Germany's Moscow and Leningrad offensives had been stopped, giving way to a slow strategic withdrawal. Kersten was treated to Wulff's conclusion that Hitler had "the same Saturn positions in his natal chart as Napoleon." Kersten's promise to show Wulff's horoscope of Hitler to Himmler caused the astrologer to blanch with horror. Wulff explained that he did not want to be clapped into prison once again. Kersten promised that no harm would come to him, insisting that he produce a horoscope of Himmler and one of himself, as well. This was a beginning of Wulff's relationship with Kersten. At least, he hoped, it would keep him out of prison and spare him further persecution by the Gestapo.[6]

Satisfied that Wulff's astrological talents were "genuine," Himmler put him in touch with Schellenberg. The two men first met in the offices of the Reich Security Main Office (RSHA) in Hamburg. Wulff's first impression of the Amt VI chief was that he was a shy man, an "almost insignificant figure." But this trait was a relief from the arrogance of most Nazi leaders. After exchanging a very few words, Wulff could see that Schellenberg had a perceptive, analytical mind and felt ill at ease in his showy SS uniform.

In preparation for this meeting, Wulff had prepared Schellenberg's horoscope and frankly told him that his birth date in 1909 produced a "hostile constellation of Neptune, Saturn, Mars, Jupiter, Uranus and the Sun." He warned Schellenberg that he should expect bad experiences. Moreover, Wulff said that his health was fragile, causing him to be excessively cautious. Schellenberg later admitted that this prediction was accurate.

Perhaps benefiting from Kersten's briefing, or perhaps because it was generally suspected in high RSHA circles, Wulff seemed to know that Schellenberg and his immediate, though nominal, superior, Kaltenbrunner, were in dangerous competition for power within the RSHA. Gestapo chief Heinrich Müller was also scheming behind Schellenberg's back. Wulff shrewdly concluded that while Schellenberg may have been genuinely motivated by humanitarian emotions and revolted by Himmler's atrocities, he was ever conscious of the need to disassociate himself from the Reichsführer's sins if he were to survive after the War[7]—and to disassociate himself from Hitler by plotting against him using Himmler as his cat's-paw.

Schellenberg suddenly popped a key question: "Do you consider that astrology is a suitable vehicle for the propagation of political concepts for the political control of a nation?" Wulff responded wholeheartedly in the affirmative, but disparaged the efforts of Goebbels's propaganda ministry and Ribbentrop's foreign ministry to use the predictions of the sixteenth-century French mystic Nostradamus for Nazi propaganda purposes during the early war years, 1939 and 1940.[8]

Schellenberg was amazingly frank in his discussion with Wulff, having been convinced by Kersten that the astrologer could be trusted. Schellenberg bluntly stated, "Hitler ought to be thrown out. . . . It is very difficult for me, holding these views, to carry out my official duties in a conscientious manner." Getting to the point, Schellenberg asked Wulff to prepare for him a comprehensive horoscope of the Führer.[9] By this time Wulff could have been under no illusions; Schellenberg wanted to use the horoscope as part of his secret campaign against Hitler.

Next, Wulff had to pass muster with Himmler himself. Escorted by Schellenberg's aide-de-camp and general factotum, Franz Göring, the astrologer proceeded to his first meeting with Himmler in the spring of 1944, at the Reichsführer's Bergwald Castle headquarters in the shadow of the Salzburg Alps. Wulff was not impressed by Himmler: the Reichsführer, "a former chicken farmer and manure salesman," was perhaps only "a political calculating machine . . . a robot with horn-rimmed glasses and a metal heart full of magical spells, which had been put there by some evil genius."[10]

Their luncheon companions consisted mainly of well-fed boors with neither manners nor apparent interest. An exception, Dr. Rudolf Brandt, said little at lunch; but, according to Wulff, "his sad, serious eyes seemed to have witnessed many terrible things. He was an idealist and a loyal, devoted servant of Himmler." With arms akimbo, "sucking his soup like a peasant," Himmler treated his guests to a strange monologue on Indian mythology. Quoting from a Hindu classic, the *Arthasastra,* Himmler tried to make a case for a ruler's need to have an effective and elaborate internal spy network. While discussing Kautilya, a mythical figure whom Himmler had obviously studied, he conceded that the use of such an all-embracing internal espionage organization was "indecent and unworthy of the German people." This, coming from the Gestapo's master, was unconvincing, to say the least. Himmler's hypocritical statement to Wulff that Nazism had provided the Germans with a "government of the people" was equally strange. Wulff's comment, as he recalled in his memoirs, was that "while the Party claimed to be a mass movement, whose every member serves as an important link in the national community," in fact the truth was that "every party member spied on every other party member." Clearly, "Himmler had organized modem methods of terror into a comprehensive system in which spying was the most important single factor." The methods that Himmler condemned in the *Arthasastra* were the methods he had introduced to Germany.[11]

Himmler apologized to Wulff for his having had to spend time in a Gestapo jail, explaining that astrology could no longer be tolerated in public. "It was causing too much mischief," Himmler reasoned. "The Nazis cannot permit any astrologers to follow their calling except those who are working for us."[12]

During lunch, Himmler discussed the horoscopes prepared by Wulff on Stalin, Churchill, and Hitler. Wulff described his work on Hitler, passed to Himmler by Kersten a year earlier, as the unvarnished account of what would certainly be a fateful—and, for Germany, fatal—end to the Führer's military ventures, and a prediction of Hitler's "mysterious" death in 1945. Wulff, in his report on Hitler, had emphasized these points "in the hope of overcoming Himmler's well-known indecision and persuading him to move against Hitler before being caught up in the general debacle."[13] Wulff added that he hoped Himmler would heed his predictions and "consider it necessary to overthrow Hitler and enter into peace negotiations," or, at least, precipitate an internal revolt that would put an end to the Nazi regime.

One must assume that Wulff's line on this subject owed its origin to Kersten's and Schellenberg's instructions. This was, of course, the line the two plotters sought to convey to Himmler, and Wulff's continuing freedom would depend on his willingness to follow their instructions, no matter what the stars told him to the contrary. Yet throughout his memoirs the astrologer, presumably for reasons of professional pride, never flatly stated that he had tailored his horoscopes to suit his controllers' wishes, instead of embracing the prescribed reading of the heavens—if indeed astrology may be accepted as an authentic science.

Suddenly, in the midst of their discussions, Himmler must have sent a chill through Wulff by saying, "You know, Herr Wulff, what we two are discussing is high treason and could cost us our lives if Hitler were to find out about our plans." Wulff must have been astonished that Himmler's comment was an unequivocal admission that he was, in fact, plotting against Hitler. This emboldened Wulff to respond, "I am convinced that foreign attitudes toward you would change if you could make peace now and put an immediate end to the concentration camps." Kersten himself could not have phrased it better! Wulff claimed to have added that Germany "would soon lose the War"—attributing this insight to the conjunction of the stars. "Your police force is still intact and you can easily take over the government," insisted Wulff. Mustering his arguments further, Wulff also added with a straight face, "Do not wait until it is too late."[14] Himmler gloomily observed that an attempted putsch would set off uprisings throughout the country; it was a very dangerous step, one that could cause serious disturbances. Wulff himself saw this as a possibility, although he did not encourage Himmler in his pessimism.

In his memoirs, Wulff recalled that a good friend, Hamburg publisher Dr. Henry Goverts, an activist in the Kreisau Circle of the Widerstand, headed by Count Helmuth von Moltke, also agreed that a putsch would set off major civil disturbances. Several others in the Kreisau Circle felt the same way. This group of anti-Nazi intellectuals would, nonetheless, be linked with the Wehrmacht military Resistance in the attempted assassination of Hitler on July 20, 1944, by Lieutenant Colonel Claus Schenk von Stauffenberg (code-named Operation Valkyrie). As predicted by Goverts and certain others in the Kreisau Circle, the attempt would fail and trigger massive retaliatory action against Resistance members by the Gestapo throughout the summer of 1944. Wulff, however, following the wishes of Kersten and Schellenberg but attributing his insight to astrological calculations, parried Himmler's pessimism concerning his own chances of staging a coup against the Führer. The astrologer argued with Himmler that chaos need not occur if he could gain the support of leading army generals in advance—in fact, a highly unlikely possibility.

Wulff's close friendship with Dr. Henry Goverts suggests that he, like the publisher, was a secret associate of the Widerstand. The Kreisau Circle had made covert contacts with the Western Allies, looking for support from them much as Himmler was seeking it through Kersten, Schellenberg, and others who were acting as go-betweens. Such Kreisau Circle leaders as von Moltke, Carl-Friedrich Goerdeler, and Hjalmar Schacht, former president of the Reichsbank and minister for economic affairs, had since early in the War been in secret high-level touch with both the British and Americans. Allen Dulles, chief of the American OSS in Bern, Switzerland, was in indirect contact with Abwehr chief Admiral Wilhelm Canaris and the Abwehr Resistance circle through its representative in Switzerland, Hans Bernd Gisevius. German Foreign Ministry officers Adam von Trott zu Solz and his brother, Theodor, at one time German chargé d'affaires in London, among others, maintained secret contact with British intelligence.[15]

Henry Goverts, while having been previously associated with Abwehr, was now working for Schellenberg, who had taken over the military intelligence agency on February 8, 1944, and joined it with the SD after Hitler fired Canaris, ostensibly for failing to anticipate several setbacks for the Germans, including the Allied invasion of North Africa and the defection to the Western Allies of three Abwehr intelligence officers in Turkey.

From November 1944 on, tensions in Germany mounted in proportion to the substantial losses sustained by the Wehrmacht on the Eastern Front. Goverts was sent by Schellenberg to Switzerland to float peace feelers through Allen Dulles. Preliminary talks held with Dulles's German-American assistant, Gero von Schulze-Gaevernitz, in the Rom Inselhotel at Constance came to nothing when Himmler got cold feet and shied away from any contact with Dulles.

Wulff, as an intelligence subagent, was probably reporting through Goverts to Amt VI on matters other than manipulating Himmler with canted horoscopes and astrological readings. Wulff mentions in his memoirs that during the month of November 1944, Goverts "needed to talk to me very often." At that time the situation on the Eastern Front had become serious for the Germans. Goverts must have been asked for intelligence on such key items as weapons and ammunition that were in short supply, declining gasoline supplies causing insufficient truck transport, and railway damage suffered as a result of Allied bombing. Then, strangely, Wulff mentions in his memoirs that Schellenberg's emissaries "were pressing for special astrological calculations concerning the military situation."

It is startling to learn that Schellenberg's Amt VI was relying on astrological techniques to help keep the German military machine running. This, however, may simply have been an exaggeration by Wulff in his postwar effort to impress people with his psychic powers and reestablish himself as a "reliable" astrologer.

Although Goverts at this time was an Amt VI intelligence agent, he had apparently worked for the SD's rival, Abwehr, where he had been part of the Abwehr circle within the Widerstand. While Goverts found himself working for Schellenberg, after the Abwehr was absorbed by the SD, his titular boss became Colonel Georg Hansen, who had replaced Canaris when the latter was removed. Interestingly, Hansen was secretly a member of the Abwehr circle of the Resistance, just as Canaris had been. Hansen and Schellenberg were thus competing putsch plotters, which fact made Goverts's position precarious.

Wulff described how good Goverts's contacts had proven to be when on an earlier occasion he secretly provided Hans Bernd Gisevius with a forged Gestapo pass immediately after the misfired July 20, 1944, bombing of Hitler's headquarters, thus enabling him to make good his escape back to safety in Switzerland in disguise and with a false identity. Despite his being wanted by the Gestapo as a Resistance activist associated with the attempt on Hitler's life, Gisevius reached Switzerland safely[16] thanks to the efforts of Goverts, who delivered to him the needed false documents provided through the underground Abwehr Resistance circle.[17]

In fact, Gisevius was Dulles's accomplice, keeping the station chief apprised of von Stauffenberg's effort to assassinate Hitler, and otherwise providing the OSS a window on Abwehr Resistance activities. It was also Dulles who had undertaken to facilitate Gisevius's secret escape by having Goverts deliver the forged identity documents, which were fabricated by the OSS in London, to Gisevius's hiding place in Germany.[18]

Wulff's description of Himmler was not flattering. The Reichsführer's "jerky movements" and habit of gesticulating as he spoke quickly suggested an innate nervousness. He was of medium height and pallid skin. Himmler's eyes were "mouse gray" with the whites of his eyelids abnormally small, while his eyelids were red as though inflamed. His temples were puffed out while his chin receded "like the jaw of a shark." The comers of his mouth were tightly drawn, "giving his face a sharp look" hiding his "basic feebleness and cruelty."[19]

Wulff saw in Himmler a man who was incredibly naive as well as mediocre when it came to political and military matters. On the occasion of Wulff's first encounter with Himmler, the Reichsführer believed, or pretended to believe, that Germany would soon make peace with the Western Allies. Once an armistice was negotiated with Britain and the United States, the entire German army, with its favorable strategic positions, could effectively prosecute the war in the East against the Soviet Union. In his discussion with Wulff, Himmler hoped that the West would join Germany in fighting Russia. He seemed woefully uninformed about the Tehran Big Three Conference; at least, he did not take seriously the agreement binding the members of the so-called Grand Alliance to remain united in purpose and avoid any temptation to make a separate peace with Germany.

Wulff sensed that he had made an impression on Himmler. The only serious point of difference that had come up had to do with Wulff's astrological interpretation of the "Battle of the Beech Tree," prophesied in ancient Rhenish and Westphalian mythology. While Wulff believed the legend would soon come true—Russia would advance and violate German soil in a kind of a replay of the Mongol invasion of Russia—Himmler was convinced that the old prophecy had nothing to do with the current war and would not come to pass if Germany was enabled to fight on only one front, the Eastern Front.

Wulff concluded he must avoid such disagreements in the future if he was to gain Himmler's complete confidence. And he vowed that his new astrological forecasts would henceforward serve Schellenberg's and Kersten's manipulative purposes.

Because of the mass arrests and a strengthened security crackdown in the wake of the failed July 1944 assassination attempt on Hitler, Wulff felt uneasy in playing his game with the wavering arch-devil himself. Could he trust Himmler? Dulles's assistant, Schulze-Gaevernitz, had in fact tipped off Goverts in advance that the SS—including Schellenberg, of course, and Himmler—knew well in advance of von Stauffenberg's July 20 bomb plot. Such omniscience increased Wulff's unease. Goverts, however, urged Wulff to stick it out and continue as a Resistance source for valuable intelligence. This indicates again that Wulff, through Goverts, was serving the Widerstand as a spy at the same time he served Schellenberg and Kersten in their efforts to convince Himmler to dispose of Hitler and make peace with the Western Allies. These two plotters were discovering that Wulff's slanted astrological reports, as well as his access to Himmler for random discussions of the psychic world so dear to his heart, would prove useful in their efforts to keep the Reichsführer on target and willing to proceed with the Zhitomir plan, despite its obvious risks. Wulff really had no choice but to play the game and be billeted at Kersten's Hartzwalde estate where he would be readily available, closely observed, and at the same time protected from Gestapo interference.

11

Himmler, the Man

In HISTORY, HEINRICH HIMMLER is defined by his atrocities in the cause of Nazism. But a picture of Himmler the man—no less egregious than his works—can be divined from his personality, and perhaps his soul, the well-spring of his evilness. Felix Kersten, whose insight is that of a doctor in almost continual attendance, has left an extraordinary record of his observations. Few people saw Himmler from such a close-up vantage point; fewer still dared to probe as deeply as he did the views of the Reichsführer SS, second only to Hitler himself as the Third Reich's most powerful leader.

On the many occasions Kersten found himself chatting with Himmler on a wide variety of matters as he massaged him to provide relief from chronic stomach distress. Himmler, with little prompting, would run on about his opinions, revealing much about himself. Strangely, perhaps, Himmler seemed to devote more time to ruminating about postwar schemes to per-petuate and glorify a victorious Third Reich, even though he had lost faith in German victory as early as the middle of 1942. He was a man of two minds: one focused on a Germany he wanted to exist, a "thousand-year Reich" created in the image of Nazi philosophy, the other all too aware of the reality of Germany's fate under the rule of a criminally flawed godhead and destined for destruction at the hands of a ruthless Bolshevik enemy. Himmler dreamed of a "utopian" future for Germany, a fantasy at odds with a reality that he recognized in more objective moments. One aspect of his utopia had to do with the role of women in it.

In mid-January 1941, Himmler treated his masseur to a monologue on the "Aryan woman"—the chosen, or *Hohenfrauen,* of the Motherland. (Hitler preferred the label "motherland" to the more traditional German reference to a "fatherland"—a departure from the norm traceable to his strong devotion to his real mother, according to the speculations of some psychologists.) Himmler's ideal Nazi woman would be well bred and would, herself, breed new members of a perfect master race. Not only would she be used as a broodmare to produce blond and blue-eyed children, but she would be a "strong, purposeful" woman such as the Romans had in their "vestals."[1]

Himmler assured Kersten that the object would not be to bestow on all German women rights "as the women's emancipation movement has demanded." A cadre of "chosen women" would, however, be selected as the nucleus of a systematic upgrading of Reich womanhood. Himmler became ecstatic as he described setting up women's "Academies for Wisdom and Culture," in which those chosen for their natural grace of mind and body— and Nordic appearance—would receive the best possible education. The fair, latter-day Rhine maidens would be steeped in Nazi philosophy, history, and foreign languages. Daily games of chess would be part of the curriculum to sharpen their minds, while training in fencing would condition their bodies.[2] But cookery and housekeeping would also be part of their curriculum.

While careers in professions such as government and diplomacy would ultimately be opened to the "chosen women," their initial purpose would be to provide proper wives for Germany's leaders, who would be "honorably" separated from their present "inferior" wives so that they might marry such proper paragons. Others would watch such elite couples and "follow their example." This variation of the holy institute of marriage may not be surprising from a man who kept a mistress—a man whose powers of rationalization in justifying wrong actions was infinite. According to Peter Padfield's treatment of this subject in his excellent biography of the Reichsführer, Himmler described what may have provided his excuse for keeping a mistress: "Too many of the top men in the Reich had married during the 'time of struggle' and the women who had been perfectly appropriate to conditions in the *Reich* then had failed to rise with their menfolk and fill their new station in life. . . . the men took mistresses; scandal was the result."[3]

In 1942, in a letter to SS Lieutenant General Oswald Pohl, Himmler proposed that women whose husbands had been killed or faced a shortage of men because of the War should be put up in a home accommodating some forty thousand women, where they would be expected to bear children sired by appropriate Aryan men. This mass-breeding enterprise would thus strengthen Germany.

Kersten, on occasion, also probed Himmler's attitude toward religion. Born and raised a Roman Catholic, Himmler, the apostate, is a study in psychological meandering. Kersten was struck by Himmler's solemn, superstitious belief in good and evil spirits. While professing some skepticism, Himmler was nonetheless addicted to astrology and would rarely make an important decision without an astrologist to advise him. This, of course, is what caused Kersten and Schellenberg to introduce Himmler to the astrologist Wilhelm Wulff, and then secretly direct the latter in constructing horoscopes calculated to influence the Reichsführer in ways congenial to their objectives.

According to Kersten, Himmler feared an invisible power and a "final accounting" he must make after death—perhaps a variation of his rejected Catholic dogma, although he would deny it and professed to feel totally hostile toward Christianity. In search of a substitute for Christianity, Himmler delved deeply into old Germanic religious ideas—not only of a Nordic nature but Indo-Germanic as well. Himmler had mastered the Hindu *Bhagavad-Gita* and other classics of the subcontinent that he found to be treasure troves of "great Aryan qualities." By unlikely extension, he was obsessed with Tibet and Lamaism. Yet he was a monotheist, believing that the "marvelous order that exists in the world of men, animals and plants can be attributed to a single god, providence, or some other description of a prime-moving force." This concept of a god, he believed, was where Marxism failed. Himmler insisted that all members of the SS must believe in a higher being. The Roman Catholic tenet that one goes to heaven or hell after dying was, as Himmler put it, "a primitive outlook, not worth discussing." He did, however, think that the "Indo-German"—as he called it—belief in reincarnation had merit.[4]

Kersten probed dangerously into Himmler's views on "evil." In response to the masseur's belief that divine grace is a concept that copes with man's evilness, if appealed to, Himmler replied: "In this life you have to pay for everything, so why shouldn't you be presented with a bill in this field too; you can settle up, even if you need one or two—or more—lives to do so."[5] Kersten pressed on, asking Himmler about his own evil deeds. "Are you not often frightened," Kersten asked, "when you reflect on the things you sometimes have to do which one day will be debited against you?" In a vain stretch of reason, Himmler fantasized about how it "may be more pleasant to concern oneself with flower beds than political dust heaps and refuse dumps, but flowers cannot thrive unless these things are seen to."

While it shocks the mind to imagine how Himmler could justify the Holocaust by such incongruous homilies, his grotesque logic says much about the man. He justified his actions by telling Kersten that "for better or worse, the present state of things demands that his role as Reichsführer SS be merged with the role of police chief." He also referred Kersten again to his favorite, the *Bhagavad-Gita,* in which it is written: "It is decreed that whenever men lose their respect for law and truth, and the world is given over to injustice, I will be born anew. I have no desire for gain."[6] This allusion, coming from Himmler, is an example of egregious hypocrisy. And few would hope for a rebirth of Himmler.

Himmler believed this passage justified Hitler, who "rose out of our deepest need." He is "one of those brilliant figures who always appears in the Germanic world when it has reached a final crisis in body, mind and soul." Himmler was convinced that "it had been ordained by the Karma of the Germanic world that he [Hitler] would wage war against the East [Russia] and save the Germanic people." Kersten, subjected to this and more of Himmler's philosophical monologue, now understood how Himmler, with his warped sense of values, considered Hitler "a person whom men would regard in centuries to come with the same reverence that they had accorded to Christ," and fantasized that he himself was a reincarnation of "Henry the Lion" of German epic history.[7]

Another retrospective assessment of Himmler was written by Schellenberg's subordinate Wilhelm Hoettl. His area of specialty was the supremely important Eastern Front, eastern Europe, and the Balkans. Hoettl had very pronounced opinions of Himmler, none of which were flattering. He described Himmler as so many have: "looking and thinking like a petty bank clerk." While Himmler had taken part in Hitler's misfired putsch of April 9, 1923, and remained a booster of National Socialism, he seemed at the outset to have little to offer. On one occasion he was temporarily fired for an unmilitary demeanor, but otherwise he hung on, attracting little attention—certainly gaining no kudos.

In Hoettl's opinion, there was but one reason that this unprepossessing man, holding the rank of Reichsführer SS but inspiring ridicule on the part of his colleagues, reached the rarified heights of Nazi leadership. He was a creature of Reinhard Heydrich; it was Heydrich who pushed him to the top. The ambitious, Machiavellian Heydrich saw Himmler as a malleable person whom he could mold to his own design despite an inferior intellect and an undistinguished appearance. Lurking in Himmler's shadow, Heydrich bided his time, waiting for an opportunity to maneuver him out of office and take his place.[8]

Heydrich had been the architect of the plan by which the Reichsführer gained control of the Nazi police and intelligence system, and enhanced the power of the SS to the point it became a state within a state, controlling a massive industrial empire advantaged by its ability to use slave labor. Heydrich's death in 1942 at the hands of Czech assassins in Prague left Himmler with the acquisitions of power engineered by Heydrich, but without the ability to promote his position much further. Although second only to Hitler within the top ranks of the Third Reich, it was by no means certain that he could ever outmaneuver Ribbentrop or Bormann at Hitler's court.

Schellenberg had learned much by watching Heydrich and aspired to replace him when he died. He also sought to fill Heydrich's place as the "power behind the Himmler throne" and, as was evident, use the Reichsführer as cat's-paw in his grand design to remove Hitler from office, negotiate peace with the Western Powers, and, in a one-front war, destroy Russia. Himmler, however, did not see fit to replace Heydrich with Schellenberg. Kaltenbrunner, instead, was made head of the RSHA, although Himmler, as we have seen, gave Schellenberg the privilege of reporting directly to him without going through Kaltenbrunner. Himmler sensed perhaps that it would be dangerous to lodge too much power in Schellenberg, thus perpetuating the Heydrich pattern in which he would be manipulated by a stronger-willed, more able subordinate. Yet Himmler had allowed Schellenberg to be his secret instrument in seeking a deal with the West. Knowledge of Himmler's dangerous plunge into high treason against his Führer gave Schellenberg a strong weapon to use over his boss should it become expedient—and, of course, vice versa. Schellenberg, all too unsure of Himmler's faint heart, fluctuating resolve, and split psyche on this matter, realized Kersten's value to him as a person with the advantages of propinquity and medical indispensability; he could help keep Himmler on track without backsliding. Kersten's influence, he believed, could also prove useful in protecting him from Himmler should the latter find it expedient to sacrifice someone to save himself.

Hoettl saw Himmler as weak and essentially cowardly, but also realized that he was a neurotic man. He hated with a vengeance the Roman Catholic

Church from which he had bolted early in life. He also hated—and feared—Freemasonry in Germany. And, of course, he was pathologically anti-Jewry, which he saw as a world conspiracy that must be wiped out. Finding a form of religious consolation in his interpretation of German history, he fantasized about various reincarnations, including his life as Prince Henry the Fowler, folk hero of the German people.

Concerned by the treatment of Jews in the Third Reich, Kersten discussed the matter on numerous occasions while giving Himmler massages. He systematically tried to convince the Reichsführer that if he wished to survive after the inevitable German defeat, he should take some action to convince the Allies that he deserved leniency. In November 1942, by which time Himmler realized that Allied victory was inevitable, Kersten had again brought up the Jewish situation.[9]

Reiterating a constant theme of his many talks with Himmler, Kersten told the Reichsführer that if he wanted to show some humanity and perhaps redeem himself in the eyes of the world, he must circumvent Hitler's orders for systematically killing all Jews. Himmler's frightened response was that the Führer "would immediately have me hanged!" He finally conceded weakly, however, that he might "let certain categories of Jews held in concentration camps go to a neutral country."[10]

On June 17, 1944, Kersten's arguments seemed to have reached their target when Himmler showed some interest in Kersten's idea that Sweden might be willing to grant a haven for Jews held in Germany and other countries under German control. Soon afterward, in the course of a lunch with his close subordinates Gottlob Berger, Rudolf Brandt, and Schellenberg, as well as Kersten, the Reichsführer announced that he had "recently given much thought to the matter . . . [and] was prepared to let Jews go abroad." His explanation for this change of heart was, however, ungracious to say the least: "extermination was a dirty business; and secondly, it aroused a good deal of ill-will as innocent people were too stupid and too ignorant to realize the necessity for it."[11] Left unsaid was Himmler's naive hope that some such eleventh-hour show of humanity might save him from the gallows when Germany capitulated to its enemies—by now a foregone conclusion in the Reichsführer's mind.

Himmler had obviously embraced Hitler's Final Solution, the implementation of which was his responsibility, although he sometimes recoiled from the future implications of his role as Germany's grim reaper. According to

Kersten, Hitler himself was the one who had set in motion serious planning for the genocidal destruction of the Jews; the masseur then paraphrased Himmler's endorsement of the Führer's idea: "The Jews . . . dominate the entire world . . . the damage which the Jews have been doing for centuries— and the future would only be worse—is of a kind so comprehensive that it can only be met by eliminating them entirely."[12]

Himmler, with tortuous reasoning, told Kersten, "If National Socialism is going to be destroyed, then its enemies and the criminals in concentration camps shall not have the satisfaction of emerging from our ruin as triumphant conquerors."[13] Such diatribes disgusted and terrified Kersten.

Assuming that Germany would lose the war, Sweden impressed Kersten as being his best haven from the dangers of a defeated Reich overrun with Russians and the forces of the Western Allies. Hartzwalde, his home in Germany, would certainly be in the path of the Red Army advancing from the east; he would not expect mercy from them. By the spring of 1943, Kersten believed that it was none too soon to make arrangements for moving his family to Sweden. He could only hope that his neutral oasis would accept him. From the early part of the war, he had shown himself willing to be cooperative with the Swedish government and had responded positively when the Swedish ambassador to Germany, Arvid Richert, had discreetly approached him during the summer of 1942. Richert had at that time appealed to Kersten to use his influence with Himmler to have released seven Swedish businessmen working in Poland who had been charged by the Gestapo with espionage on behalf of Sweden.

12

Enter the OSS

O N A TRIP TO SWEDEN in September 1943, Kersten met with Swedish foreign minister Christian Günther, who discussed on a confidential basis several subjects of mutual interest. Kersten's stock had risen in Günther's opinion after the masseur had expressed his willingness to try and talk Himmler into freeing a significant number of Swedish prisoners languishing in German custody, including particularly the seven businessmen mentioned by Richert. Kersten had used the argument with the Reichsführer that good relations with Sweden would help Germany, which depended on various important imports from Sweden such as iron and ball bearings in prosecuting the War.[1]

Relations between Sweden and Germany were suffering because of Hitler's perception that the Swedes were not cooperating with Germany to the extent they could. Kersten confidentially revealed to the Swedish foreign minister that in July 1942, Himmler had told the Finnish foreign minister, Rolf Johan Witting, in his presence that Hitler had become so angry with Sweden that he regretted not occupying that country at the same time as he had occupied Norway in 1940. Hitler was particularly intent on keeping an uninterrupted supply of Swedish iron ore for Germany's defense industries and would let nothing stand in his way in getting it.[2] Kersten also confided that during Himmler's July 1942 visit to Finland, the Reichsführer had described to Foreign Minister Witting Hitler's plan to carve up Sweden between Germany and Finland after the War—assuming, of course, that Germany would win. Finland would be awarded the northern half of Sweden while Germany would annex central and southern Sweden to a greater Reich.

Günther, grateful for Kersten's offer to help in the freeing of the seven so-called Warsaw Swedes, took the occasion to ask Kersten's help in convincing Himmler to accept a plan he had drafted to free Scandinavian subjects kept in German concentration camps. The centerpiece of Günther's request was a long list of specific Swedish nationals, including Jews, whom his government was anxious to have released. Taking full advantage of his relationship with Günther and the positive aura of their discussions, Kersten felt the time was right to rent an apartment in Stockholm, a haven of safety where he could keep his family if things went badly for him in Germany. The eminent Swedish banker Jacob Wallenberg was of considerable help in preparing the way; he discreetly cut through the bureaucracy to obtain the necessary permits for his friend's new home. By mid-June 1943, a flat was partly furnished and waiting for Kersten to move in.[3]

On September 30, 1943, Kersten made his own move to Sweden. He flew to Stockholm documented as a Finnish courier, thanks to the Finnish ambassador, T. M. Kivimäkki. In this way Kersten could take with him his highly secret and compromising papers, including cryptic notes from which he could flesh out his diaries and personal correspondence in the relatively safe environment of Stockholm, free from the Gestapo's prying eyes.

The Finns had made it clear that they expected Kersten to continue his role as their eyes and ears within Himmler's domain. The Swedish government and the Dutch underground also would profit by having their "friend" within commuting distance of the heart of the Third Reich as Kersten still responded very frequently to Himmler's summons. Kersten's position remained precarious, however. Ernst Kaltenbrunner of the RSHA and the Gestapo's Heinrich Müller would continue to keep their eyes on him.

Relations between Finland and Germany were strained. In its efforts to loosen the ties binding it to Germany, Finland hoped that the United States might still prove helpful, even though an earlier effort to use the Vatican as an intermediary in negotiating an agreement guaranteeing Finland's territorial integrity had failed.[4]

The Finns also had heard reports originating with the Russian envoy in Stockholm, Mme. Aleksandra Kolantay, that, as documented in the British record office, "Stalin was considering a Finnish-Soviet peace formula calling for a return to the 1939 borders as they existed before World War II broke out."[5] In fact, there had been reports that the Soviets were dangling peace offers before the Nazis in the hope, if not assumption, that Hitler's reverses along the Eastern Front would make the Führer consider a negotiated settlement.[6] The United States at this time had been generally in favor of extracting Finland from Nazi Germany's grip in order to provide Russia some relief as it reeled before Hitler's panzers.

The question of Finland would acquire a new dimension in October 1943 when Kersten was introduced to Abram Stevens Hewitt, an American "businessman" recently arrived in Stockholm. It had soon become rumored in that city that Hewitt was a friend of Franklin Roosevelt's who had been sent to Sweden to report to the president on events from this neutral vantage point. In fact, Hewitt was in Stockholm under the aegis of OSS, although he was close to Roosevelt. Hewitt's meeting with Kersten would prove fateful.

During the autumn of 1943, the OSS in Sweden had come under new management. Dr. Bruce Hopper had been replaced by his deputy, Wilho Tikander. In addition, a new Special Operations team had been created, headed by George Brewer, a former Yale professor who had gained fame as a Broadway playwright who wrote the hit play *Dark Victory,* starring Tallulah Bankhead.[7]

Aware of Hewitt's connections with Roosevelt, Kersten had great hopes that his discussions with the American would prove useful to his and Schellenberg's plan to prod Himmler into seeking peace with the West. Hewitt, a graduate of Harvard and Oxford and socially well connected in the United States, seemed to be just the person he needed as a contact. Kersten noted in his diary that Hewitt's good friend Holger Graffman had brought them together. While the American initially spoke of needing massages for a "bad back," his conversation with Kersten quickly made it apparent that he was interested in talking politics, just as Kersten was. The first subject discussed was Finland. Himmler's therapist noted in his diary that he considered himself fortunate to have been put in touch with a man well placed in the United States. Kersten expressed his hope that an occasion would soon arise to make it possible for Finland to make peace with Russia. But, Kersten stressed, "it must be peace with honour."[8] At their next meeting, Finland again dominated their conversation. Kersten, in an October 8 entry in his diary, noted that Hewitt believed it possible that President Roosevelt would be willing to intervene in arranging peace between Finland and Russia since "America still has great sympathy for Finland."[9]

Kersten responded to Hewitt by volunteering that Finland essentially disliked Nazi Germany, noting that it was only Finland's despair over its winter war with Russia on the eve of World War II that drove it into alliance with Germany. Kersten cryptically noted in his October 25 diary entry that he was summoned to Finland to give the new Finnish foreign minister, Dr. Henrik Ramsay, information on his conversations with Hewitt.[10] Kersten said while talking with Hewitt that he intended to visit Finland soon and would take up the matter with the Finnish government. The American told Kersten that he was prepared to act as an intermediary between Finland and Russia, but only if Finland "made the first move."[11] Progress had been made.

The OSS had made earlier efforts to help Finland divorce itself from Germany's control. In June 22, 1942, it had sent to Helsinki an astute and attractive American agent named Therese Bonney under cover as a war reporter for *Colliers* magazine. Her daring mission was to make secret contact with the great Finnish leader Marshal Carl Mannerheim, a friend from the dark days of the Russo-Finnish War when she covered the action as a freelance correspondent. Bonney reached Mannerheim for secret discussions despite Gestapo efforts to interdict her. Speaking for the United States government, she tried to convince the marshal to use his influence to have Finland withdraw from its close relationship with Germany. But her mission failed; the Finns could not yet hope to shed their country's vassalage under Hitler.[12]

OSS chief William Donovan had also sent to Finland as "special agent" Stanton Griffis, chairman of the board of Madison Square Garden and owner of the Brentano's book chain. Arriving in Helsinki in December 1942, he set about establishing an intelligence network throughout Scandinavia targeted mainly at Germany's Eastern Front forces.[13]

Kersten did in fact spend mid-October 1943 in Helsinki as he had promised Hewitt, and discussed the latter's offer to act as intermediary between the United States and Ramsay, but serious complications became apparent and soon spoiled this plan. In March 1943, Secretary of State Cordell Hull had instructed the U.S. envoy in Helsinki, Robert McClintock, to query the Finnish government as to its willingness to have the United States act as mediator between Finland and Russia toward breaking Finland's tie with Germany and reaching a peace agreement with Stalin. Ramsay, it seems, somehow learned that Germany had broken U.S. diplomatic ciphers and had been reading State Department correspondence, so he felt compelled to tip off the Germans as to the American overtures. This soured American relations with Finland and for the time being ended any possibility of U.S. mediation.[14] A disappointed Hull informed President Roosevelt that the State Department "had unmistakable evidence that the Germans, learning of our approach, brought increased pressure on the Finns not to enter into any discussions with us with a view to any contact with the Soviet Government."[15]

Kersten's actions in October 1943 with regard to Finland give further insight to his role for the Finnish government at that time. In a memo of meeting with the new Finnish foreign minister on October 25, after returning to Stockholm, he wrote for his own personal records:

> I explained to him [Ramsay] that the German military situation was hopeless and that Germany could hold on at the most another one or two more years. In my opinion a total breakdown would follow. I considered it absolutely necessary for Finland to put out peace feelers now in order to extricate itself from German clutches which, I thought, was not weighing as heavily on Finland any more. Furthermore, I told Ramsay that in case he wished to use it, I had a direct connection to Roosevelt. There was in Stockholm at present a special representative, Mr. Hewitt, who was a patient of mine and whom I could use as a point of liaison. I told Ramsay that I thought, however, it advisable that the Finnish Minister in Stockholm, Griepenberg, should conduct these negotiations. Ramsay was much pleased to learn about this connection and asked me to bring about the connection Griepenberg-Hewitt.

Kersten had welcomed his new relationship with Hewitt as it concerned the Finnish problem, but he saw in the OSS agent an even more important role. He believed that Hewitt could provide him and Schellenberg with a link to the West in their efforts to encourage Himmler to act against Hitler as discussed at Zhitomir in August 1942.

Kersten asked Graffman how best to deal with the Americans in such a scenario. Graffman was as frank as he was realistic in warning Kersten that the United States, bound by its pact with Great Britain and the USSR, would never unilaterally negotiate any deal with the Third Reich nor have anything to do with Himmler—or any other Nazi leader. Nonetheless, Kersten persisted in explaining his and Schellenberg's intentions to overturn Hitler, although he was purposely vague about Himmler's role and, more broadly, the role of the SS in their thinking. Kersten, of course, knew that if Himmler mustered the courage to proceed with the plan agreed upon with Schellenberg at Zhitomir, he would, if successful, insist on his prize: to become the ruler of Germany.

On October 24, Kersten again sought Graffman's advice. Graffman, whom he described in his diary entry of this date as a very intelligent and farsighted person, expressed to him his convictions that Germany could not win the war because "American technology and aircraft production are on a scale that will overwhelm Germany. . . . Germany will break up in another six months." Graffman added that this would mark the end of Hitler's Third Reich, but would ensure dark days in Europe. He told Kersten, "For that reason the sooner peace is made the better."

When Kersten complained that the West underestimated the danger emerging from the East, Graffman retorted, "That's why it is so urgently necessary to make peace [with the West] in good time." Graffman also pointed out that the West would not make peace with Hitler; he and his regime "had to go first."[16]

Notwithstanding Graffman's counsel, Kersten began discussions with Hewitt. They had several long talks, all of which seemed to have gone well. Hewitt was not reticent about discussing such things. Indicative of the interest, or at least curiosity, aroused in Washington can be seen by the fact that the essence of the exchanges were passed as aide-mémoire to the British and Soviet partners in the Grand Alliance.[17]

On October 24, 1943, Kersten wrote Himmler from Stockholm describing his conversations with Hewitt and their informally agreed upon seven-point proposal, "which might have the greatest significance for Germany, for Europe, even for the entire world." They offered "the possibility of an honorable peace." The specific points were, to say the least, amazing:

1. Evacuation of all territories occupied by Germany and restitution of their sovereignty.
2. Abolition of the Nazi Party: democratic elections under American and British supervision.
3. Abolition of Hitler's dictatorship.
4. Restitution of the 1914 German frontier.
5. Reduction of the German army and air force to a size excluding the possibility of aggression.
6. Complete control of the German armament industry by the Americans and British.
7. Removal of the leading Nazis and their appearance before a court charged with war crimes.

Kersten concluded his message to Himmler with an impassioned plea: "Herr Reichsführer, fate and history have placed it in your hands to bring an end to this terrible war."[18]

Kersten wrote to Hewitt after he had discussed their meetings with Himmler, saying that "Himmler . . . knows that the War is lost and is anxious to arrive at an arrangement with the Americans and British [note the absence of "USSR"] which would leave something of Germany." Kersten declared further that realizing it would be impossible for the Americans and British to deal with Hitler, "Himmler was now quite prepared to bring about his overthrow."[19]

It should be noted that Kersten, well aware of the U.S. and British attitude, omitted any mention of the fact that Himmler considered himself Hitler's replacement. While this was perhaps implicit, Kersten's message obviously sought to dodge the issue. Also avoided was explicit mention of Himmler's intention to continue the War against Russia. Hewitt, however, had little doubt about Himmler's intentions. Hewitt's old acquaintance Jacob Wallenberg had discussed this with him in August 1943, and had asked him if he would be willing to meet a representative of the Resistance.[20] When Hewitt pursued the matter again with Wallenberg in October, the latter explained that the Resistance, meaning the Widerstand, weighted in favor of Wehrmacht and Abwehr dissidents, had been effectively neutralized; therefore, the only possible replacement for Hitler now would have to emerge as the result of a full-scale German army revolt or a move by Himmler and the SS to remove him.[21]

Kersten's plea to Himmler that he send Schellenberg to pursue with Hewitt further possibilities of peace was approved by the Reichsführer after much soul-searching. Schellenberg, using the cover name Schellenkampf and pretending to be a German businessman, arrived in Stockholm on November 9, 1943. Kersten noted in his diary that he wished that Schellenberg's conversations with Hewitt would lead to peace. Having returned to Berlin from Stockholm on December 4, Kersten continued to urge Himmler to act: "The German people and Europe await your decision. . . . Don't hesitate, Herr Reichsführer; grant peace to Europe if you really want to appear before history as a great Germanic leader. In Stockholm Mr. Hewitt is waiting for your decision so that he can take it to Roosevelt."[22]

Schellenberg's version of what transpired, as gleaned from his postwar interrogation in mid-July 1945, is interesting. It can be guessed that he did his best to impress Hewitt with his sincerity—and his innocence as far as war crimes were concerned. He described Hewitt as an American patient of Kersten's in Stockholm. No specific mention was made of Hewitt's affiliation with the OSS, nor was there any hint that Hewitt's "medical reason" for meeting Kersten was mainly for cover purposes, although Hewitt, in fact, had a sore back at the time. Schellenberg described the object of his meeting as enabling "an open discussion of the best and quickest means of ending the War . . ." Significantly, Schellenberg noted realistically that "from the very beginning, Germany was to be tacitly regarded as the party seeking to make a compromise [peace settlement]." This surely would not have been a convincing assumption as far as the ever-suspicious Stalin was concerned. And, considering Stalin's access to the Western Allies' intelligence apparatus through spies serving Russia, such as Britain's Kim Philby and others, he must have been duly informed of this drama from the beginning and as it unfolded.

Schellenberg justifiably let it be known to the Western Allies through Hewitt that he had incurred "considerable risk by having . . . such a conversation with Hewitt." He claimed, in the first place, that he had no authorization to talk with representatives of a hostile power, and that he had no authorization to discuss Germany's peace plans; it was in fact forbidden. He said that he knew nothing of Hewitt; he might have been an agent provocateur as far as he knew, and his conversation might be used against him in a press campaign. Moreover, he could not predict how the volatile Himmler would react when told of the conversation.

These may well have been pro forma disclaimers. As his narrative, acquired under interrogation, unfolds below, it is clear that Schellenberg knew quite a bit about Hewitt, including his closeness with President Roosevelt, since Kersten had briefed him well:

> In conversation Hewitt was represented as a man of no small importance in America, especially in circles close to Roosevelt. Hewitt was represented to me by Kersten as an emissary of the U.S. President and the U.S. Secretary of State, especially commissioned to examine and study the German question, in the post-war period as well. Hewitt was a wealthy and independent man, in whom I could have complete confidence. His first wife was a Vanderbilt, his present wife was a Huchesson. He was also well-known socially to Mrs. Roosevelt.

Schellenberg continued:

> I visited Hewitt in his hotel, and the conversation took place in the sitting room of his apartment. Kersten did no more than introduce us, and then left us alone. Hewitt came to meet me in a very friendly manner; he was a quiet, pleasant man with whom I soon felt on good terms. We very soon agreed not to waste time in diplomatic fencing, but to come to the point clearly and directly. From the beginning Hewitt was

at pains to make it clear that he had no official function and was not a diplomat, and that on that account our conversation was valuable only from the point of view of information. This attitude agreed entirely with my own, so this question was settled in advance for both of us.[23]

Schellenberg then presented an overview of the situation in Europe as seen by him:

> With complete frankness, . . . I explained to Hewitt my view of the general situation in Germany, mentioning especially the ever-increasing internal difficulties; the very critical position in state, party and economics; the ever-increasing war-weariness of the entire population with all its consequences; the widespread radical feeling in the working classes; and the gradual relaxation of effort, the almost systematic lowering of resistance—in strength and willpower—of the Wehrmacht, with the exception of a few special troops and the Waffen SS. My plan was to persuade Himmler as soon as possible to make a proposal of compromise to the Western powers—but *I deliberately left it vague whether this would be with or without Hitler's consent* [author's italics].[24]

In the meantime, Kersten, now in Berlin, became depressed by Himmler's vacillation. The Reichsführer could not yet bring himself to take the big step; he could not yet bear to betray his Führer: "Everything I am, I owe to him." Finally, on the morning of December 9, Himmler told Kersten that he had come to the end of his inner conflict and was ready to allow Schellenberg to negotiate seriously with Hewitt, but he added: "America should make an effort to understand Germany and should show signs of good faith."[25]

Himmler told Kersten to let Hewitt know this, but stressed that "the utmost secrecy should be observed." Kersten had done all he could do in bringing Himmler around to agree; and Schellenberg now had held what he considered encouraging talks with Hewitt.

As he headed back to Berlin, Schellenberg was euphoric. The head of the SD sensed another achievement in the making to add to his string of operational successes.

In discussing the Hewitt meeting immediately upon Schellenberg's return, Himmler seemed to be eager to proceed with serious negotiations with the American, who could perhaps be smuggled into Berlin for secret talks with him. But to the dismay of Schellenberg, Himmler again lost his nerve, protesting that he could not bring himself to betray his Führer. Arguing with Himmler, Schellenberg stressed that Hewitt was potentially too valuable to drop. Still the Reichsführer hesitated. Nursing a false state of denial, an anguished Himmler added ingenuously, "Am I to become a traitor?" What seemed to bother Himmler the most, however, was the point that had been discussed and informally agreed upon by Kersten and Hewitt stating that Nazi leaders would be held accountable for "war crimes."[26]

Finally, however, the mercurial Himmler soon seemed to have had another change of attitude. Schellenberg noted in his memoirs that in late December 1943, Himmler told him that he now realized that some steps had to be taken if Germany was to be saved from total destruction. To Schellenberg's astonishment, Himmler blurted out: "For God's sake, don't let your contact with Hewitt be broken off, . . . I am ready to have a conversation with him."[27]

But it was too late; Kersten heard from sources in Sweden that Hewitt "had fallen from favor because of his talks in Stockholm with Himmler's representative, Walter Schellenberg, and had retired from political life altogether, devoting himself to horse breeding."[28] In fact, Hewitt had not fallen from favor, but Washington did not want to pursue further the Reichsführer's overtures because of solemn commitments made to Stalin and because Himmler was in such disrepute.

The scene must now shift to Washington as OSS chief Donovan passes on to President Roosevelt Hewitt's report—his version and views of his talks with both Kersten and Schellenberg.

13

Hewitt Reports to President Roosevelt

ON MARCH 20, 1944, General William ("Wild Bill") Donovan, director of the Office of Strategic Services, passed on to President Roosevelt a memorandum sent to him by Abram Hewitt (code designation number 610), OSS agent in Stockholm, under cover of the United States Commercial Company. Hewitt's message, which summed up his conversations with Felix Kersten and Walter Schellenberg, emissaries of Himmler, must surely have caught the president's attention. Not only were its contents startling, but the report had been sent by Hewitt, his longtime friend whom he had sent to Stockholm under the aegis of OSS to get a feel for the role and significance of Scandinavia.[1] The report is excerpted in the following pages to provide an authentic account of Hewitt's version of his talks with Schellenberg.

William Donovan's position and his personal relationship with the president gave him easy access to the White House. Hewitt's report, however, was more important than most communications that required Roosevelt's personal attention: it concerned a secret proposal proffered by Heinrich Himmler, and iterated by Schellenberg and Kersten, for ousting Hitler and negotiating peace with the Western Allies as a first step in fighting a one-front, one-enemy war with the Soviet Union—with or without help from the United States and Britain. As head of the Waffen SS forces and czar of

Nazi security and intelligence matters, Himmler had power in his own right, but his power flowed even more convincingly from that fact that he was among the most trusted of Hitler's acolytes. Yet the import of Reichsführer SS Himmler's proposal, as transmitted by Kersten and Schellenberg, unmistakably bespoke Himmler's high treason against the Führer.

In a brief introduction to the OSS agent's report, Donovan wrote: "Here is a statement made by Abram Hewitt, whom I think you know. He was in Sweden for some time and these notes represent a meeting with Dr. Kersten, attending physical therapist of Himmler, and the efforts of Felix Kersten to induce Hewitt to go to Germany [for talks with the Reichsführer himself]." Donovan assured President Roosevelt that he had told Hewitt "not to do this as I assumed you would not care to have Americans in Germany on such a basis."

It is curious that Donovan's introductory note features Kersten and makes scant reference to Schellenberg, who had delved more deeply into arranging the meeting and devising the means by which Hewitt could be brought into Germany clandestinely. Perhaps Donovan sensed that the masseur had the

General William ("Wild Bill") Donovan, World War I hero and head of the Office of Strategic Services (OSS) in World War II, received secret peace overtures from Schellenberg and Kersten. (Courtesy of Elizabeth McIntosh, OSS operative)

greater influence on the Reichsführer. Hewitt's version of his meetings with Kersten and Schellenberg provide a rare glimpse of an OSS covert political action involving someone of Himmler's rank and power.

Hewitt described how he met Kersten in October 1943. Feigning a "bad back" to provide him cover for frequent meetings with the masseur, and realizing that Kersten, too, was interested in the meetings for political reasons, Hewitt got right down to business—but always mythically insisting that he was not speaking for the U.S. government. Dubious about any such liaison with emissaries from the Devil's domain, OSS officers had usually brushed off earlier efforts by the Nazis to make contact. Among other reasons, the Americans were concerned lest Stalin resent and protest any apparent machination that left him out of the picture. Throughout the War, the Soviet dictator feared that in the end, as Germany realized that defeat was imminent and inevitable, the Western Allies would cook a deal with the Nazis and turn on Russia. Roosevelt, particularly, did not want to aggravate Stalin's paranoia by creating an appearance of weakening the solidarity of the Grand Alliance. But seeing a political action opportunity to sow discord among the Nazi leaders, Hewitt was not reticent about responding positively to Kersten. He sensed that the therapist was a victim of circumstances beyond his control; he was not a Nazi, nor was he irrevocably bound to Himmler, witness his having begun the process of moving to Sweden. He believed Kersten was eager to establish his own relationships with the West rather than be compromised by his link to the Reichsführer when the Third Reich crumbled in defeat and its evil paladins were judged by the victors.

As background, Hewitt's report described the prevailing local attitude in Stockholm toward the War, particularly on the part of Swedish industrialists: "While in a political sense the Swedes are freedom-loving people . . . there is in Sweden a very deep-seated fear and distrust of Russia and the motives of the existing Russian government [under Stalin]. The Swedes, therefore, are looking for a counterweight to Russia after the War. They believe that the only effective counterweight for them is Germany." Hewitt added: "On this account and due to the fact that a very big proportion of Swedish foreign trade is conducted with Germany, the Swedes are anxious that Germany should not be totally destroyed. In fact, the Swedes would like to see . . . the least possible destruction of Germany."[2]

Hewitt elaborated on Swedish-German industrial and banking ties. He described the influence wielded by Enskilda Banken, a bank dominating Sweden's mining and manufacturing sector of the economy and controlled by the powerful Wallenberg family. Jacob Wallenberg handled the bank's dealings with Germany and the rest of continental Europe, while his younger brother, Marcus, was responsible for relations with the English-speaking world, including South Africa.

Hewitt explained that he had first met Jacob Wallenberg in 1932 while in Stockholm representing a trustee in the bankruptcy of the International Match Corporation, an American holding company for the Ivar Kreuger interests. In the course of reorganizing the company, the Wallenbergs had assumed control of the Swedish Match Corporation and its far-flung international subsidiaries. Clearly, Hewitt was no stranger to Sweden and had many influential contacts there.

More than a decade later, in August 1943, as war raged in Europe, Hewitt made contact again with his old acquaintance, Jacob. Aware that Hewitt was well connected in the United States and was even a friend of President Roosevelt, Wallenberg, secretly tied in with the German Resistance, confided freely in him.[3] Explaining that he was "in touch with a cross-section of the high ranking German financial and manufacturing interests," Wallenberg told him that Resistance "cells were forming in Germany for the purpose of overthrowing Hitler." He asked Hewitt if he "would be willing to meet with representatives of such cells." Because of the highly sensitive political nature of this information, Hewitt informed Herschel Johnson, the American minister in Stockholm, who telegraphed it to the State Department.

In commenting on Hitler, Wallenberg explained to Hewitt that "his friends" in Germany—a euphemistic reference to Resistance members he knew—were somewhat perplexed about the Reichsführer's true motives. While Himmler was supposed to be entirely loyal to Hitler, certain changes were taking place in Germany that could only raise questions in the minds of intelligence observers. Hewitt drew the conclusion that Wallenberg, though vague on this score, meant that Himmler's intention was to oust Hitler and take over Germany's government himself as a prelude to reaching a peace agreement with the Western Allies. It was Wallenberg's opinion that by the summer of 1942—if not before, in December 1941, when the United States entered the War—Himmler was convinced that Germany would lose, and so he had begun searching for ways to ingratiate himself with the Western Allies, using the SS and the Nazi Party security apparatus as bargaining chips in an unrealistic scenario in which Germany, governed by him in alliance with the Western Powers, would turn their guns on the Russians and defeat the mutually hated Communist bogey. Strangely insensitive to the revulsion felt toward him by the West for atrocities he was known to have committed, but well aware of his fate if the Russians were to capture him upon Germany's ultimate capitulation, Himmler was sending out feelers to the Americans in Sweden and other neutral countries through a variety of go-betweens. But his principal point men in this treacherous enterprise were Walter Schellenberg and Felix Kersten. As Hewitt himself discovered, Schellenberg, responsible for foreign intelligence, was useful because of his professional contacts and ability to hide his special tasks for Himmler within his organization. And Kersten, who traveled often to Sweden, where he was establishing a permanent home, was able to make contact with the American OSS without attracting attention.

In Stockholm, Herschel Johnson had not yet received a response to the message he had sent to the State Department concerning Himmler's indirect feelers to Hewitt, nor did Hewitt soon hear again from Wallenberg. Three months would go by before the two men would meet again. In the meantime, Himmler had been named the interior minister by Hitler, making him still more powerful. When Jacob Wallenberg finally appeared—having been in Germany or elsewhere in Europe—he reported that the Resistance situation had changed in Germany because of increased focus by the Gestapo on the military—particularly Abwehr dissidents and certain prominent civilians with whom they were allied in the Widerstand. According to Hewitt's report, Wallenberg gave as his opinion that the only alternatives to Hitler were Himmler, backed primarily by the Waffen SS and the Gestapo, or the Wehrmacht secret opposition cells if they could survive Gestapo harassment and rally the main body of the army before Hitler became aware of what was going on and destroyed them—not an easy thing to do in the midst of mortal combat with enemies on two fronts. What Hewitt and presumably Jacob Wallenberg did not know at this time was that Hitler's deputy, Martin Bormann, and Gestapo chief Heinrich Müller had found a way to establish secret contact with the Soviets, on whom they were placing their bets for determining the fate of Europe after the War.[4] It had become clear to Hewitt, however, that the secret "organized" opposition to Hitler was a complicated matter.

There were those in Stockholm who believed that Hitler and the German war effort were not doomed to fail anytime soon. Hewitt described the logic used to reach such optimism on the part of certain of his other Swedish contacts: "The Germans, perhaps, could not win the war, but they did not feel that the German position was hopeless, and they would continue to fight." Such Swedish hopes were based on (1) A successful resistance to the

Russians after shortening their lines somewhere near the German border, (2) the belief that they [the Germans] would be able to repulse the invasion launched from England, and (3) the devastating effects of their [the Germans] so-called secret weapon when used. Gossip had it that this weapon would only be used when the invasion from England was launched.[5]

In the second part of his report, Hewitt provided some additional background on the still somewhat enigmatic Kersten. Hewitt explained that it had been in early October when a Swedish friend, Holger Graffman, who held a key position in Wallenberg's business organization, had urged him to make contact with Dr. Felix Kersten, who had the exalted rank of Medizinalrat in Finland. Graffman explained: This title, the highest Finnish honor awarded to medical doctors, was held by only three living men. This honor was recognized as prestigious in Finland and Sweden, and permitted its holder to use the title "doctor." While it was considered a valid medical rank, it did not confer the right to practice standard medicine.

Although Hewitt's Swedish friend was not acquainted with Kersten personally, he had been told that the therapist was one of the most powerful men in Germany—an exaggeration, perhaps, but Kersten had by then acquired a remarkable influence over the Reichsführer SS. Himmler had become dependent on Kersten because of the masseur's unique ability to alleviate his chronic, sometimes unbearable, stomach pains. A distinguished British World War II intelligence officer and eminent historian, Hugh Trevor-Roper, after the War knighted as Lord Dacre of Glanton, observed that Kersten was able to "manipulate the conscience as well as the stomach of that . . . inhuman, but naive, mystical tyrant of the 'New Order.'"[6]

During his sessions of "back therapy," his cover for the meetings with Kersten, Hewitt was able to learn much about the Finnish masseur's background and pick up some interesting observations concerning Himmler as well. The Reichsführer was fanatically anti-Russian, one of the many traits attributed to his Nazi racism. He had "a great fear of the consequences of the high Russian birth rate." Disliking the threatening mixture of Slav blood with German blood, Himmler was determined to do almost anything rather than see Stalin win the War. Himmler had a preference for the Anglo-Saxons because of the similarity of their blood and racial characteristics with the Germans. By way of impressing Hewitt with the Reichsführer's power, the doctor reported that there were over two million men in the SS and about three hundred thousand men in the Gestapo by October 1943, all under Himmler's control and command.

Hewitt reported that the climax of Kersten's several conversations with him was a startling overture urging collaboration with the Western Allies in ousting Hitler and joining forces with a Germany led by Himmler and the SS to destroy Russia. To quote Hewitt's report: "The doctor [Kersten] urged me to come to Germany to discuss Himmler's position with him, and to see whether a settlement might be possible. He indicated clearly that, on certain conditions, Himmler was prepared to overthrow Hitler and that he was the only man who had power to do so in Germany."[7]

An aide-mémoire based on Hewitt's report, given to the British and Soviets by the Department of State and dated January 22, 1944, is revealing— although it could contain an exaggeration by Kersten. According to the aide-mémoire, Kersten had said, "Himmler . . . knows that the War is lost and is anxious to arrive at an arrangement with the Americans and British which would leave something of Germany." Kersten was quoted as adding that "realizing it would be impossible for the Americans and the British to deal with Hitler, Himmler was now quite prepared to bring about his overthrow."[8]

Sticking to his cover story for the record—however transparent—Hewitt cautiously replied to this astounding proposition: "I told him that I did not represent the American government, and that I did not even know what the current policies of the American government were, and that on this account, it would be pointless for me to talk with Himmler. The doctor then suggested that I return to Washington, familiarize myself with the position of the American government, and come back to Europe." Adding detail, Hewitt wrote: "He [Kersten] mentioned to me that Himmler was organizing his own [shadow] government within the SS and that his two chief advisors on foreign affairs were Oberfuhrer Walter Schellenberg and Dr. Braun, and that he would be glad to get one of these men to come to Stockholm to confirm what he had been saying to me." Despite Hewitt's cautious reaction, Kersten told him two days later that Schellenberg had just arrived in Stockholm and would like to see him.

It is important to note that Hewitt's report revealed that Kersten, in an aside and speaking confidentially for himself, urged Hewitt to act quickly because the German minister to Sweden, following the debacle at Stalingrad, had brought to the SS offices in Stockholm a copy of a Russian peace proposal for Hitler's consideration. Moreover, at roughly the same time, the German ambassador to Turkey, Franz von Papen, had received from the Russians in Ankara the same proposal. According to these identical overtures, Germany was offered "about one half of the Baltic countries to the north of East Prussia; and Poland would be divided according to the 1939 lines." The Soviets were clearly demanding the lion's share: "the whole coast to the Black Sea—including the mouth of the Danube, extending as far as Constantinople and Salonika—and a port on the Adriatic Sea." Kersten added that although Ribbentrop and Goebbels had been in favor of accepting these proposals, Himmler and Hitler were against them.

Himmler's resistance to the Soviet proposals was, of course, consistent with his intense hatred of the Russians—and his intense fear of them should he fall into their hands after a German surrender. According to Hewitt's report, Kersten stressed again Himmler's strong preference for an alliance with the Western powers against the Russians. Realizing that a coup by Himmler could spark a revolution within Germany, the masseur pointed out that it would be Himmler's policy as Hitler's replacement "to keep order in Germany under the existing [i.e., Nazi] government as long as possible. . . ." As Himmler became ever more irrational while fantasizing about this mad Machiavellian scheme, Kersten claimed that the Reichsführer explained to him that when the time came that he believed further military resistance would be futile, he would destroy all the private property in the occupied countries and in Germany to order to produce a mass reactive wave of Communism. Kersten recalled that Himmler then claimed he would "announce himself a Communist, and throw his lot in with the Russians," arguing that "with superior technical ability and organizing capacity, they [the Germans] would succeed in dominating the greater Russian population and obtaining control of the vast Russian resources," a line of reasoning reeking of apocalyptic fantasy.[9] It all sounds much like the wasp that deposits her live larvae in the guts of a tarantula, where they feed and soon undergo metamorphosis, killing their unhappy host in the process.

Kersten, in his postwar memoirs, stated that on October 24, 1943, he had written Himmler from Stockholm recounting his conversations with Hewitt, the centerpiece of which was an informally agreed-upon seven-point proposal, offering "the possibility of an honorable peace."[10] It should be noted that in Hewitt's report to Donovan, passed to the president following his conversations with Kersten and Schellenberg, he did not itemize his and Kersten's seven-point informal agreement.

In the report to Donovan, Hewitt assured him that he had made no promises to Kersten or Schellenberg beyond stating that he "would try to get back to Washington and see that the matter was brought to the attention of the President." Hewitt expressed what he considered positive arguments in favor of meeting Himmler: "While it is obvious that conferences with Himmler are loaded with potential dynamite, nevertheless, I believe that there are enormous possible advantages in such a trip." He listed these:

1. A great deal could be learned about the German frame of mind, and the relations of the important Germans with each other. The weak links in their armor in a material, psychological and personal sense could be better explored in this way than in any other.

2. The possibilities of provoking a "putsch" or civil war in Germany could be explored at first hand. It is possible that this, if successful, might save hundreds of thousands of lives in connection with the coming invasion [of western Europe by the Western Allies].

In concluding his report, Hewitt admitted: "The disadvantage of such a trip would be the capital which the Germans could make out of it in their own press and radio. However, they are in a position to do that anyway if they choose to lie about it. An untruth is a consideration which has never yet weighed with them."

Not specified here was the damage that such an operation would have on American and British relations with Stalin. The United States had an important stake in keeping Stalin friendly—certainly until the Japanese as well as the Germans were soundly defeated. Hitler's eleventh-hour, last-ditch strategy as the Third Reich slid toward defeat would be an effort to break up the Grand Alliance that the West had with the Russians. Hewitt was, of course, oblivious to the several penetrations at top levels of the Western Allies by spies, such as British Secret Intelligence Service officer Kim Philby, who were keeping Stalin informed of efforts by Western intelligence to establish contact with the various factions of the secret German opposition.[11] In fact, the U.S. Department of State, faithful to the spirit of the Grand Alliance with the USSR, and doubtless fearing Stalin's reaction if the OSS was caught dealing behind his back with Himmler, kept the Russians as well as the British generally informed of Hewitt's talks with Kersten and Schellenberg.[12]

Hewitt closed his report to Donovan and the president with a plea for action: "I hope that full consideration will be given to the possibilities of such a trip. I am, of course, ready to discuss the matter and amplify this report in any way that is desired."

Judging from his memoirs, Schellenberg was distressed and disappointed by the breakdown of the U.S. relationship. Clearly, dealing with Himmler had not been easy. "I was lucky not to be arrested [by Himmler]," he wrote.[13] "Nothing can break the spell which Hitler still exercised upon those around him." Schellenberg was also disappointed because he had naively believed that the Americans were willing to reach an agreement with a successor government in Germany and end the War without the participation, much less the agreement, of the Russians. He attributed to Nazi foreign minister Ribbentrop the failure of an earlier, officially endorsed effort to find a formula to split the Grand Alliance by making a bilateral deal with Stalin for a separate peace at British-American expense.

When the Soviet minister to Sweden, Mme. Aleksandra Kolantay, sent a "final" peace proposal to Ribbentrop by way of a go-between, Bruno Peter Kleist, during the summer of 1943, Hitler was furious, allegedly shouting "Soviet capitulations, yes, negotiations, no!" With the news that Hewitt had been called home, Schellenberg concluded that the Americans seemed to have abandoned his and Kersten's initiatives for peace. He could see the irony of an American motive for rejecting Himmler's advances based on Roosevelt's refusal to break his pledge to Stalin, while the Soviet dictator had no qualms about exploring with the Germans their willingness to surrender without reference to his American and British partners in the Grand Alliance.

Schellenberg should probably have known better than to presume that the Western Allies would join forces with a successor German government, particularly one led by another Nazi leader, against Stalin. Unconditional surrender meant just that, and the United States and Britain had with good reason solemnly agreed to keep their commitment to the trilateral agreement inviolate. But in the minds of several German political scientists—and Schellenberg considered himself one—there was logic in attacking Soviet Bolshevism and denying to the USSR postwar hegemony over much of central and eastern Europe. Moreover, throughout the War Stalin had taken several actions that seemed to be in preparation for his immediate postwar power grabs in Germany as well as elsewhere in middle and eastern Europe. Kersten, from the beginning, had been schooled by Holger Graffman in matters of realpolitik, particularly the Soviet threat, and doubtless had passed his advice on to Schellenberg.

While Calvin Hoover, director of Scandinavian operations at the OSS's Washington headquarters, did not approve of Hewitt's plan at the time for policy reasons, he expressed himself personally after the war in his memoirs. He admitted that the Stockholm OSS officers were, in fact, actors in a charade: "We [the OSS] did not for an instant really intend to deal with the Himmler government as the successor to Hitler and certainly the U.S. Government would not have done so." But, Hoover somewhat wistfully added, "I felt sure that if Himmler tried to arrest Hitler, he would fail; the effect on the morale of the Nazi Party and the German Army would be shattering." In hindsight, Hoover claimed to have serious regrets that the United States had not pursued further the Himmler connection. If a serious split between Hitler and Himmler could have been achieved, "the resulting disorganization might have resulted in the collapse of Germany before it did, in fact, occur. The lives of at least a million people would have been saved." As for the sensibilities of Stalin, Hoover wrote, "the exclusive occupation of Poland, Czechoslovakia and Eastern Europe by the Soviet armies would have been averted [and] the division of Germany might have been avoided."[14]

Hewitt also described his reaction to this possible opportunity lost: "In spite of my assurances, American Government circles could see in Kersten only an agent of Himmler. They did not believe in the humanitarian reasons for his actions that so many proofs have since confirmed. I remain convinced that much suffering and loss of life could have been avoided if they had taken into account the very laudable efforts of Kersten."[15]

It is interesting to note that in the spring of 1944, the OSS Morale Operations unit, working out of Stockholm, littered German-occupied Europe with propaganda leaflets whose purpose was "to hold out hope to German businessmen that if they acted to throw out the Nazis, Allied business interests would cooperate with them in building a bulwark against Bolshevism"—obviously a line at odds with U.S. and British overt policy toward its wartime ally, Russia.[16]

In the course of one of his interrogations by the Western Allies at the War's end, Schellenberg attributed the following views to Hewitt:

> Hewitt . . . emphasized especially the great danger to Germany that a bolshevizing of the masses would mean, and considered it essential that the SS should be strengthened as a stabilizing factor inside the country and on the Eastern Front. The essence of his proposition was that Himmler should take a firm grip of the reins and as far as possible change the Wehrmacht troops in the West to the Waffen SS, and divert them to the East. If this were done, Europe would be saved from bolshevisation and this, in his view, decides the future of the continent of Europe. To achieve this object, Germany must understand that a compromise would mean considerable concessions by the Western powers. A tangible expression of this would mean the cession of the occupied territories in the West, with the withdrawal of the Wehrmacht toward the East. There was no question as yet of a final establishment of the

frontiers in the West, since the Western powers had not yet determined the fate of France; here possibly there was an opening for further discussions of various districts [e.g., Alsace]. Regarding the acquisition of territory in the East as well, Germany must have no illusions, although from natural causes there were more possibilities than in the West, and some small hope might be cherished—but this question must be left as a matter for more concrete discussions.[17]

It should be noted that Hewitt's report to Donovan and Roosevelt did not always refer to the ideas attributed to him by Schellenberg. It is likely that the sentiments expressed above are essentially those of Schellenberg, not Hewitt. While Hewitt might have amiably agreed with some of Schellenberg's remarks, he would have done so in the interest of gaining rapport with him because he saw in Schellenberg's link with Himmler an opportunity to sow dissension within the ranks of Nazi leaders. But considering that Schellenberg was in Allied custody when interrogated, and was striving to impress favorably his custodians lest he be tried as a major war criminal, his remarks about Hewitt may well have exaggerated or twisted what the American had actually said in order to suggest that the two men had been in complete agreement.

Schellenberg may have been more frank when he discussed Himmler under interrogation. He expressed his frustration with the Reichsführer's vacillation in the matter of meeting with Hewitt. He also described in some detail how Ernst Kaltenbrunner, using all the power he had as Himmler's deputy, repeatedly tried to discredit him. A hard-line Nazi, Kaltenbrunner believed that Schellenberg could not be trusted. He knew only too well that Schellenberg was trying to keep the vacillating Himmler focused on efforts to remove Hitler from power.

There were other voices of disapproval contributing to Washington's rejection of Hewitt's initiatives as described in his report. The U.S. minister to Sweden, Herschel V. Johnson, was, for one, strongly opposed to the whole matter. Indicative of his attitude in general, it will be remembered that Johnson had warned Bruce Hopper, the first representative in Sweden for the U. S. Office of Coordinator of Information (COI)—soon to become the OSS—that any clandestine operations attempted by him would result in his removal from Stockholm. Moreover, it was Donovan himself who had recommended to Roosevelt that Hewitt not pursue the Schellenberg-Himmler overture.

In a memorandum sent to the Department of State dated January 10, 1944, from Stockholm, Johnson described the position and role of Kersten as he understood it from Hewitt.[18] Then, on January 19, the department received from Minister Johnson a memorandum incorporating parts of Hewitt's memorandum to Donovan and Roosevelt and voicing his displeasure.[19] Obviously distressed by Hewitt's acts, Johnson gave as his strong opinion that Hewitt's contacts with Kersten and Schellenberg were "extremely dangerous," and ended his memorandum with a recommendation that minced no words: "He [Hewitt] should be got out of Sweden as soon as possible." So urgent were Johnson's concerns that he suggested that the British be requested to provide Hewitt with a special high priority to fly on a British transport aircraft, which was solidly booked for two weeks in advance. Hewitt was able to leave on February 2, 1944, for Washington via London.

Johnson's strong reaction was in part stimulated by a Moscow *Pravda* dispatch from Cairo, datelined January 18, 1944, concerning alleged British overtures to Nazi foreign minister Ribbentrop regarding a separate peace agreement behind Stalin's back. The *Pravda* article claimed that "two Englishmen had conferred with Ribbentrop about a separate peace." Erik C. Boheman, secretary-general of the Swedish Ministry of Foreign Affairs, told Johnson that he "considered it a typical Russian maneuver and in his view linked with the case of Poland." Boheman suspected it was "a form of blackmail on Anglo-Saxon Powers warning them to keep hands off of Eastern European questions and carrying an intimation that Anglo-Saxon advice and interest in this area are not desired in Moscow." He added, "It is basically a stupid statement but one which Russians probably consider clever."[20] Boheman thought that the article "may be a part of Russian design to alarm the British by making his charge against them and thus indirectly suggesting that Russia might possibly make a separate peace, if events do not develop according to her liking."[21]

In his January 19 message to the State Department, Johnson declared that whatever the final explanation of the Soviet article in *Pravda* may be, it "emphasizes in my opinion the danger of activities of government agents similar to those of Mr. Hewitt."

While the Department of State had in January 1944 sent an aide-mémoire to both Great Britain and the USSR keeping these allies apprised of peace feelers from the enemy taking place in Stockholm,[22] the Russians had been far from conscientious in abiding by the unconditional surrender agreement. But the United States considered it important to play it straight with Stalin, who Roosevelt hoped would work with him to forge a new, more peaceful world after the War. In a memorandum to President Roosevelt dated January 14, 1944, Secretary of State Cordell Hull passed on earlier comments made by W. Averell Harriman, the U.S. ambassador in Moscow, in response to Soviet foreign minister Molotov's remarks on the definition of "unconditional surrender," and asked what the U.S. opinion on this should be.

Harriman had reported that it was his understanding that the Soviet interest in this matter "is not based on any desire to weaken the principal of unconditional surrender or to offer milder terms to enemy countries, but rather on the belief that the present undefined term 'unconditional surrender' affords enemy propaganda an opportunity to play on a fear of the unknown in the minds of their people and consequently stiffen their will to fight." Harriman added, "As I understand it, the Soviet government believes that some definition, however general . . . would deprive the enemy of this propaganda advantage and consequently weaken the morale of their armed forces and people.[23]

In a very balanced memorandum to the secretary of state on January 17, 1944, President Roosevelt gave his views on this subject:

> Frankly, I do not like the idea of conversation to define the term unconditional surrender. Russia, Britain, and the United States have agreed not to make any peace without consultation with each other. I think each case should stand on its own merits in that way.
>
> The German people can have dinned into their ears what I said in my Christmas Eve speech—in effect, that we have no thought of destroying the German people and that we want them to live through the generations like other European peoples on condition, of course, that they get rid of their present philosophy of conquest. . . ."
>
> Secondly, the German people and Russia should also be told the best definition of what "unconditional surrender" really means. The story of Lee's surrender to Grant is the best illustration. Lee wanted to talk about all kinds of conditions. Grant said that Lee must put his confidence in his [Grant's] fairness. Then Lee surrendered. Immediately Lee brought up the question of the Confederate officers' horses, which belonged to them personally in most cases, and Grant settled that item by telling Lee that they should take their horses home as they would be needed in the Spring plowing.

Roosevelt concluded: "Whatever words we might agree on would probably have to be modified or changed the first time some nation wanted to surrender."[24] The president's philosophy contains infinitely more wisdom than Minister Johnson's adamant opposition to political action or clandestine maneuvering of any kind based in Sweden. The Italian surrender under Marshal Pietro Badoglio had been welcomed by the Western Allies, who most likely gave assistance and encouragement behind the scenes. A British intelligence officer, John Lockhart, head of C branch of the British military in Italy, provided safe shelter for Badoglio at a critical time during the coup.[25] Later, Allen Dulles's successful 1945 secret negotiations with SS General Karl Wolff led to the surrender of all German forces in Italy to the Western Allies and resulted in the saving of many lives, Allied and Axis, even though it infuriated Stalin, who suspected Allied trickery and saw his plan for postwar expansion threatened. Nonetheless, it was approved by Great Britain as well as the United States despite rabid complaints and implied threats by Stalin. Sometimes criticized by certain war historians for provoking Russia to pursue a policy of postwar aggression, this confrontation with Stalin in fact gained a valuable dividend for the Western Allies to the extent it illuminated with frightening clarity the Soviet dictator's attitude and telegraphed his already well-advanced plans for postwar domination over much of Eastern and Middle Europe, which would become known as the Cold War.

Hewitt's efforts to exploit Himmler's flirtation with high treason and encourage his self-seeking efforts to get rid of Hitler and surrender to the West without conditions were fraught with complications, but possibly the OSS agent's initiatives were cut short by Donovan too soon. Himmler was in trouble, veering perilously close to being found out by his own police and intelligence services, his rivals Bormann and Ribbentrop, and, soon, Hitler himself. Himmler's irresolution and vacillation was also his enemy. If he had been encouraged to support Kersten's and Schellenberg's efforts and thus enticed further into the swamp of treachery and deceit by Hewitt, the Nazi monolith might well have cracked before it did. Contestants for postwar leadership were already struggling senselessly among themselves for power that could never be theirs. A strong symptom of things to come was the game being played by RSHA chief Kaltenbrunner and Gestapo chief Müller. Kaltenbrunner himself was attempting a variation of Schellenberg's and Kersten's game with Himmler. With an eye to his own future, he was secretly exploiting growing Austrian sentiment that their country's future would not prosper under a Hitler who was leading the Third Reich to imminent and certain defeat. Trying to gain Himmler's support in this enterprise, Kaltenbrunner did all he could to discredit Schellenberg, his rival in attempting to use Himmler for treasonous action against Hitler. Rats leaving the sinking Nazi ship of state scurried in different directions in their efforts to rescue themselves from drowning. Hewitt, working with Kersten and Schellenberg, would have had a fertile field for intrigues calculated to hasten the death of the Third Reich.

It can be argued that by recalling Hewitt and breaking contact with Schellenberg and Kersten, an opportunity was missed to exploit Himmler's vulnerabilities and create chaos within the Third Reich. But it is perhaps just as persuasive to argue that such covert action operations could have broken up the Grand Alliance—exactly what Hitler wanted to achieve as his last hope to avoid total defeat.

As it was, a hypersuspicious Stalin feared throughout the War that the Western Allies would abandon him and make a deal with the Third Reich to Russia's detriment—witness his strong reaction to Churchill's consideration in 1943 of opening the second front and attacking Germany through the Balkans, Stalin's sphere of influence, rather than through France. As seen before, Stalin also voiced angry complaints to both Roosevelt and Churchill for permitting Dulles to launch Operation Sunrise, in which SS General Wolff, the ranking military officer in Italy, surrendered all German forces on that front on April 29, 1945. Earlier that same month, Hitler's propagandist, Joseph Goebbels, gave a vicious speech on Hitler's birthday, accusing the British and Americans of "running amok" and threatening a "flood of Bolshevism" in an attempt to cause the Western Allies to turn against their Soviet allies. Moreover, with an Asian war against the Japanese still to be won, this was no time to alienate Stalin.

Himmler had too much to worry about without lamenting Hewitt's hasty departure. He was walking an ever-slackening tightrope. His own Gestapo, using intercepted Allied messages, had compiled a damning record of Carl Langbehn's seditious discussions with Allen Dulles in Bern. Following the massive Gestapo crackdown on all dissidents in the wake of Claus Schenk von Stauffenberg's abortive attempt to bomb Hitler on July 20, 1944, Langbehn was indicted and faced a drumhead trial. Himmler, fearing that his own involvement with Langbehn would come out, did everything he could to distance himself from his old friend, making him take the rap for his own treasonous actions. Himmler saw to it that the trial was a quick one, without the Gestapo having the time or opportunity to extract a formal confession from Langbehn that might fatally implicate himself.

While Himmler escaped disaster by a small margin, Schellenberg and Kersten, also involved with Langbehn, were still in jeopardy. Kersten had in fact tried hard to convince Himmler that he should save Langbehn from being executed, but he failed. It was too late. Langbehn's execution took place in October 1944. This intervention further convinced Kaltenbrunner and Müller that the masseur was guilty of high treason and had been able to survive only because of Himmler's protection. But would the Reichsführer's protection always be extended; would Himmler one day throw Kersten and Schellenberg to the wolves to save himself as had been the case with Langbehn? And in this weird rondo of accuser chasing accused, Kaltenbrunner's efforts to destroy Schellenberg would frequently require Kersten's intervention, influencing Himmler to save his colleague-in-treason from the shadow assaults of the RSHA chief and Müller. By now the latter two predators were convinced that both Kersten and Schellenberg were agents of the Western Powers and had implicated their boss, Himmler, in their plot.

As early as August 1942, when Kersten began his collaboration with Schellenberg in the course of their treasonous discussions with Himmler at Zhitomir, the masseur realized that Schellenberg's position was precarious. In a memorandum of conversation written by Kersten for his own personal diary-like records after a late-night, heart-to-heart talk, the masseur noted: "Schellenberg is in a very difficult position. The old Party bosses distrust and hate him. They consider him an outsider. The only one to stand by him is Himmler. But, even in Himmler's circle they are already working against Schellenberg as Brandt told me yesterday. I will support Schellenberg by influencing Himmler in his favor. It is necessary for him to keep Himmler's confidence. Only then can Schellenberg help me in my fight for human rights."

Since midsummer 1943, there had been several accusations levied by Kaltenbrunner against Schellenberg. Kaltenbrunner predictably alerted Himmler to what he believed Schellenberg's game was—and he was right. An embittered Schellenberg stated during his postwar interrogation that because of Kaltenbrunner's actions, Himmler in a fury had rejected a report he had circulated on the grounds it was "defeatist," and threatened to jail those responsible (meaning Schellenberg himself). Schellenberg stated that he had been "spared imprisonment owing only by the intervention of

Brandt [Himmler's secretary] who secured for me an interview with Himmler at which I succeeded in clearing myself of the charges."[26] Behind the scenes, Kersten, not wanting to lose a friend and fellow collaborator, had been even more influential in saving Schellenberg on this occasion.

But just as Kersten made every effort to save Schellenberg then, a time would come when Schellenberg would save Kersten from a ruthless effort by Kaltenbrunner to have him murdered. Kersten would have a very close call.

14

Murder Plot Puts Kersten at Risk

FOLLOWING THE JULY 20, 1944, attempt on Hitler's life by Claus Schenk von Stauffenberg and his Resistance associates, the Gestapo went into high gear, ferreting out anyone remotely connected with the plot. Even family members of those under suspicion were held. The scouring of Germany for traitors was stressful for Himmler; Hitler had given him an arbitrary quota to fill of persons suspected of being accomplices of von Stauffenberg, even though it would mean jailing or executing perfectly innocent people.

The failure of Operation Valkyrie provoked a mystical Himmler to exclaim: "By saving the Führer, Providence has given us a sign; the Führer lives; he is invulnerable. It is the will of Providence that he shall survive for our sake and that we shall bring the War to a victorious conclusion under his leadership."[1]

This crisis made Kersten's efforts to obtain the release of prisoners in Nazi concentration camps all the more difficult. The near-death of Hitler restored, for the time being, the Reichsführer's almost fanatical attachment to him. The orgy of bloodletting that resulted from Himmler's sudden zeal made his bowel spasms worse. As was his custom when such attacks struck, Himmler called for Kersten to minister to him. On August 1, from his advance headquarters at Hochwald in East Prussia, Himmler summoned

Kersten by phone, suggesting he drive to Berlin and take his private train that same afternoon.

In an August 3, 1944, entry in his diary written two days after the event, Kersten made note of a frightening close call.[2] It all began when Kersten ordered his official automobile and driver at 3:00 P.M. on August 1. They were planning to take their usual route from Hartzwalde to Berlin via Oranienburg, but at the very moment of departure an SS motorcycle courier roared into view and thrust an urgent note from Schellenberg into Kersten's hands.

The terse message began with a startling warning: "Look out" Schellenberg's message continued with an alarming explanation for Kersten which, in effect, said that Kaltenbrunner had murder on his mind: "The danger is imminent. Kaltenbrunner had decided to kill you in spite of Himmler."[3] Almost overlooked was another scrap of paper that had fallen out of the envelope in which Schellenberg had scratched some advice as to what route to take to avoid an ambush set along the highway. It told Kersten that he must not travel by way of Oranienburg. Instead, Schellenberg advised him to take another route, which he specified.

Ernst Kaltenbrunner, Himmler's deputy and chief of the Reich Security Main Office (RSHA). Kersten feared Kaltenbrunner, particularly after the RSHA chief tried to have him murdered. (U.S. National Archives)

In a reflection of the atmosphere of terror that permeated the country, Kersten had doubts about whether he should follow Schellenberg's advice. Could this be a trap of his making? For all his reliance on Schellenberg and their mutual interest in manipulating Himmler, Kersten knew that Schellenberg was ambitious and calculating—his own survival came first. Somewhat ashamed of his mistrust, Kersten nonetheless plotted his route carefully. The alternative route suggested by Schellenberg might really be where the ambush had been set. Taking no chances, he took a third route of his own choosing. Armed with a revolver, Kersten reached Himmler on schedule and without incident.

Kersten immediately had his friend at court, Rudolf Brandt, do some checking. Brandt proved to Kersten's satisfaction that Schellenberg had told the truth; Kaltenbrunner had set the trap in collaboration with Gestapo chief Heinrich Müller. Taking advantage of his order from Hitler to track down ruthlessly all dissidents, Kaltenbrunner believed this to be an opportune time to rid himself of Kersten, thereby removing a man whose influence on Himmler was too great for his liking.

By early August 1944, even Colonel General Georg Hansen, Admiral Canaris's successor as head of Abwehr, who was now serving under Schellenberg because the military's intelligence agency had been absorbed by the Sicherheitsdienst, was arrested and jailed for collaborating with the Resistance. More alarming, SS *Generaloberst* Fritz Lindemann, with whom Schellenberg had secretly discussed Hitler's assassination in 1943, was imprisoned and interrogated. Also worrisome for Schellenberg was a message in early August from Müller, who was passing on instructions to arrest personally Wilhelm Canaris on suspicion of high treason. The admiral's standoff with Himmler, in which by tacit agreement neither had wanted to betray the other for all their overt rivalry, was clearly at an end following von Stauffenberg's attempted assassination of Hitler. If Himmler was going to survive Hitler's ire, he had to exhibit extreme zealousness in cutting down the Resistance in whatever form it appeared.

Then there was the case of Lieutenant General Fritz Thiele, chief of Wireless Security, who had briefly replaced General Erich Fellgiebel as overall chief of Hitler's Signals and Communications following the abortive July 20 plot, but had himself been arrested for complicity on orders of Müller and Kaltenbrunner on July 24. Schellenberg feared that he might be vulnerable to charges of having been an accessory to the crime; under Allied interrogation after the War, he stated that in conversations with Thiele and Hansen he had received "indirect if somewhat confusing warning of a possible coup-de-main by certain military elements in the Reich." Worse, Schellenberg received a telephone call from General Thiele at 6:00 P.M. on the day of the attempted coup. The general inquired "whether Schellenberg was still in his office and then, hardly waiting for a reply, blurted out that 'everything had gone wrong!'" This conversation, which could have been monitored, seriously alarmed Schellenberg. Fearing to be compromised, he took the precautionary measure of ringing Gestapo Müller "informing him that he had just heard from Thiele that there was a tremendous uproar in the Bendlerstrasse where firing was taking place." Müller replied ominously, "Fancy that, from your friend, Thiele."[4] According to Schellenberg's interrogation report, "Not long afterwards Thiele telephoned, tactlessly announcing that everything had quieted down and that Himmler had been appointed Commander in Chief of the *Ersatzheer* [replacement troops], naively adding that he thought this would be 'a good thing for them both,' whereupon Schellenberg, alarmed by Thiele's lack of caution, replaced the receiver."[5]

Hansen, after being arrested on July 25, protested that "he had played no greater part in the attempted rising than had Schellenberg himself," a statement that must have sent shivers down Schellenberg's spine. But for all his unease, Schellenberg survived, probably because of Himmler's implicit protection of him motivated by his own involvement with Schellenberg's plotting. Kaltenbrunner even seemed to have shown his confidence in Schellenberg by putting him in charge of military security, perhaps because he, too, felt vulnerable to charges of high treason. He had recently been used by Himmler to make treasonous feelers to the Americans. He could not afford to have Schellenberg as an enemy.

Kaltenbrunner, however, must have thought he could do away with Kersten by setting an ambush for him on the highway. He was wrong. Kersten promptly complained to Himmler about his close call with death arranged by Kaltenbrunner. Kersten showed Schellenberg's warning letter to the Reichsführer.[6] When Himmler had Rudolf Brandt check out the validity of Schellenberg's information, it proved to be accurate. The Reichsführer, who imagined his own predicament if he no longer had Kersten to ease his intestinal pains, was incensed to hear of Kaltenbrunner's intentions.

Over a lunch organized by Himmler and Kersten, the Reichsführer at first toyed with Kaltenbrunner before charging him directly with the intention of murdering his masseur. Kersten, too, joked with Kaltenbrunner, saying something to the effect that he must no longer suspect him of being a secret British spy because he had been recently fired by them for lack of performance. A puzzled Kaltenbrunner began to look uncomfortable, then panic-stricken, when Himmler announced sternly, "My dear Kaltenbrunner, if anything were to happen to Kersten, not only would my life be in danger, but yours too. I fear that you would only survive Kersten by a few hours!" Kaltenbrunner's hand shook as he held his wineglass while Himmler drank a toast to Kersten's "long life."[7]

Schellenberg later described Kaltenbrunner's plan in more detail to Kersten. On the road between Kersten's home, Hartzwalde, and Berlin, the attack was to occur in the forest bordering Ruppin. Kersten's car would have been flagged down by Gestapo agents and the masseur, with his chauffeur Otto Boehn, would have been summarily shot. The police would have been notified that the car had refused to stop on signal and the two men had been shot as they tried to speed away.[8]

Kaltenbrunner's humiliation at his dark plan being uncovered, and discovering that the "Boss" himself blew the whistle on him in front of Kersten, the intended victim, served to make him even more bitter about the masseur's seemingly privileged position with Himmler. This incident, however, did not deter Kersten from his objectives. In fact, he accelerated his campaign of influence in an effort to convince the Reichsführer that in the cause of humanity he must find a means to spare the remaining Jews in Germany who had thus far evaded death in the Holocaust. Himmler himself faced the strong probability of death in defeat; if he died, it would be as retribution at the hands of the Allies for the enormity of his atrocities against humanity, particularly his genocidal killing of Jews.

The World Jewish Congress (WJC), alarmed at the specter of accelerated bloodletting ordered by a vengeful Hitler who wanted to finish the Final Solution before defeat, was spurred to action. After several false starts, the congress would find in Kersten a willing ally, able to provide effective help.

15

Jews in Jeopardy

JEWISH COMMUNITIES throughout the world were understandably
extremely concerned by the fate of their coreligionists held in Hitler's death
camps as the end of the War grew nearer and rumors began to circulate in
Germany that Hitler would have all remaining Jews under his control executed before the Allies could liberate them. An effort was made in September 1944 by the World Jewish Congress (WJC) to find some way to rescue
them. The congress's representative in Sweden, Hilel Storch, approached
one Edgar Klaus, an Abwehr Russian expert and a close contact of the
Soviet envoy to Sweden, Mme. Aleksandra Kolantay, who had been using
him as a conduit to the German government to float proposals for reaching
a "separate Russian peace" with Hitler as early as September 1941.

On September 20, Storch met Standartenführer Peter Kleist, an eastern
Russia expert serving as chief of the Central Office for Eastern Europe in the
Foreign Ministry's "special bureau," with whom Klaus had arranged contact.
(Kleist was in secret a member of the German Resistance and had long been
an agent of Resistance patron Admiral Canaris.) In making his proposition
to Kleist, Storch stated that the World Jewish Congress was willing to offer
the SS $500,000 per person for the release of an estimated forty-five hundred
non-German Jews of various nationalities, but mainly Czech, Dutch, and
Belgian Jews at risk in concentration camps at Tallinn and Kretinga.

Kleist appeared to bridle at the proposition with its assumption that he or any "half-civilized Central European" would be a party to "such a filthy traffic in human beings." In trying to strengthen his case, Storch hinted— true or not—that President Roosevelt might consider helping along any negotiations for the lives of suffering Jews in Nazi Germany, involving as many as 1.5 million of Hitler's victims. Impressed with this possibility, Kleist informed Kaltenbrunner, who in turn informed Himmler.

While Himmler was somewhat intrigued by this possibility at first, Schellenberg apparently advised him not to deal with Kleist, whose connections with Ribbentrop, his bête noir, essentially disqualified him. Schellenberg also advised Himmler to keep Kaltenbrunner out of the picture. Himmler apparently took Schellenberg's advice because Kaltenbrunner, on instructions, told Kleist to abandon his Stockholm contact.[1]

Schellenberg's eagerness to keep Ribbentrop himself at arm's length was shared by Himmler, who considered the foreign minister a complication in his pursuit of a plan for some eleventh-hour action to help the Jews that might provide him with some absolution from the Western Allies after the War—a plan that had been seeded in Himmler's mind by Kersten.

Kersten had learned on August 3, 1944, that a group of Swiss businessmen were collaborating with the Swiss Red Cross to free some twenty thousand Jews from Nazi concentration camps. They hoped to be able to transport these Jews upon their release from death camps to detention camps in the south of France by way of Switzerland, pending an end of the War and complete liberation by the Allies. A former patient of Kersten's asked him to extract from Himmler official permission for this project of mercy. Himmler, however, showed little interest in it because, as Kersten discovered, the Reichsführer and Schellenberg, without his knowledge, were involved themselves in a variation of the Swiss businessmen's plan. Himmler, in his approach, demanded of the Swiss Red Cross a bounty on each Jew as prerequisite for his or her release. In an effort to justify such crass commercialism, Himmler specified that the proceeds would be used to purchase tractors needed to cultivate food products used in supporting the Jews until the War's end. Kersten remonstrated with Himmler, pointing out that despite such flimsy excuses, he would be internationally accused of "trafficking in human lives."

Himmler and Schellenberg nonetheless proceeded, gaining momentum when Jean-Marie Musy, former federal counselor and president of the Swiss Confederation, became involved. Schellenberg's contacts in Switzerland were many, but this one of whom he relied upon for cooperation from the

Swiss government. Schellenberg described Musy as "an utterly selfless man" whose aim was "saving as many as possible of the hundreds of thousands concentration camp inmates."[2]

On October 29, 1944, Musy discussed the fate of the Jews with Schellenberg. On November 3, he was able to gain an appointment with Himmler himself. Traveling with Schellenberg to Breslau, Musy met the Reichsführer, whom he accompanied to Vienna on the latter's private train. Musy explained to Himmler that he had been empowered to act on behalf of the Joint Jewish Rabbi's Organization of the United States and Canada by its representative in Switzerland, a Dr. Sternbuch. Musy pleaded that all Jews should be set free, arguing that such an act of mercy would gain international accolades. Always fearful of Hitler's reaction should he hear of such negotiations, Himmler was cautious. Finally, however, he agreed that all Jews still alive, including a list of specific, well-known figures to be later identified, would be given asylum in Switzerland until the Swiss government could send them on to the United States. Himmler, however, still insisted that per capita payments be made in the form of tractors and trucks to be used for agricultural purposes. Musy again talked with Himmler on January 21, 1945, to fine-tune the plan. The former Swiss president stipulated that about twelve hundred Jews would be permitted to enter Switzerland twice a month. But rather than making payment in agricultural vehicles, difficult to find because of wartime shortages, the two men agreed on a sum of 5 million Swiss francs per transfer, to be deposited in a Swiss bank account. But Kersten again warned Himmler that souls-for-cash would be hard to justify in the eyes of the world.

Schellenberg believed that Himmler could not comprehend that freeing Jews was important to German foreign policy at this stage of the war, when he hoped that a deal with the West might permit Germany to fight the Soviet Union with the full force of the Wehrmacht. Himmler was also blinded by his concern with the reaction of Hitler and certain Nazi Party stalwarts should they hear of such discussions. And, complained Schellenberg, the Reichsführer could not believe how necessary it would be for his own postwar survival to cleanse himself of his genocidal reputation by some major act of contrition, and distance himself from the policies of his Führer by shifting most of the blame onto him.[3]

Practical problems arose during the transport of the Jews, particularly in the winter weather. Moreover, hard-liners Kaltenbrunner and Müller were able to subtly sabotage the logistics of the operation. Nonetheless, by February 1945, the first trainload of some twelve hundred freed Jews crossed into Switzerland. Unfortunately, publicity in American newspapers would provoke Hitler to issue a total ban on further transfers of Jews.

On March 11, 1945, the U.S. secretary of the treasury, Henry Morganthau, Jewish himself, expressed concern over the remittances from U.S. Jews to help cover the fees being charged. He feared that American Jews might be compromised by anti-Semitic publicity stimulated by coreligionists in Europe who accused them of dealing with the Devil. When the first contingent of released Jews successfully reached Switzerland, however, 5 million Swiss francs were duly paid to Musy as trustee at the end of February 1945. The *New York Times* ran an article on this landmark event. But more explosive was an intercepted and deciphered message making reference to the matter from one of Charles de Gaulle's centers in Spain, which was shown to Hitler. The message also stated that Himmler had negotiated a deal with Musy through Schellenberg, securing asylum in Switzerland for 250 Nazi leaders. This was a false allegation which in Schellenberg's opinion had been secretly circulated by Kaltenbrunner to discredit him. The whole project foundered when Radio Berlin announced the chilling edict that all Jews in Germany would be executed, and Hitler threatened death to any German helping Jews escape.[4]

World Jewish Congress representative Hilel Storch had in the meantime made contacts with Ivar Olson of the American Legation in Stockholm, where he functioned as the representative of the U.S. Refugee Committee of Northern and Western Europe. Storch's hope was that help for the Jews would be forthcoming through high-level political intervention by the Western Powers rather than having the Jews' freedom bartered or bought. Musy did not disagree with this principle. More specifically, he felt that "Switzerland should be recognized by the U.S. as a place of transit for Jews who would eventually emigrate [to the United States]."[5]

While Olson's ability to help was limited, Storch was not willing to give up. New hope, in fact, appeared when Kersten wrote Storch in Stockholm on March 24, 1945, describing the progress he was making in solving the dire crisis of the Jews; he had discussed with Himmler new formulas by which to rescue the Jews from certain death. Kersten reported that Himmler had informally agreed to do what he could and, in fact, had released some twenty-seven hundred Jews to Switzerland in December 1944 with no fees paid.

As the collapse of the Third Reich drew closer, the tempo of events quickened. Kersten met with Storch in Stockholm in February 1945, having been introduced by Ottokar Von Knieriem, a senior officer of the Dresden

Scandinavian Bank. Storch, speaking for the World Jewish Congress, expressed alarm at Hitler's announced intention to annihilate all Jewish prisoners before they could be liberated by the rapidly advancing Allied armies. He asked Kersten if he could arrange for Himmler to intervene with Hitler to prevent him from perpetrating this final, almost inconceivable assault against humanity. In a follow-up letter to Kersten, Storch wrote: "We are aware of your deep humanitarian feelings and thank you for everything you have achieved. . . . And we hope that you will be as successful now in aiding us in this very desperate situation."[6]

What followed as the Third Reich faced certain, imminent defeat was a drama of incredible proportions, casting Kersten in his finest role.

16

Negotiations
with the Devil

KERSTEN ACCEPTED THE CHALLENGE that Storch's plea placed before him. He warned Himmler that further destruction of the Jews before they could be liberated by the advancing Allied armies would cast him, as well as Hitler, in the roles of supervillains whose atrocities would eternally define them in history. But Himmler temporized; his often-used argument was "If National Socialism is going to be destroyed, then its enemies and the criminals in concentration camps shall not have the satisfaction of emerging from our ruin as triumphant conquerors." Kersten persisted, arguing that the slaughter proposed by Hitler was senseless.

Finally, on March 12, 1945, Kersten extracted from a very nervous Himmler his agreement not to pass on Hitler's instructions to concentration camps to kill all of their prisoners rather than relinquish them to the Allies. Kersten had overcome a seemingly impregnable barrier. He had finally made progress. On a written agreement that they cosigned he wrote by hand that step one has been achieved "in the name of humanity."[1]

Despite Himmler's grudging agreement to block Hitler's inhumane order, it was by no means certain that the Reichsführer would—or could—do much about it. Schellenberg was skeptical and conveyed his doubts to Jean-Marie Musy, who was still searching for a solution by which to save the

Jews. The aging statesman prevailed on Schellenberg to approach Himmler with a new proposal. This required the Western Allies to call a four-day truce in hostilities during which time all Jews and foreign political prisoners could be conducted through the lines as a gesture of German goodwill. Himmler weakly agreed but could not muster the courage to present it to Hitler, who he knew would reject it out of hand. As Schellenberg recalled after the War during his interrogation, Himmler was only willing to promote Musy's proposal that no further camps be evacuated in view of the rapidly deteriorating military situation—that is, their inmates would not be taken away out of Allied reach and killed. Schellenberg was convinced that this partial concession had been made as a result of Kersten's intervention with Himmler in response to Storch's pleading with him.

On April 7, 1945, Schellenberg informed Musy of Himmler's decision and wanted it "to be transmitted without delay to General Eisenhower." But, unfortunately, Kaltenbrunner, fully aware of Himmler's timidity in this matter, and being fearful of Hitler's reaction, blocked the Reichsführer's instructions. The battle to save Jewish lives was not yet won. More pressure would have to be exerted.[2]

A new player entered the scene with the arrival of Count Folke Bernadotte, a Swedish nobleman closely related to the Swedish royal family and a high-ranking Swedish Red Cross official. The purpose of Bernadotte's visit was a mission of humanitarian concern on the part of the Swedish Red Cross, which feared for the fate of Swedish inmates in Nazi death camps on the eve of Germany's defeat. The meeting between Bernadotte and Himmler was attended by Schellenberg, who had briefed the Swedish nobleman in advance. He also briefed RSHA chief Kaltenbrunner, whom Himmler wanted included in the proceedings to cover himself and avoid any suggestion that he was freewheeling. For the same reason, Himmler had Schellenberg brief Foreign Minister Ribbentrop on what transpired to prevent the Foreign Office from complaining about Himmler's "meddling" in foreign affairs. Ribbentrop jumped to the unjustified conclusion that Schellenberg had secretly arranged Bernadotte's visit. In fact, it had been Kersten who arranged it. That was the sort of backdoor diplomacy that Schellenberg often indulged in to the distress of the foreign minister. Kaltenbrunner, too, was frequently maddened by Schellenberg's actions in bypassing him by invoking his privilege of reporting directly to Himmler.[3]

According to Count Bernadotte's account of his mission, he was "to meet Himmler and obtain his consent to the internment in Sweden of all Scandinavian prisoners held in German prison camps."[4] The Swedish government had agreed, as had the president of the Swedish Red Cross, Prince Charles of Sweden, whose idea it had been to include Norwegian and Danish prisoners as well as Swedes. Bernadotte knew that the task would be difficult, perhaps impossible, but he considered Himmler the best person with whom to discuss the matter. Not only was he interior minister and Reichsführer SS, but he had been made commander of all German forces on the Oder sector of the Eastern Front. Himmler, moreover, would be best equipped to handle a project requiring the discreet liberation of Scandinavian prisoners. What Bernadotte did not write in his memoir, *The Fall of the Curtain*, was the fact that it had been Kersten whose influence on Himmler made the mission possible.[5] Kersten and Schellenberg had the additional, more secret motive of hoping to use Bernadotte as a go-between with the supreme commander of Allied forces on the Western Front, Dwight D. Eisenhower, in arranging the ouster of Hitler and negotiating a peace with the Western Allies to the exclusion of the Soviet Union.

Responding to a secret request made by Swedish foreign minister Christian Günther, Kersten had tried to convince Himmler before his meeting with Bernadotte that he should agree that all Scandinavian prisoners be repatriated immediately to Sweden. The Reichsführer, however, had his usual last-minute qualms, knowing the inflammatory effect it would have on Hitler. A compromise was reached calling for a gathering of Scandinavian prisoners in one camp chosen for its proximity to Sweden, so that when the war ended, if not before, they could be quickly transported by a fleet of buses provided by the Swedish Red Cross to Sweden and safety. On behalf of the Swedish Red Cross, Bernadotte would be in charge of the bus evacuation when the time for action came.[6]

For all his timidity and ingrained Hitler worship, Himmler was increasingly conscious of the wages of defeat that now seemed certain and near. He seemed to realize that even bolder action was required on his part in cutting a deal with the Western Allies if he was going to survive after a German surrender. In a diary entry of April 21, Kersten recorded how Himmler had asked him if he would undertake to get into contact with General Eisenhower and "open discussions with him about the immediate cessation of hostilities." Kersten refused, saying that he was not a man of politics. He urged Himmler instead to discuss this matter himself with Count Bernadotte. This idea had appealed to Himmler, although he knew that it would enrage Hitler if it came to his attention. When Kersten attempted to convince Himmler that he should talk frankly to the Führer himself about arranging a surrender of German troops in Norway, Denmark, and

Holland, the only response he received was a shudder of horror; Himmler knew how Hitler would react if he found out.

Kersten, who was secretly keeping Sweden's foreign minister fully informed of all Scandinavian developments, was told by Günther that Bernadotte would not be permitted to proceed to Eisenhower's headquarters without a formal request being made through the Swedish foreign office. Matters of this magnitude could not be handled through covert political action, and this was no time for Sweden to become involved with any secret scheme in which the Western Allies enabled the Wehrmacht to turn its undivided attention to Russia and the Eastern Front.[7]

Himmler had been miffed that the Swedish government had heralded Bernadotte's mission of arranging for the release of Scandinavian prisoners through formal diplomatic channels, although he had no choice but to have the count received by Ribbentrop. That would involve Kaltenbrunner as well, since the latter was being used by the foreign minister as his point of contact within Himmler's domain. Making matters worse for Himmler, Kaltenbrunner, to protect himself, informally and circuitously notified Hitler himself through SS Gruppenführer Hermann Fegelein, whose wife was the sister of Eva Braun, the Führer's mistress. Hitler's reaction was to forbid the meeting, shouting, "One can do nothing in this war with such fools!"[8]

But before this rejection was transmitted to Himmler, Bernadotte had called the Reichsführer to ask him for a meeting as "as a gesture of friendship that would be of assistance in solving certain technical questions." Meant as a broad hint, Bernadotte added that a meeting "might well be politically interesting." Himmler, with much trepidation, agreed, but for protocol reasons he told Bernadotte that he should first meet with Ribbentrop and Kaltenbrunner. Himmler did not tell Ribbentrop of Hitler's outburst of rage when rejecting the idea of any meeting with Bernadotte by anyone.

Schellenberg, orchestrating the whole encounter for Himmler, took the occasion to have his own discussion with Bernadotte. Ribbentrop would discuss Scandinavian prisoner releases, but Schellenberg was determined to talk confidentially with Bernadotte about serving as the mediator for Himmler in arranging a compromise peace with the United States and Britain, by which Germany would be relieved from waging war on the Western Front.[9]

Intent on seeing Himmler, Bernadotte also worked though the Swedish Legation to reach Schellenberg and have him arrange a working-level discussion that would include Kaltenbrunner. Schellenberg artfully manipulated the meeting by giving Kaltenbrunner star billing—and after it was over, lavishing compliments in praise of the gullible RSHA chief for "the splendid way he handled the discussion." Schellenberg recalled how at first Kaltenbrunner was hostile to the idea of negotiating with Bernadotte, but he was won over by the latter's charm and Schellenberg's flattery. Kaltenbrunner telephoned Himmler after the meeting strongly supporting Bernadotte's request to meet personally with the Reichsführer. As Schellenberg put it in his memoirs, flattery caused the slow-thinking Kaltenbrunner to "take the bait so eagerly that I could hardly hold him. . . . He became the most ardent protagonist of the proposed meeting between Himmler and Bernadotte."[10]

Bernadotte's account of his meeting with Kaltenbrunner and Schellenberg assessed the RSHA chief, describing how his "eyes, which he fixed on me, were cold and enquiring." Anxious to impress Himmler's second in command by flattery, as Schellenberg had done, Bernadotte pursued his principal purpose, to gain an audience with Himmler. But he took careful note of Kaltenbrunner's character. He painted him as the man who "murdered an unknown number of Czech patriots" in retribution for Heydrich's assassination in Prague. It was obvious to Bernadotte that "Kaltenbrunner could have little understanding for any humanitarian action in connection with the German concentration camps."[11]

The astrologer Wilhelm Wulff, who had been introduced to Himmler by Kersten and Schellenberg for the specific purpose of crafting horoscopes that supported plans and ideas that the manipulating duo wanted Himmler to embrace, was in the wings during the Bernadotte mission. Some of his observations add a slightly different slant on events. Schellenberg told Wulff that while talking about a relatively unexceptional exchange of prisoners, he sought to use the occasion to "broach the all-important question of peace negotiations." Wulff added that Schellenberg had told him that Bernadotte wanted a personal meeting with Himmler: "If I [Wulff] were to give precise astrological information as to the possibility of a peace, this vital issue would have to be dealt with first."[12] Soon after his conversation with Schellenberg on this subject, Wulff met his friend—and perhaps his real controller—Dr. Henry Goverts, who had just returned from Stockholm. It will be recalled that Goverts was apparently a member of the Kreisau Circle of the anti-Nazi Resistance movement, which gives added meaning to Wulff's statement in his memoirs that he and Goverts "were able to make the journey to Hamburg together and *exchange news on the way*" (italics added). It is also interesting to note that Wulff claimed that he and Goverts found out in Hamburg that Himmler was suffering from a nervous breakdown and was recuperating at his Hohenlychen headquarters.[13] The cause of Himmler's problem was his increasingly stressful relationship with Hitler, although the public was being told that the Reichsführer simply had a touch of the flu.

Wulff relates in his memoirs that Goverts had not bothered to get in touch with Schellenberg at this time since "he preferred to discuss his news with me." But, related Wulff, "neither of us was particularly interested in the course of events anymore. Because of Himmler's continual vacillation, the moment for action—for deposing Hitler and forming a new government— had been missed."[14]

Schellenberg had an occasion to speak privately with Bernadotte following the Swedish Red Cross official's meeting with Ribbentrop.[15] Not surprisingly, Bernadotte was unimpressed with the German foreign minister. "He had been extremely voluble" and had done most of the talking. Ribbentrop gave his view: "if the Western Powers did not have consideration for Germany, she would lapse into Bolshevism." This was a frequently heard argument given by Nazis naive enough to think that in seeking an honorable, negotiated peace, Germany could play off the USSR and the Western Powers against each other. In this way Hitler could choose whichever side promised the best deal. Ribbentrop stupidly bragged that he had earlier attempted to discuss peace with the Western Powers through an intermediary named Hesse in Stockholm, who talked with the British envoy in Stockholm, Sir Victor Mallet. Ribbentrop also tried to make contact through Dr. Peter Kleist with Hilel Storch of the World Jewish Congress—who was also in touch with Kersten, acting as intermediary with Himmler.[16]

Count Bernadotte tried to listen patiently to Ribbentrop, whose monologue reminded him of a "gramophone record." However much nationalistic bombast came from this "ridiculous" man of small mental capability, it was clear to Bernadotte that Ribbentrop realized that the war was lost. He could romanticize his "accomplishment" in 1939 when he had forged a pact with Russia, but now could only dream of blazing a new trail to Moscow, leading to a pact in which Russia and Germany would turn their guns on the Western Powers.

Immediately after his talk with Ribbentrop, which accomplished nothing, Bernadotte at last met with Himmler. But before the meeting started,

Schellenberg talked alone with the count to brief him. Schellenberg described some of the Reichsführer's idiosyncrasies and warned him not to complicate the meeting by suggesting that Danish and Norwegian prisoners be interned in Sweden. The most viable proposal, Schellenberg thought, would be the establishment of a central camp in which all political prisoners in Germany would be held pending the end of the war.

Bernadotte expected more from Himmler when he met with him on February 12, 1945. This man, supreme head of the SS, the Gestapo, the whole German police and concentration camp structure and now commander in chief of the Home Army, had through terror "stained politics with crime in a manner hitherto unknown." Now Bernadotte would try to extract from him wide-scale humanitarian concessions.[17]

It would be a curious experience for Bernadotte to attempt to gain humanitarian concessions from someone who had sent millions of human beings to their deaths in the cruelest way possible. The Swedish count later concluded: "Nothing can . . . exonerate Heinrich Himmler from the terrible guilt which rests on his shoulder . . ."[18]

Apparently the meeting between Himmler and Bernadotte went relatively well. Himmler seemed pleased and urged Schellenberg, who had also attended, to monitor carefully how their plans to rescue remaining Scandinavian death camp prisoners were proceeding, realizing that Ribbentrop, Kaltenbrunner, and Müller could be relied upon to sabotage the whole plan if they could. And, indeed, when Schellenberg informed Kaltenbrunner and Müller that it had been agreed that Danish and Norwegian prisoners, as well as Swedish prisoners, would be collected from the various camps and placed at Neuengamme under the surveillance of the Swedish Red Cross, Kaltenbrunner accused Schellenberg of unduly influencing Himmler in attempting to implement an impractical plan.

In the course of his postwar interrogation, a summary of Schellenberg's testimony stated: "The first objection raised by Kaltenbrunner concerning the use of German lorries and petrol was countered by Schellenberg with a proposal that the Swedish Red Cross should supply both; and a further criticism proffered by Müller that the refugees on the roads could not be expected to watch the Swedish Red Cross lorries driving past them with prisoners, was met by the proposal that the transportation take place by night and that Schellenberg himself would supply personnel from his own department for the observance of the agreement." Finally, the outline of the project to rescue prisoners of Scandinavian nationality was accepted by all parties at the meeting.[19]

In the course of his interrogation, Schellenberg made the point that he had been careful to assign reliable men on whom he could count. Despite this, the transportation of Danish, Norwegian, and even some Polish and Jewish prisoners brought about so much uncertainty in the issuing of orders that many instructions issued by Kaltenbrunner and other officers, purporting to be those of the Reichsführer, would not be acted upon. It would also not always be possible for Swedish Red Cross personnel to visit certain camps, despite the agreement allowing them to do so.

Schellenberg's assistant, Hauptsturmführer Franz Göring, under interrogation by the Western Allies immediately after the end of the War, testified that by April 16, 1945, "the Russian offensive had already advanced so far that on the following day there no longer existed any communication link between North and South Germany. Conditions in Germany became daily more hopeless, and one could feel the approach of complete collapse. Berlin had been declared a fortress and the Russians had almost closed the ring around the town" (see Appendix 7, paragraph 2).

Thanks to the advance work done by Kersten and Schellenberg, Bernadotte had achieved limited success on behalf of the government of Sweden in granting protection to Scandinavian inmates in certain concentration camps. Nevertheless, there still remained the more challenging problem of saving the large, vulnerable population of Jews who were awaiting execution in Hitler's death camps. Still facing Kersten was the plea of the World Jewish Congress, conveyed by Hilel Storch, that Himmler be induced to give the proper orders permitting Red Cross relief trucks to evacuate Jewish prisoners—thus negating Hitler's order that all Jews be killed before Allied invaders could reach and rescue them. While Himmler had promised Kersten on March 12 that he would accommodate Storch's request—albeit for self-serving motives—more convincing would have to be done by Himmler's therapist to translate the Reichsführer's promise into action.

17

Eleventh-Hour Rescue of Jewish Captives

FELIX KERSTEN'S GREATEST ACHIEVEMENT was to arrange a secret meeting between Himmler and a representative of the World Jewish Congress for the purpose of negotiating the rescue of death camp prisoners marked for execution as Nazi Germany faced imminent defeat. With difficulty Kersten managed to talk the Reichsführer into a meeting, fraught with danger for both parties, at his Gut Hartzwalde estate near Berlin. Hilel Storch had been the designated spokesman for the World Jewish Congress, but a variety of reasons caused him to bow out at the last minute. He was replaced by Norbert Masur of the Stockholm branch of the congress.

Storch explained his reasons for this in 1955, long after the event. The World Jewish Congress rescue committee and Professor Marcus Ehrenpreis, chief rabbi in Stockholm, had decided that Storch should not travel within Germany for this purpose unless he could get a Swedish passport and on condition that it was absolutely necessary that he go. These terms could not be met, and Storch also believed that it would be politically unwise since he might be too conspicuous because of his March talks with Kersten. Moreover, since Himmler might be considering him as an intermediary with the Western Allies, Storch did not want to damage a prospective peace project by his prior involvement in negotiating the liberation of the imprisoned Jews. Foreign Ministry officer Peter Kleist had taken the initiative to suggest that Storch consult with Foreign Minister Ribbentrop with regard to possible peace overtures to the Western Powers. But Himmler did not want to inform Ribbentrop of his plans, much less involve him in the possibility of holding a secret meeting with a representative of the World Jewish Congress to discuss rescuing Jews, Storch and his principals did not want to endanger the rescue activities by his presence inside Germany becoming known. On April 19, the Swedish foreign office declined to issue Storch a Swedish passport, which settled the matter. Storch later had the grace as well as the conviction to declare that it inevitably was Kersten, not an emissary from the World Jewish Congress, who could best convince Himmler to act. The identity of the World Jewish Congress representative attending would thus not be so important. Storch expressed himself as sorry that he had not been able to attend what had turned out to an historic conference. He did express his opinion that it was "an heroic act of Mr. Masur" to have undertaken the mission to meet Himmler.[1]

On April 19, shortly before the meeting at Hartzwalde, Schellenberg had commiserated with Kersten over Himmler's last-minute hesitation to deal with Masur.[2] The next morning it was still uncertain whether Himmler would show up as hoped—but he did. Schellenberg met him upon his arrival at nearby Wustrow at 9:00 P.M. on April 20. Despite lingering doubts—or fears—Himmler had finally agreed to sit down with Masur. The two men, along with Kersten, began this epic meeting, on which the lives of countless Jews depended.

In a private meeting with Himmler before the conference began, Kersten urged the Reichsführer to be "magnanimous" with Masur. It was important, said Kersten, to keep in mind that this would be an opportunity "to show the world, which had been so disgusted by the harsh treatment accorded to the Third Reich's political enemies, that this had been reversed and humanitarian measures undertaken."[3] He must grant Masur's request to rescue the Jews in the death camps whom Hitler had ordered killed before they could be liberated by the Allied enemy, and Hitler's order, itself, must be canceled. Kersten knew that this would be difficult for the Reichsführer. Himmler had previously told Kersten of Hitler's explicit command to liquidate all the concentration camp prisoners so that they could not enjoy the sight of Nazi German's defeat. The Reichsführer had told Kersten that he thus had to see the complete execution of this order from the Führer.

Himmler, Masur, and Kersten got down to business late at night on April 20. At stake were the lives of countless Jews, many of whom were already near death. Kersten's description of the meeting—a meeting of two contestants representing diametrically opposed points of view—reveals much about Himmler. The Reichsführer, a petty schoolmaster by instinct, could not resist delivering a lecture on why Germany historically felt as it did toward the Jews. He also tried to justify the Nazi concentration camp system. Obviously this did not sit well with Masur, who nonetheless valiantly kept his temper and concentrated on the object of the meeting. As direct as Himmler was convoluted, Masur pressed the basic point that all Jews in Germany and Germany's conquered neighbors must be spared death and be quickly released.

When Masur specifically demanded a test run as an earnest of intent to indicate that Germany would release the inmates of the Ravensbrück camp, something that Himmler had promised Kersten in March, Himmler was hesitant. But after nudging by Kersten, he again agreed to release immediately a thousand Jewish women prisoners, providing they be described as Polish, not Jewish.[4]

After two and a half hours of discussion, the night meeting ended in a far-reaching agreement. Himmler accepted Masur's basic points:

1. That no more Jews would be allowed to be put to death.
2. The present number of Jews, which was certainly not accurately known and was disputable, should, whatever happened, be kept in the camps (until liberated by the Allies) and no longer be evacuated by the Nazis (thus hidden from Allied access).
3. That all camps in which there were still Jewish prisoners should be cataloged and made known.

Himmler promised to carry out these terms expeditiously, although he pointed out that he could well run into trouble with Hitler should the Führer learn of what was happening.

The conversations and decisions were to be kept secret. And both Schellenberg and Himmler's secretary, Brandt, promised Kersten privately that they would raise the number of Jews to be released to Swedish Red Cross trucks and discreetly position them on Germany's northern border for quick transfer to Sweden and safety as soon as the Third Reich surrendered. Kersten and Schellenberg tried to assure Masur that there would be no orgy of killing Jews in the concentration camps as the victorious Allied forces approached them as liberators.

According to Dr. Shmuel Krakowski, director of archives at the Holocaust Martyrs and Heroes Remembrance Authority in Sweden, Kersten had written in his diary that an agreement had been reached between Himmler and

Masur after exhaustive negotiations.[5] According to Hugh Trevor-Roper, a British intelligence officer during World War II and a historian whose coverage of the last days of Hitler has been widely recognized, Himmler had made certain general promises to Kersten in March 1945, but it took Masur's presence to bring these promises "into clear, practical form."[6]

Kersten made a full report of the meeting between Himmler and Masur to Swedish foreign minister Günther. Storch was also informed, but he remained skeptical that Himmler would remain true to his word. By April 22, the day after the agreement was signed by Himmler, it was in fact put to the test. When Schellenberg's representative ordered that the women at the Malchow concentration camp be transferred to a location where Red Cross buses would meet them preparatory to driving them to safety as soon as the official surrender of Germany was signed, the camp commander refused to obey. He claimed that Kaltenbrunner had already passed on Hitler's order that all prisoners be "liquidated," so he was obliged to comply. A phone call to Brandt in Himmler's office, however, set things straight. The women were released to the Swedish Red Cross representatives and moved to the safety of the Swedish buses. More would follow.[7]

Schellenberg accompanied Himmler back to Berlin after the meeting. The traffic to Wustrow airport was terrible. Schellenberg recalled: "We got into great traffic difficulties in Loewenberg as numberless troop movements had become mixed up with endless columns of refugees." Despite low-flying enemy aircraft, Himmler was deep in thought during the drive, but aroused himself to comment to Schellenberg: "I dread all that's still to come."[8]

According to Schellenberg's autobiographical memorandum after the War, his conversation with Himmler was devoted largely to comments regarding the just-concluded meeting with Masur. Schellenberg referred to "the great guilt of Kaltenbrunner in continually nullifying the orders issued since the Musy business." This seemed to have struck a sensitive chord in Himmler. He replied, "Yes, yes, Schellenberg, if only I had listened to you earlier." But Himmler admonished Schellenberg not to be too harsh in his judgment of him: "Hitler must have been furious for days that Buchenwald and Bergen-Belsen were not evacuated a hundred per cent [before the Allies could reach them]." Schellenberg replied impishly, "But in this case Hitler's Parkinson's illness must have developed very far."[9] It made Himmler uncomfortable at this point to be reminded that he had justified his secret opposition to Hitler on the grounds that the Führer was too ill to rule, but had been afraid to take decisive action to unseat him. Was it now too late?

· · ·

Having been housed at Kersten's Hartzwalde estate, the astrologer Wilhelm Wulff was a peripheral witness to the presence there of Norbert Masur of the World Jewish Congress as he closeted himself with Himmler and Kersten to negotiate the rescue of Nazi death camp Jews. Wulff's views were sometimes biased, but his powers of observation were often acute. He had, for example, realized how sick Himmler was during the crucial spring of 1945, and noticed how frequently he had asked for astrological reports on a variety of persons and situations. The Reichsführer, worried by Hitler's progressively cool relationship with him and concerned by what the future might hold when Nazi Germany collapsed, was in the throes of a nervous breakdown, according to Wulff.

Wulff had also been well aware of Kersten's contacts with the World Jewish Congress representative, Hilel Storch, and his efforts to bring Storch into contact with Himmler. Kersten had described to Wulff how important Storch was in the Zionist movement[10] and how he had been charged by the Jewish Congress with saving imprisoned Jews in Germany from eleventh-hour execution as ordered by Hitler before they could be rescued by the Allies—a daunting mission. Wulff, somewhat cynically, minimized the likelihood of Kersten succeeding in his efforts to energize a timid Himmler to free a significant number of Jews.

Storch had sought Kersten's help from the outset. He had met Kersten in February 1944 through a friend, Mr. Ottokar von Knieriem, representing the Dresden Scandinavian Bank in Stockholm, and a patient of Kersten. Storch had realized that he must personally deal with Himmler, rather than rely on intermediaries such as Folke Bernadotte, despite the count's prominence as vice president of the Swedish Red Cross. Kersten had, therefore, taken it upon himself to convince the Reichsführer to negotiate with Storch, a Jew, with all the dangers that implied in Nazi Germany. In his postwar memoirs, Wulff noted that Kersten had been distressed when he found that he would be introducing to Himmler as negotiator for the World Jewish Congress "an unassuming Jewish gentleman who looked about him with frightened eyes" and whose name was Norbert Masur, not Herr Storch.

Wulff noted in passing that ever since early 1943 he, Dr. Goverts, and Schellenberg had been working toward mounting a putsch against Hitler as preparation for persuading Himmler to take over the government and negotiating peace with the Western Allies, so they took a lively interest in Kersten's role in bringing a World Jewish Congress representative to Himmler. The Wulff-Schellenberg team, like the Kersten-Schellenberg team, had as their secretly declared object to free the inmates of the Nazi concentration camps and repatriate all foreign political prisoners, particularly Jews, thereby gaining acceptance by the United States and Britain. Himmler, Wulff claimed, had known about and approved these plans since early 1944, and had even discussed them personally with him in May 1944. Wulff's comments revealed another of the several intrigues Schellenberg hatched in implementing his August 1942 secret agreement with Himmler following their meeting in Zhitomir.[11] It also reveals the early association of Goverts with Schellenberg in anti-Hitler Resistance activity, and Goverts's connections with Allen Dulles, OSS chief of station in Switzerland, and Dulles's assistant Gero von Schultze-Gaevernitz. Schellenberg understandably had other partners in treason, compartmented one from another, although Kersten, he knew, provided him with the best and all-important access to Himmler, which was vital not only to his plans but to preserve his standing within the Reichsführer's inner circle and for protection against serious rivals such as Kaltenbrunner.

Schellenberg had been taken aside by Himmler in a meeting with him at his Hohenlychen headquarters on April 21, following the meeting at Hartzwalde. Masur, too, was scheduled to meet with Himmler, with Count Bernadotte present, to discuss operational details. Himmler intended to keep working on Bernadotte in an effort to get him to fly to General Eisenhower's headquarters and convince the supreme commander to negotiate a peace on the Western Front with Himmler behind Hitler's back. Bernadotte, however, confided in Schellenberg before they parted: "The *Reichsführer* does not see the real situation any more. I cannot help him any more; for that he would have had to take things in the Reich entirely into his own hands after my first visit. I can hardly allow him any more chances, and you, my dear Schellenberg, would be more sensible to now think of yourself" Upon hearing this, Schellenberg described himself as feeling "extremely sad."[12]

Hitler, beyond governance but holed up in his Berlin bunker, a remnant of a man wracked by Parkinson's disease, was the stumbling block. While deals could be concluded behind his back to rescue certain specific categories of Jews in limited numbers, any semblance of an orderly surrender and a total rescue of Jews required his death or removal. Despite the rapid fading of the "Twilight of the Gods," Himmler still found it impossible to take decisive action as urged by Schellenberg. Specifically, Schellenberg's hope that Himmler would agree to use Bernadotte as a go-between with General Eisenhower to convey a message of capitulation met with continuing resistance on the part of the Reichsführer. Himmler still temporized. A frustrated Schellenberg almost daily engaged him in a struggle of minds in which he "wrestled for his soul."[13]

When Himmler next met with Schellenberg, it was clear to the latter that Hitler's relations with Himmler were badly strained. The Führer, annoyed that Himmler's actions did not show due diligence in defending the Third Reich, had gone so far as to order his bodyguard to have the stripes removed from the sleeves of Himmler's uniform as a mark of dishonor. Schellenberg recalled Himmler's agonizing; he did not feel he could shoot Hitler, the Führer to whom he had pledged allegiance; he could not poison him, nor could he arrest him in the Reich Chancellery using SS troops. Any such action would cause the whole military machine to come to a halt. That would never do if Germany hoped to resist—even defeat—the Russians. Himmler complained that if he tried to talk Hitler into resigning, the Führer would become enraged and shoot him out of hand.[14]

After an hour and a half of discussion and persuasion, Himmler managed to muster a daring idea as the bold side of his psyche suddenly asserted itself. He would take aside his old schoolmate and friend, SS *Obersturmbannführer* Dr. Ludwig Stumpfegger, Hitler's doctor at the time, as well as Schellenberg's friend and accomplice in treason, Professor Max de Crinis, a psychologist, and make it clear to them that since the Führer was no longer physically fit to govern he should be killed. Perhaps they could talk over this problem with Bormann. Schellenberg discovered that despite Himmler's exhortations—which perhaps were delivered too timidly to make any impression—Stumpfegger and de Crinis had refused to face Bormann with such an indictment of the Führer, much less intimate that Hitler should under some pretense be given a lethal injection. Their rejection of his suggestion frightened Himmler, and he "begged" Schellenberg to maintain total silence about the whole matter. A dejected and desperate Himmler could only comment that he would attempt to devise some way to solve this problem.[15]

Hitler and Himmler had met face-to-face for the last time on April 20, 1945, before Himmler's meeting with Masur at Hartzwalde. The meeting, demanded by protocol, was to give Hitler birthday greetings. Himmler had seized the occasion to talk alone with Dr. Stumpfegger. What passed between them is not reliably known, but Amt VI intelligence officer Wilhelm Hoettl later claimed in his postwar memoirs that his boss, Schellenberg, had told him: "Himmler tried to persuade his friend [Stumpfegger] to get rid of Hitler by means of a lethal injection."[16]

Under postwar interrogation, Schellenberg stated that on the night of April 24–25, during a meeting between Himmler and Bernadotte, the Reichsführer formally asked the count to convey to the Swedish government for onward transmission to General Eisenhower a message expressing his willingness to order a cease-fire on the Western Front so that any further "senseless fighting and unnecessary bloodshed may be spared."[17] But Himmler's statement, as remembered by Schellenberg, made Allied acceptance impossible because of its special enmity shown toward the USSR. The text read: "To the Russians it is impossible for us Germans, and above all for me, to capitulate."[18]

Schellenberg considered another comment made by Himmler to Bernadotte on this occasion as being highly significant in the context of the Reichsführer's recent meeting with Dr. Stumpfegger on April 20. According to Schellenberg's interrogation report, "Himmler also declared that he had the authority to make these declarations to Bernadotte for further transmission at this time since it was only a question of one or two, or at the most three, days before Hitler gave up his life in this dramatic struggle." Hoettl confirmed this, asserting that Himmler made this statement to Bernadotte during the night of April 24–25. Hoettl later also confirmed that "Schellenberg considers that there is a connection between the Himmler-Stumpfegger conversation and the statement to Bernadotte; and that Himmler had Stumpfegger's promise to give a lethal injection within that specified period."[19] Hoettl added in his memoirs that immediately after his talk with Bernadotte, "Himmler had a long telephone conversation with Stumpfegger in Berlin."[20] Hoettl's point, however, was that while all the evidence pointed to the conclusion that Hitler committed suicide in his bunker as the Russians invested Berlin, Himmler and Stumpfegger may have had a plan—obviously unnecessary and never carried out—to murder the Führer![21]

Air raids provided fitting background music as the Third Reich crumbled. After hypocritically describing how he had remained loyal to the Führer, Himmler had rationalized that now Hitler was on the edge of death, it was up to him to act soon to save what was left of Germany. That was why he asked Bernadotte to send a message from him to the Swedish government for transmittal to Supreme Allied Commander Dwight D. Eisenhower surrendering German forces on the Western Front.

Bernadotte's version of these events appeared in his 1945 book *The Fall of the Curtain*, rushed into print as the War ended. In it, he told how he had been awakened by a telephone call at 3:00 A.M. on April 23. Bernadotte found Schellenberg on the phone line, wanting to arrange a meeting that afternoon to discuss a most urgent matter. When they met, "Schellenberg lost no time in letting off his bombshell: Hitler was finished! It was thought that he could not live more than a couple of days at the outside."[22]

Hearing from Schellenberg that Himmler wanted him to see Eisenhower and tell the Allied commander that the Reichsführer was prepared to assume command of German forces in the West and order them to capitulate, Bernadotte insisted that German forces in Norway and Denmark be ordered to surrender as well. And he warned Schellenberg that the Western Allies would never recognize Himmler in any capacity except war criminal—certainly not as Germany's head of state. There were many things to talk about, so a meeting between Himmler and Bernadotte took place.

Bernadotte balked when Himmler explained that he wanted to save as much of Germany as possible from Russian occupation, and so was prepared to capitulate only on the Western Front, permitting the Allies to

Adolf Hitler and Hermann Göring, with Mrs. Göring, attend a state funeral for a Luftwaffe ace killed in action. Göring vied with Himmler for Hitler's favor during much of the War; both sought to replace a discredited Hitler on the eve of Germany's defeat. (Courtesy of Angus Thuermer)

advance more rapidly into Germany at Russian expense. Doubtful that the Western Powers would accept Himmler's proposals, Bernadotte agreed only to submit a letter from Himmler to the Swedish foreign office.[23] Predictably, neither Roosevelt nor Churchill was interested in the deal proposed by Himmler, a deal which seemed to be but one more effort by the already-beaten Germans to divide the Grand Alliance by separating Russia from the Western Powers.

On April 28, the British news agency Reuters broke the story of Himmler's overture to the Western Allies and their rejection of it. News of Himmler's treason reached Hitler in his underground bunker in Berlin when Goebbels sent him the Ministry of Propaganda clipping from Reuters, which described the Reichsführer's "negotiations" with the West through Count Bernadotte. Hitler, mustering all his remaining strength, erupted in rage, shouting that "even faithful Himmler" had been untrue to him. Göring, who had just telegraphed Hitler his willingness to assume the mantle of power, had at least sought the Führer's concurrence. Nonetheless, Göring by his insensitive actions had, in effect, implied that Hitler was no longer fit to rule.* For his presumptuousness he had been clapped into jail at Mautendorf. Himmler could expect no less for his own more egregious act of trying to seize power, in his case without prior communication with the Führer. Hitler by then may have been only a fragile shell of the man he had been, but he was not yet dead—his venom was still deadly. He was in a frenzy. During the night of April 28–29 he declared Himmler's act to be the "worst act of treachery" he had ever known.[24] Himmler had betrayed him and must be shot as a traitor. On April 29, Hitler wrote in his last will and testament: "Before my death I expel from the Party and from all his offices the former Reichsführer SS and Reich Interior Minister, Heinrich Himmler."[25]

---

*The following is a translation of the core of Göring's message to Hitler announcing his intention to take over the Third Reich, which provoked the Führer to order Göring's arrest:

"My Führer, in view of your decision to remain at your post in the fortress of Berlin, do you agree that I take over at once the total leadership of the Reich, with full freedom of action at home and abroad, as your deputy, in accordance with your decree of 29 June 1941? If no reply is received by 10:00 tonight I shall take it for granted that you have lost your freedom of action and shall consider the conditions of your decree as fulfilled and shall act to the best interest of your country and our people. . . ."

Himmler's efforts to establish contact with the West to achieve a negotiated peace at Russia's expense had been more than Hitler could ever have
imagined, nor could the Führer have fully realized that Himmler's political
flirtations with the West included getting rid of him in the process. Certain
of his actions had been imprudently taken on his own, without the benefit
of advice from Schellenberg or Kersten. One of Himmler's more interesting
plans to reach the Western Allies arose when Resistance leader Carl Goerdeler
was arrested by the Gestapo for his participation in the July 20, 1944, bomb
plot against Hitler. Rather than have him executed immediately, Himmler
waited four months and had Goerdeler write Jacob Wallenberg in Stockholm, asking the Swedish tycoon to feel out the British as to some possible
peace formula. Goerdeler was also importuned by Himmler to write to his
friend Chaim Weizmann, the prominent Zionist leader, and ask that he
work on Churchill in bringing the War to an end. Nothing came of these
initiatives. Churchill, in fact, was furious that Himmler had the gall to try to
reach him. Neither was Wallenberg interested in serving as a bridge between
Himmler and the West. Himmler was not the kind of man with whom Wallenberg wished to deal, nor did he want to be associated with any Nazi in
such a sensitive matter."[26] Since early 1944, Himmler had also used Dr.
Franz Six of the Foreign Ministry to make contacts in Stockholm, and as the
War drew to an end he even tried to use Göring's good friend Birger
Dahlerus in an effort to reach Churchill with peace offers.[27]

While it is true that Hitler had encouraged Himmler and others of his
inner circle to seek Western contacts as a means of splitting the Grand
Alliance and isolating the Soviets as a common enemy, he would become
furious when he began to suspect such contacts were being approached
with the secret proposition that he be removed from power as a condition
for any peace agreement. Himmler was walking a frayed tightrope and was
in ill-humor when Schellenberg came to call on him.

Schellenberg dreaded his first face-to-face encounter with Himmler at
Lübeck following the failure of Bernadotte's April 27 mission. He feared the
possibility of being executed by an enraged Himmler. Hadn't Langbehn
taken the fall for Himmler when he was executed by the Gestapo for his
secret contacts with Allen Dulles? Schellenberg was so worried that he summoned the astrologer Wulff to accompany him to see the Reichsführer.

The meeting took place on April 29. Schellenberg's charm and Wulff's
astrological predictions calmed Himmler a little. Himmler even gave Schellenberg authority to continue discussions with Bernadotte regarding the
surrender of German troops in Norway—and possibly soon in Denmark as

well. Moreover, he gave Schellenberg the authority—even if it wasn't his to give—to negotiate with the Swedish government for a peaceful solution in the "Northern Sector." Himmler still deluded himself in believing that he would become the Führer's successor at any moment—as soon as Hitler died or fled. Then, he fantasized, everything would work out all right.

Wulff's version of this meeting with Himmler and Schellenberg painted a scene of utter despair. He remembered that Schellenberg seemed to have thrown off the despondency he had exhibited earlier in the day by the time Himmler walked in with a cigar in his mouth. Himmler's face was swollen and flush; he had liquor on his breath. It was clear that the Reichsführer was very distressed by the Reuters article and knew he was in trouble. According to Wulff, Himmler turned toward him and said: "I now realize, Herr Wulff, that in urging me to arrest Hitler and enter into peace negotiations through the English you were giving me honest advice. Now it is too late. Last year, when you warned me, the time was ripe. You meant well."[28]

Wulff tried to bring up the point that Schellenberg wanted him to convey; that is, he should give Schellenberg permission to go to Sweden to conduct fresh negotiations. But Himmler was too concerned about himself to focus on Schellenberg's plan. He ranted and raved: "What's going to happen, what's going to happen!" Wulff pointed out that if new negotiations proved impossible or came to naught, Himmler might be able to find haven abroad. He suggested two possibilities: a half-Finnish countess who was in debt to him would probably hide him on her estates in Finland or Lapland, and an employee of his was willing to hide him on an estate in the Oldenburg district in northern Germany. Himmler continued to smoke his cigar with trembling hands, saying in despair that he must take his own life.

Finally, Himmler did give Schellenberg permission to go soon to Sweden, but for a moment he clung to him, rather regretting that he had done so, having thereby given him an opportunity to jump ship and save himself.[29] Wulff also made plans to extract himself from the mess by returning at the earliest possible moment to his home in Hamburg.

On April 30, the world later learned, Hitler made his longtime mistress, Eva Braun, his wife in a makeshift ceremony in the Führer's bunker before they both committed suicide. Some details were learned by the OSS through the interrogation of a German nurse assigned to the bunker who gave her simplistic description of the event that had occurred shortly after Berlin fell to the Russians:

The marriage of Hitler to Eva Braun took place on the 28th of April. When I learned about it, it was immediately clear to me that this signified the end of the Third Reich, for if Hitler had believed a continuation of it possible, he would never have taken this step. Now, with death facing him, he wished to thank this woman for her self-sacrificing loyalty by giving her his name. . . . This incident was of little importance to us; at any rate, we saw nothing unusual in it, for Eva Braun was a completely colorless personality. When she was with a crowd of stenographers, she was in no way conspicuous among them . . . The fact that Hitler had poisoned his wolfhound somehow affected us more. The dog received in Hitler's presence a large dose of the poison with which later others were also poisoned. He was very fond of his dog, and took his death to heart."[30]

Just after Hitler's death, news reached Schellenberg that RSHA chief Kaltenbrunner had fired him. Schellenberg, now in jeopardy, found at least temporary refuge under Count Bernadotte's protection in Sweden. Admiral Dönitz had been named to head the German government long enough to conclude a cease-fire and surrender all German forces. Himmler's fantasies of supreme power as he led his Nazi legions against the Bolshevik foe were no more. The "thousand-year Reich" had ended sooner than Hitler had planned.

18

Schellenberg Tries to Negotiate Surrender in Scandinavia

ALTHOUGH KERSTEN HAD LEFT Germany by air for Sweden on September 28, 1944, followed by his wife and children the next day, he spent much of his time tending Himmler's pains in Berlin. Nevertheless, he found solace in the fact that his family was now safely settled in Stockholm as chaos and danger mounted in a dying Germany.

With Germany collapsing, Schellenberg faced his own prospects with considerable trepidation. If captured by the Russians, he could expect the most ruthless treatment because of his position as head of Nazi foreign intelligence, and because he had acted as a point man for Himmler's treachery in plotting against the Führer and making secret overtures to the West for a negotiated peace excluding the Soviets.

Although kept officially informed by the Western Allies, who shared some of their intelligence on this matter with the Soviets, Stalin was generally skeptical; he never ceased to be suspicious of Churchill's and Roosevelt's intentions toward the USSR once the War was won. His own spies, especially Harold A. R. ("Kim") Philby and John Cairncross, both of whom were well placed in British Secret Intelligence (MI-6), doubtless kept him even better informed.

If captured by the Western Allies rather than the Russians, Schellenberg could expect thorough interrogation and, more seriously, indictment by a tribunal certain to be set up by the victors to try Nazi war criminals. Thus a personal invitation extended by Swedish Red Cross senior official Count Folke Bernadotte to be his guest in Sweden gave Schellenberg hope that he could avoid accountability for his service in the SS and his propinquity to Himmler, whose sins of inhumanity would surely taint him as well after the War. The official attitude of the Swedish government, however, might not be as hospitable.

Schellenberg could only hope that chances of his acceptance by Sweden would be improved if he could bring about an early surrender of German forces in Norway—in the Wehrmacht's Northern Sector. The possibility of having to endure fully armed German troops retreating from Norway through Swedish territory was not appealing to the Swedes, who had to date staunchly refused transit rights to German forces whose objective was to rejoin the war against the Soviet Union in the defense of Germany.

During Schellenberg's discussions about this with Himmler at the Danziger Hof in Lübeck in late April 1945, the Reichsführer, as usual, was timid about making decisions of such magnitude on his own. But, as Schellenberg recorded in his autobiographical account of his wartime activities written in Sweden at the War's end, he was visited by "unbelievable luck."[1] They had talked about the Western Allies' refusal to deal with Himmler regarding general surrender along the Western Front. Himmler voiced his bitter disappointment at this and his shock occasioned by the disclosure in the world press of his surrender discussions with Count Bernadotte. Schellenberg expressed his own fear that a letter he had written to the Swedish foreign minister, Christian Günther, would be leaked to the press. Schellenberg also described his concern that his responsibility as a moving spirit in Himmler's unauthorized contacts and actions would provide a difficult basis on which to carry through the plan for arranging a peaceful surrender in the Northern Sector—that is, Germany's Scandinavian theater of military operations—particularly in Norway.[2]

With evident pride, Schellenberg described how he had braced Himmler on this matter—with help from astronomer Wilhelm Wulff, whom he had brought along—and how the Reichsführer had finally given him authority to continue talks with Bernadotte. The discussions included suspension of Germany's occupation of Norway and the consequent internment of unarmed German troops in Sweden until a normal general armistice could be reached. Himmler further nominated Schellenberg as his representative to "negotiate a peaceful solution to the North" with the Swedish government. Schellenberg believed that Himmler's willingness to accredit him was based on his assumption that he, the Reichsführer, "would be in a position, as Hitler's successor, to make these decisions." Pleased with the final result of his conversations with Himmler, Schellenberg proceeded to Flensburg, Germany, for discussions with Count Bernadotte.

The meeting, which included an official of the Swedish government and Dr. Werner Best, the German minister in Denmark, took place in Copenhagen on April 29, at a hotel appropriately named D'Angleterre. The Swedish government requested that the German government, through Schellenberg, produce a clear and definite proposal for a plan by which Germany would peaceably end its occupation of Norway and Denmark.

At nightfall on May 1 in Flensburg, Schellenberg met with his friend and colleague, Dr. Wirsing, who had just flown in from Munich with news that there had been a profound shuffle of power—or whatever was left of power in the near-moribund Third Reich. Hitler, disillusioned by Himmler's disloyalty, had removed the Reichsführer from office and had, of course, simultaneously removed him from consideration as his heir to power. Instead, Hitler named Admiral Karl Dönitz as his successor. This startling development caused Himmler to seek a meeting with Dönitz in Plön.

Schellenberg was pleased that Himmler was at least able to convince Dönitz he should oust Ribbentrop as foreign minister and name as his replacement Graf Lutz Schwerin von Krosigk. Himmler also persuaded Dönitz to name Schellenberg as Schwerin von Krosigk's deputy. But Schellenberg found Himmler deeply depressed by his own bad fortune; his dream to take the helm of his government had vanished and his future seemed grim. He was in fact considering suicide. Events were moving quickly. With much difficulty Schellenberg made his way to Plön where he met with Schwerin von Krosigk, Dönitz, and Himmler, as well as army leaders Wilhelm Keitel and Alfred Jodl. Himmler and Schwerin von Krosigk favored surrender of German forces in the Northern Sector, but Dönitz, Keitel, and Jodl did not agree. They unrealistically could not bear the thought of surrendering Norway without a fight. With the help of Dr. Wirsing, Schellenberg drew up a draft memorandum with his recommendation that the Northern Sector be given up and German forces withdrawn, heralded by appropriate announcements made over the radio.

May 2 found Schellenberg in Denmark. By this time the prospect of total German capitulation to the Allies was so imminent that the Swedish government had lost interest in Schellenberg's plans for a special surrender in Scandinavia. Schellenberg, nonetheless, returned to Plön for further discussions with the new German government. That he had been removed from his position as chief of intelligence by Kaltenbrunner did not deter him from his mission, nor did it seem to have made any difference in Himmler's reliance on him. But then Himmler was also without a position and would soon become a fugitive.

Schellenberg still wanted to see the Allied commander, General Eisenhower, about the large problem of overall surrender of German forces along the Western Front. But he was not yet ready to give up the idea of immediate surrender in Norway. On May 4, Schellenberg was given plenary powers to negotiate with the Swedish government on this matter by Dönitz, so he headed back to Copenhagen.

Denmark's capital was in an uproar with large crowds filling the streets in celebration of the imminent collapse of the interim Nazi government and the end of the War. So crowded were the streets with jubilant people trying to mob his car that Schellenberg was late in arriving at the Swedish Legation. On May 5, still in pursuit of his—by now—lost cause, Schellenberg flew to Stockholm in a Swedish military aircraft. There he was met by Bernadotte and escorted by the count to his home.[3] After long discussions with two Swedish government representatives, the latter decided they must talk over the question of a German surrender in Scandinavia with representatives of the Western Powers in Stockholm. But after the matter had been referred to Eisenhower's headquarters, a response was received in Stockholm that a special commission had been set up by the supreme commander himself to examine existing problems in Scandinavia.

In fact, events soon moved beyond this; on May 7, Germany declared total capitulation and negotiations for its surrender were already under way. Because of this, the Swedish government saw no useful purpose in conducting separate discussions regarding the Northern Sector. Nor were the Allies interested in having Sweden play any role in the total surrender of all German forces.[4] Schellenberg, too, realized that he no longer had anything to say, or do, with this matter.

According to the Allied interrogators who processed Schellenberg's autobiographical memorandum, prepared in Sweden while under the protection of Count Folke Bernadotte, Schellenberg gave himself up willingly to Allied Headquarters at Frankfurt on Main after the cessation of hostilities. In the company of Count Bernadotte, he was flown by military aircraft to Frankfurt for a preliminary interrogation, and on July 7, 1945, he was sent on to London for further questioning.[5]

According to Kersten, Schellenberg felt that Bernadotte had deceived him by letting him believe that he would be protected by him and that he would

Walter Schellenberg while held in U.S. custody as a witness testifying at the International Tribunal at Nuremberg with his guard, Lieutenant Jack ("Tex") Wheelis of the U.S. Army. (University of Texas at Austin, Center for American History, Wheelis Papers)

be permitted to return to Sweden after the interrogations. This, however, was not to be the case, and so Schellenberg felt betrayed.

Schellenberg was not tried by the Allies at the Nuremberg Tribunal as a major war criminal. He did, however, appear as a witness in the trials of the principal defendants—including Göring and Ribbentrop, among others.[6] And he was brought before a lesser American tribunal in January 1948, along with nineteen other defendants in the Wilhelmstrasse Case—*United States vs. Ernst von Weizsaecker et al.*[7] Not until April 1949 was a sentence rendered. Schellenberg was acquitted on all but two charges: that he was a member of the SS and, more specifically, the Sicherheitsdienst, considered by the Allies as criminal organizations; and for complicity in the execution of a number of Russian prisoners recruited for an SD intelligence operation code-named Zeppelin.[8] The purpose of this operation was to air-drop a large number of Russian prisoners who had gone over to the Germans and would wear Wehrmacht uniforms. Their mission was to conduct espionage and attempt to disrupt Russian partisan operations. Russians discovered to be counterspies still loyal to Russia were summarily executed.

Because of a long-suffered stomach malady, Schellenberg had been treated by Kersten's "magic hands" from time to time. During his stay in prison after the War without benefit of treatment his conditioned worsened. His sentence had been considered a light one imposed in consideration of his role in seeking peace with the Allies and for having helped to save many still-imprisoned Jews toward War's end. For these reasons he was released long before he had served his full six-year term in confinement.

Schellenberg's wartime contacts in Switzerland—Colonel-Brigadier Roger Masson, head of the Swiss secret service (more formally, chief of Swiss army intelligence), and General Henri Guisan, commander in chief of the Swiss army—offered him haven in Switzerland. From there he visited Spain, hoping to obtain financial relief from former colleagues who had gone there to avoid Allied arrest for suspected war crimes. He finally died in Italy on March 31, 1952, of what was probably cancer, while staying with an old friend as he wrote his wartime memoirs for publication.

19

Himmler's Demise

FOR HEINRICH HIMMLER, perpetrator of genocide and ruthless policeman of Nazi Germany, the curtain suddenly came down on the last act of
his misbegotten life when the War ended. He fled ahead of SS units determined to carry out Hitler's last instructions: kill the Reichsführer on sight.
And he fled from Allied invaders intent on retribution and determined to
put him on trial as a major war criminal. His last role as a fugitive engulfed
in the confusion of a dying war and the exultation for a budding peace
would attract scant public attention abroad. The thousand-year Reich envisioned by Hitler had been either a Nazi fanatic's fantasy or a catchy slogan
calculated to excite nationalistic pride among demoralized Germans
ground down by World War I and the ensuing Great Depression. But whatever the thousand-year Reich was meant to be, it was no more.

There was no curtain call, much less a Wagnerian finale. There was only
the detritus of a superheated Hot War to be cleaned up, and intimations of
what would soon be called a Cold War, featuring the United States arrayed
with its European Allies against their erstwhile wartime ally, Joseph Stalin.
The Soviet dictator had long been preparing in secret for this opportunity
to grab greater power and extend the USSR's hegemony throughout a tired,
vulnerable postwar world.

New weapons of war held by the United States included the atomic bomb, an ever-threatening instrument of Armageddon soon to be possessed by the Soviets as well. And still in Stalin's arsenal, although long held in reserve following his pact with Hitler on the eve of World War II, was the "gospel according to Marx," now fully resuscitated to give an ideological aura to raw Russian nationalistic aggression. True peace at World War II's end would be chimeric.

Nazi leaders scurried for cover or killed themselves. Hermann Göring, who aspired to succeed Hitler, cheated death by taking poison in his cell at the Allies' Nuremberg trials. Joseph Goebbels killed himself by taking cyanide in Hitler's bunker. And in what must be one of Nazi Germany's most cruel and selfish examples of murder by a family man, Hitler's propagandist made his wife and six young children take cyanide pills and die with him. Foreign Minister Joachim Ribbentrop tried to hide but was found by the Allies in bed with a girlfriend in a Hamburg apartment. He was sentenced to die by hanging at Nuremberg, as were most other major Nazis. Schellenberg's nemesis, Ernst Kaltenbrunner, hid out in a forest cabin until found by the Allies. He was found guilty of major war crimes, and hanged.

Having killed themselves in the underground command bunker, the corpses of Hitler and his hastily wedded mistress, Eva Braun, were doused in gasoline and set afire in the courtyard. No martyr dying on the ramparts, fighting to the end against the Russian invaders of Berlin, was he. His death was ignominious, not glorious.

Heinrich Himmler was among those seeking to escape. His psyche split between wishing to die on the one hand and, on the other, joining a band of Nazi underground guerrilla fighters called "Werewolves," yet to be formed, Himmler set out for Bavaria. Damned by Hitler in his dying hours for high treason and breach of trust, Himmler was a broken and frightened man. Because of his betrayal, he was in jeopardy from roaming SS vigilante groups, as well as from a victorious enemy that wanted to bring him to trial for major war crimes. With Hitler dead, Himmler remained the symbol of Nazism against whom Allied retribution was focused. He was war criminal number one, the Nazi who best embodied the regime's crimes of genocide and vicious assault against humanity. He would be the principal target of Allied punitive action, but also a scapegoat for other Nazi defendants at Nuremberg who would try to shift their blame onto him.

Vainly trying to exit with some semblance of dignity, Himmler addressed his inner cadre of officers on May 5, 1945, the date of Germany's cease-fire. In his farewell speech, he indicated that he might go into hiding and fight a guerrilla war against their occupiers from the fastness of the Bavarian Alps.

Grand Admiral Dönitz, who would briefly govern the remnant of a beaten Germany and sign the peace accords, would have none of Himmler. The Reichsführer, second most powerful man in Germany, had become a man without a country, without friends and in deadly peril. But before setting out, he suggested to his closest officers that they, too, join the still mythical Werewolves.

Himmler did, in fact, try to drop from sight. He took the identity of a dead Geheime Feldspolizei officer—executed for "defeatism"—named Heinrich Hitzinger. He shaved off his mustache, donned a black patch over his right eye, and made other minor adjustments to his face, including taking off the small, narrow-rimmed glasses that had always identified him to the general public. He seemed to cling to a hope, if not a conviction, that the Soviet Union would split with the Western Allies. With simplistic reasoning, he hoped that he could muster enough Germans, particularly military men from the SS, for underground action. In his dream, such a force would rise and provide a balance of power between East and West within central Europe.[1]

Himmler, immersed in the lore encasing his concept of "eternal" Germany, found it difficult to conceive of permanent defeat. Yes, he knew Germany would lose this war, and had believed this to be its fate since mid-1942. But he dreamed that the Germans would rise from the ashes and one day rule the world.

In a secret speech he delivered to an elite cadre of SS officers in Poznan, Poland, early in 1943, Himmler had treated his incredulous audience to his tortured logic and implausible optimism, stating: "For us the end of this war will mean an open road to the East, the creation of the Germanic Reich in this war. . . . We shall have fetched home 30 million people of our blood so that still in our life time we shall be a people of 120 million German souls!" With the industrial prowess of Germans and the success of the Final Solution in cleansing the race, an invincible Germany would emerge victorious, he seemed to promise.[2]

In his talk, Himmler promised that a Nazi rebirth would begin in the troubled interim of an Allied occupation. He predicted that Germany would soon marshal its strength with the guerrilla force he referred to as the "Werewolf" movement, led by his friend Hans Pruetzmann. An Allied presence in Germany would only spawn partisan warfare on a great scale, he predicted. But any apparent faith he had in his plan was contradicted when he had a hole drilled in one of his molars to hide a cyanide vial with which he would commit suicide if captured.

Along with most other Nazi leaders, Himmler was formally dismissed by Dönitz after he took over the government—at least that had been the admiral's intention as divined by a letter of dismissal found in his desk. It is doubtful that Himmler ever knew of the letter he might have received if he had not fled. The simple, unembroidered missive informed him that his services were no longer required and his offices had been abolished.[3]

Himmler and his closest officers—Rudolf Brandt, Otto Ohlendorf, Professor Karl Gebhardt, Heinz Macher, and a military aide, Werner Grothmann—set out by automobile on May 10 for Bavaria with the intention of joining any units of Werewolves they could find. Because of British guards at the bridge over the Elbe, the little group felt it prudent to leave their automobile and split up before crossing the river. They continued on foot, hoping to blend in with the crowds.

On May 21, Himmler and two adjutants were captured by a British patrol that had been alerted to be on the lookout for the former Reichsführer. The Danish government had received intelligence that Himmler would try to make his way circuitously to Bavaria and had passed the information to the British. Himmler and his two adjutants were, however, picked up at a British control point near Bremervord, midway between Hamburg and Bremen, under the impression that they were deserting Geheime Feldpolizei officers. Himmler was not recognized at first for who he was. But his vanity perhaps caused him to bridle at being treated as a common policeman when he was brought into an interrogation center at Barfeld on May 23, since he soon volunteered his true identity to his captors.[4]

Himmler's early comments included a curious defense: "Am I responsible for the excesses of my subordinates?"[5] This was a reversal of the usual plea of Nazi war criminals, who would often claim that they only carried out orders from their superiors. Before Himmler could be interrogated to any meaningful extent, he bit the cyanide capsule lodged in his molar and died almost instantly. The former Reichsführer SS, destined to be remembered in history as the devil incarnate, was no more.

It is poetic justice that Zionist Chaim Herzog, destined one day to become president of the new state of Israel, was among the British intelligence officers present when the sergeant major stunned his commanding officer, a Captain Selvester, by introducing to him their captive as Heinrich Himmler.

After the War, Kersten summarized his assessment of Himmler, with whom he had worked so long: "Fate gave him a position which he was not able to manage. . . . his character was weak [but] he preached toughness. . . ." Kersten claimed that he had been able to influence Himmler in ways egregiously in contradiction to the orders of the Führer. At first Kersten had only been able to arrange for the release of individual Jews, but with the reception of a senior World Jewish Congress representative, the masseur had been able to get Himmler to prevent the execution of an estimated sixty thousand Jews during the course of 1944 and 1945.

By giving relief to Himmler's recurring stomach cramps, Kersten had made himself indispensable. But beyond lessening the Reichsführer's sometimes almost unendurable pain, he could reach those more remote niches of his psyche that were otherwise inaccessible. Kersten wrote in his memoirs that Himmler seemed to have been "happy to have a man beside him who had no connection with the Party hierarchy—somebody who was simply a human being." For that reason Kersten's appeals to him often elicited positive responses. Kersten knew Himmler to have been a vacillating figure, "something in him of a Wallenstein, something of a Robespierre." He had the respect of military men, but because of his power he inspired terror. With regard to Himmler's split psyche, and his sometimes ambivalent view of Hitler, Kersten wrote, "His head contained both the plans of a Faust and the schemes of a Mephistopheles; it was the head of a Janus, for one side showed strains of loyalty, while the other revealed nothing but a skull." Himmler spouted phrases such as "The preservation of the Germanic race justifies cruelty." As for his capacity for cruelty, he believed that "the needs of the state transcended any human destiny."[6]

Still another example of Himmler's meandering mind and penchant for unrealism can be seen in a letter he sent to Charles de Gaulle through the Red Cross as Germany crumbled: "Agree, you have won. Considering where you started from, one bows low indeed to you, General de Gaulle; but now what will you do? Rely on Americans and the British? They will deal with you as a satellite, and you will lose all the honor you have won. Ally yourself with the Soviets? They will restore France to their laws and liquidate you. . . . Actually, the only road that can lead your people to greatness and to independence is that of an entente with a defeated Germany. Proclaim it at once."[7]

Kersten looked back on his last conversation with Himmler, a conversation that had taken place during the night of April 20–21, upon the conclusion of the fateful meeting between Himmler and Norbert Masur of the World Jewish Congress at Kersten's home, Gut Hartzwalde, and remembered that Himmler had shed tears as he climbed into his auto; he thanked Kersten for having bestowed on him the benefits of his medical talent.

Burdened with the knowledge of the evil deeds his patient had perpetrated, Kersten reflected after the War that however one looked at Himmler, one must not ignore the fact that for "countless human beings, his sole significance was death and destruction."[8]

Epilogue

N OW THAT THE WAR WAS OVER, Kersten's future was of even greater concern to him. The attitude of the Finnish government toward him would be important even though he had no wish to seek his fortune in a country whose citizenship he held but which he had not considered his homeland. And the prospect of residing in a country that gave every evidence of falling under Soviet domination did not appeal to him. But he knew that because of his secret services to Finland during World War II, he enjoyed the respect and gratitude of its current government. He might even need its help toward disabusing those in Sweden, the new homeland of his choice, of suspecting him of being a Nazi. In fact, a diplomat in the Finnish Legation, Mr. E. Lundstrom, helpfully revealed in July 1949 that Kersten had been asked by top officers of the Finnish Legation at the beginning of the war to accept Himmler's request—virtually an order—that he become his masseur. Kersten had not wanted to be in thrall to Himmler, but the legation officers made it clear that "it would be of considerable service to the Finnish Government if a Finnish citizen, such as Kersten was, could place himself in such close relations with the Reichsführer SS."[1] Such a statement unambiguously made it clear that the Finnish government considered Kersten not only philosophically and ethically opposed to Himmler and the

Nazi Party, but that he was helpful to his country as an inside source and point of influence reporting on Himmler and his entourage.

Kersten was a true cosmopolitan. Raised in Baltic countries, he felt akin to both Russia and Scandinavia but was culturally a Baltic German.[2] Because of his services to Finland, Kersten had been awarded the title of medical counselor (Medizinalrat), a title given by parliamentary decree, previously granted only four times. Immediately after World War II, Kersten was made "Commander in the Order of the White Rose" by a grateful Finnish Government for having been instrumental in protecting Finnish Jews from Nazi extradition and for arranging for Finland to receive much needed German grain supplies during the War.[3] Finland helped Kersten relocate in Sweden, a first step in distancing himself and his family from possible harassment by enemies such as RSHA chief Ernst Kaltenbrunner and Gestapo chief Heinrich Müller. Specifically, the Finnish government had provided Kersten with an excuse that he could use to gain Himmler's approval for the move.

It was the Swedish government, however, with which Kersten knew he must make friends if he were to settle there after the War. Fortuitously, Kersten's relationship with Swedish foreign minister Christian Günther was firmly established when the masseur had intervened with Himmler and Ribbentrop to have seven Swedish businessmen released from Nazi imprisonment on charges of spying against the Third Reich in Poland. Günther had been duly impressed with Kersten's influence and saw in him a useful agent for conducting humanitarian operations in Sweden's behalf. Specifically, Günther recognized Kersten as an ideal person to help Sweden in its efforts to negotiate with Himmler for the transportation to Sweden by the Swedish Red Cross of many Scandinavian Jews and other citizens arbitrarily held by the Nazis. If Sweden with its Red Cross could perform humanitarian acts by freeing Nazi-held Jews, it might be able to dramatize its usefulness as a neutral and thereby assuage Allied antagonism engendered by Sweden's brisk wartime trade with Germany in such needed commodities as ball bearings and other steel products.

Hearing of Kersten's humanitarian efforts, beginning modestly with securing the release of specific individuals or small groups from concentration camps, we have seen how the Swedish branch of the World Jewish Congress (WJC) had secretly solicited Kersten's services in effecting a mass rescue of Jews awaiting their execution as part of Hitler's Final Solution. Kersten proved himself worthy of WJC hopes by ultimately saving the lives of countless Jews marked for "extermination" during the final days of the European War. Gratitude for this remarkable achievement appeared in a letter from the

World Jewish Congress to Kersten dated August 15, 1945. And in a postwar letter to Dutch historian N. W. Posthumus dated August 1, 1955, WJC executive Hilel Storch affirmed that, "on the basis of Kersten's negotiations 6500 Jews had been rescued and given asylum in Sweden and on the basis of Kersten's arrangements for the handing over of the concentration camps there have been another 60,000 Jews saved." Moreover, according to Professor Posthumus and the *Report of the Dutch Parliamentary Commission of Enquiry into the Government's Conduct of Affairs, 1940–1945, of the Second Chamber of the States General,* published in 1950 by the Dutch government, the number of Dutch people saved by Kersten was approximately 1,900.

Kersten had been able to convince Himmler that such action not only would help mitigate the evil reputation he earned for having perpetrated genocidal pogroms against the Jews of Germany and German occupied territories, but would make it possible to bring a ranking officer of the Swedish Red Cross, Count Folke Bernadotte, together with the Reichsführer. Although Bernadotte needed to discuss secretly the details of delivering to Sweden by Red Cross trucks those released from the death camps, Himmler saw another use for such a meeting. He saw Bernadotte as a useful neutral intermediary between his office and the Western Allies' supreme commander, General Eisenhower, in achieving a negotiated German surrender on the Western Front.

The genesis of this thinking predated Bernadotte's involvement. In a December 8, 1944, letter to Himmler, Kersten confirmed an agreement they had reached between themselves. He thanked Himmler for his cooperation in reaching the agreement and expressed confidence that the Swedish government would be willing to accept for repatriation Dutch, Danish, Norwegian, and Swedish prisoners held in German concentration camps. Kersten also promised to inform Swedish foreign minister Günther of the agreement when he returned to Stockholm.

Kersten also took the occasion to remind Himmler of their earlier discussions with regard to freeing Jews, during which the masseur had recommended releasing some twenty thousand Jews and permitting them to be transported to Switzerland. Now, however, Himmler temporized. The "Great Rescue Operation," in which 150 white buses of the Swedish Red Cross were involved in rescuing Jews, would not begin until April 1945— and Bernadotte would not be able to act as an intermediary for peace. Kersten, however, had paved the way and had brought Bernadotte together with Himmler in launching the daring Red Cross rescue operation behind Hitler's back—no easy accomplishment.

Almost immediately after the European War ended, Bernadotte published a memoir of this event, entitled *Slutet* (The End). The book described the Red Cross role, emphasizing his own personal contribution, in saving the lives of the Nazi death camp inmates. Kersten, who had hoped to receive Swedish citizenship at war's end, was distraught. Instead of providing him with accolades that would help him ingratiate himself with the Swedish government so he could obtain Swedish citizenship, Bernadotte's book gave him no credit for his prime role in the operation—in fact, it did not even mention his name, nor was Sweden's wartime foreign minister, Christian Günther, who had played an important part in the genesis of the operation, mentioned. And the important role played by Norbert Masur, emissary of the World Jewish Congress, was also conspicuously omitted.

Of more immediate concern to Kersten, the Swedish government refused his pending request for Swedish citizenship. While it was a relief that the European War had ended, Kersten felt vulnerable. He was still a man without a country. While he held Finnish citizenship, tighter Soviet control of Finland now made it an inhospitable place—even a dangerous one—in which to settle. Kersten still had his Gut Hartzwalde estate, but it was located in what would become a Soviet zone of control—soon to become East Germany, a Soviet satellite. Kersten had ominous news that the Soviet secret police, either directly or through Germans working under the guidance and control of the USSR, wanted to interrogate him.

There were those, unaware of the circumstances of his employment as the Reichsführer's physical therapist, who leaped to the conclusion that he was a Nazi. The albatross of "guilt by association" was dangerous. It was understandable that Kersten sought laurels upon which he could rest for a while and enjoy his postwar freedom—relatively speaking. He feared criticism and welcomed accolades for his services in behalf of humanity because his future and that of his family were at stake.

Fortunately for Kersten, he had friends who were grateful for his services to the Netherlands and Sweden, as well to the Allied cause. Dr. J. E. H. Baron van Nagell, previously the Dutch minister in Stockholm, responded to an appeal from Kersten, whom he had known well, by obtaining from Günther promises that Kersten would not be harassed by the Swedish government. Günther's influence, however, had been lessened when he was replaced by Osten Unden as foreign minister in July 1945.

The Dutch had much to thank Kersten for, and those in Holland who were knowledgeable about Kersten's wartime activities were critical of what appeared to be Sweden's overly reserved attitude toward him. On November

22, 1945, the Dutch information officer in Stockholm reported that the new Swedish government had stated that "Kersten's presence will be tolerated by the Swedes only if he keeps himself in the background." Later, the new government, according to the Stockholm paper *Aftonbladet* on April 23, 1953, would not even reimburse Kersten for traveling costs incurred by him in behalf of the Swedish government.

On the initiative of Professor N. W. Posthumus, director of the Netherlands Institute of War Documentation, the Dutch government in 1948 set up a special investigating panel to look into the Kersten case. Called the Commission of Enquiry into the Government's Conduct of Affairs, 1940–1945, of the Second Chamber of the States General, this body made a thorough investigation of Kersten, interviewing scores of persons acquainted with the man and his actions during the war, as well as looking up Dutch Foreign Office records and combing other archives.

The commission's report, completed in 1949, essentially upheld Kersten's reported accomplishments in saving lives, and, in the case of the Dutch, saving property and national treasures from Nazi destruction. Reference was made to reports pertaining to Holland that Kersten had talked Himmler into issuing an order that countermanded instructions implementing Hitler's eleventh-hour scorched-earth policy just before Germany's fall. Himmler's adjutant, Rudolf Brandt, recalled that Hermann Fegelein, Himmler's communications officer attached to Hitler's headquarters, had transmitted the order sparing The Hague and other important centers, and ordering that they be surrendered in good condition to the invading Allies. The message specifically stated that the strategic Yselmeer (Zuider Zee) Dam under no condition should be blown up, despite Hitler's still existing orders to do so. Baron van Nagell, describing himself as having been in close touch with Mr. Lundstrom, an adviser to the Finnish Legation in Berlin and a friend of Kersten's in Berlin,[4] testified for the record that he had overheard a telephone conversation in Stockholm during which Brandt alluded to Himmler's instructions not to implement previous orders calling for widespread destruction in Holland—particularly Western Holland. But it is probable that there were others besides Kersten who had brought influence to bear in an effort to prevent Hitler from carrying out his scorched-earth policy, not least of whom was Albert Speer, Hitler's minister of munitions.

The commission, looking back to another accomplishment credited to Kersten's intervention with Himmler in 1941, in which Hitler's project to resettle in the East a large number of the Dutch people was canceled, believed it "very probable" but not proven that credit for this success should be given exclusively to Kersten. The following comment made by Hitler was preserved in the book *Hitler's Table Talk, 1941–1944,* in which Martin Bormann in his role as Hitler's "Boswell" customarily took notes on the Führer's remarks while dining with senior officials: "we must attract the Norwegians, the Swedes, the Danes *and the Dutch* [italics added] into our Eastern territories."[5]

In the interests of objectivity, the Dutch Commission of Enquiry concluded that while Kersten exerted his influence in this matter as well as to prevent the Nazi destruction of The Hague, the blowing up of Yselmeer Dam, and the removal of Dutch art treasures by the Nazis, it could not be demonstrated that such atrocities should be attributed solely to Kersten's intervention. But the commission also concluded that "a great amount of tact and diplomacy was needed to manage so unbalanced a man as Himmler in such a way that the end aimed at might be achieved,"[6] suggesting that Kersten stood high in these qualities. In sum, Kersten's acts at least contributed to the end result, if not single-handedly caused them to occur. Whatever the case, mainly as a result of the commission's report Felix Kersten was made a Grand Officer of Orange-Nassau and given the Silver Medal of Merit, a high award given by the Netherlands government and handed personally to him in August 1950 by Prince Bernhard of the Netherlands.[7] Moreover, a grateful Netherlands nominated Kersten for a Nobel Peace Prize on nine occasions after World War II.[8]

It was perhaps not surprising that following the War there were those among the victorious Allies, unaware of the true circumstances, who leaped to the unfair conclusion that anyone as close to Himmler and as influential as Kersten must have participated in at least some of Himmler's crimes against humanity. But for the Swedish government, on occasion a beneficiary of Kersten's influence, to have long delayed granting citizenship to him after the War was a source of wonder and worry to the masseur.[9]

Kersten's greatest achievement had been to obtain Himmler's agreement and arranging the details for the fateful secret meeting between the Reichsführer and Norbert Masur of the Swedish branch of the World Jewish Congress held at Hartzwalde on April 20–21, 1945, to deal with imminent Jewish jeopardy and to confirm the earlier agreement he had negotiated calling for the transport of Jews to Sweden under the auspices of the Swedish Red. Cross.[10]

While credited by the World Jewish Congress with saving the lives of some sixty thousand Jews, one historian would claim that Kersten, by his influence on Himmler, saved the lives of some eight hundred thousand Nazi

Felix Kersten was made a Grand Officer of Orange-Nassau and was awarded the Silver Medal of Merit of the Netherlands Red Cross, handed to him by Prince Bernhard for humanitarian services rendered to the Netherlands during World War II. (Courtesy of the Kersten family)

prisoners in all, of various nationalities, who might otherwise have been killed rather than left alive for the Allies to free at the end of the War.[11]

A latter-day confirmation of Kersten's accomplishment in causing Himmler to release the Jews still remaining in death camps at the War's end despite Hitler's order that they all be killed was contained in a message to Kersten's widow on August 2, 1988, by Moshe Erell, the Israeli ambassador to Sweden. Ambassador Erell relates how he approached the Holocaust Martyrs and Heroes Remembrance Authority in Jerusalem to compare its information with what he had been able to discover in Stockholm as a result of further research. Erell then stated that he had "been mandated" to pass on the conclusions based on an article, "now given confirmation as an authoritative account, by Dr. Shmuel Krakowski, director of archives at the Holocaust Martyrs and Heroes Remembrance Authority, . . . and present it to you by virtue of its obvious interest to Dr. Felix Kersten's family, and in homage to his memory." Krakowski's account stated:

Kersten wrote in his diary that, on March 5, 1945, Himmler had told him of Hitler's explicit command to liquidate all the concentration-camp prisoners so that they would not enjoy the sight of Nazi Germany's defeat. Himmler told Kersten that he considered himself obliged to see to the exact and complete execution of the Führer's instruction. Kersten goes on to say that, after exhausting and dramatic negotiations, he succeeded on March 12, in coming to an agreement with Himmler. The agreement contained four paragraphs:

1. Hitler's instruction was not to be passed on to the concentration camps.
2. The camps were to be transferred to the Allies in an organized manner.
3. The killing of Jews was to be stopped. The Jews were to be treated the same as the other prisoners.
4. The evacuation of the camps [to remove their inmates out of reach of the Allies] was to cease.

This is the record. In transmitting it to you as an act of formal recognition the Israeli ambassador tendered his own respectful sentiments as well.[12]

In light of the considerable evidence shown above and elsewhere in the written record, concerning Kersten's major role in causing Jews and other nationalities to be freed rather than executed as the Allied forces approached Hitler's concentration camps, it is curious that the book published very soon after the end of the European War by Count Folke Bernadotte (the English-language edition is titled *The Fall of the Curtain*),[13] which narrated his and the Swedish Red Cross's role in the liberation of prisoners, seemed so incomplete.

Bernadotte may have felt constrained so soon after the European war from mentioning Kersten because of the latter's close and very discreet relationship with the Swedish foreign minister, Christian Günther. The war crimes trials were in preparation at the time the book appeared, and this also may have given the count pause. Sweden as a wartime neutral found itself criticized by some in the West for having succumbed too readily to Nazi pressure. The Nazis, to the contrary, felt that Sweden had been too accommodating to the Western Powers. Hitler was furious with the Swedes for permitting the Americans and British to use their country as a platform for espionage and propaganda against the Third Reich and seriously considered occupying Sweden as he had done Norway

There was Bernadotte's government to consider, not to mention the Swedish royal family to which he belonged. Sweden would also benefit from his humanitarian efforts and those of the Swedish Red Cross, and may not have been eager to see most of the credit going to a somewhat enigmatic physical therapist.

Kersten, however, believed that Bernadotte's motive had been to gain kudos for himself as an act of personal vanity. Kersten claimed that his own motives were based on wanting to be accepted by the Swedish government as a resident and citizen, free to ply his profession as a physical therapist; he was not interested in public acclaim. He was, however, conscious of needing recognition for his achievement in the eyes of the Allies in order to mitigate suspicions that he harbored Nazi sentiments and financially benefited by his propinquity to Himmler. He also wanted to be known as a humanitarian, which he believed he was, not an adjunct to Himmler's inhumanity. He was simply a victim of circumstances who had not wanted to work for the notorious Nazi leader, but had no choice except to make the best of it.

What did Kersten's partner in nudging Himmler toward surrender, Walter Schellenberg, think of all this? Because he was, in the first place, trying to avoid conviction as a war criminal at Nuremberg, he, too, tended to blow his own trumpet. But under secret interrogation in England at the War's end he was honest in stating that it had been Kersten, not Bernadotte, who exerted the most influence on Himmler.[14]

While testifying at the Nuremberg trials, Schellenberg again tried to take credit for saving the "seven Swedes" jailed in Poland for crimes against the Third Reich by prevailing on Himmler, but it became clear during the trial that the person who deserved the credit was Felix Kersten, who was virtually unknown by those present.

Schellenberg enjoyed good relations with the Swedish government, and Bernadotte was not hesitant to refer to him in his postwar memoir. On the basis of his interrogation after the European War, it became clear that Schellenberg enjoyed a good relationship with the chief of the Swedish Secret Police, Commissioner Lundquist. In Berlin, Schellenberg also maintained good relations with Swedish ambassador Arvid Richert, who was very pleased with "the fight that Schellenberg was carrying on for Richert's countrymen who were condemned to death." They had much to discuss about Richert's efforts to free Scandinavian prisoners held by the Nazis. It is interesting to note that Schellenberg spoke with him very frankly; he even "initiated him into his plans regarding the cessation of the war." And Richert seemed to know about "Schellenberg's close contact with Count Bernadotte."

German-Swedish relations had become difficult with the rupture of economic relations, a rupture that, as Schellenberg had heard from Himmler, was being seriously considered from the German side as well.[15] Schellenberg claimed during his interrogation that he had used all available means and given Himmler his formal promise to do everything possible to avoid a break with Sweden. All of this suggests that the Swedish government—and by extension, Count Bernadotte—was well disposed toward Schellenberg even if it had publicly seemed to ignore Kersten. Schellenberg's interrogator felt that "there was no doubt that Richert was convinced that in Schellenberg he had found a silent helper."

Kersten had a strong supporter in British war historian H. R. Trevor-Roper. Having completed a thorough examination of the last days of Hitler and the Third Reich,[16] Trevor-Roper became aware of the Felix Kersten story and took it upon himself to set the record straight. Like Professor Posthumus, who managed the Dutch commission's inquiry into Kersten's role, Trevor-Roper believed that what little information about Himmler's therapist had surfaced during the War or its immediate aftermath was incomplete and often wrong. In various publications, particularly the *Atlantic Monthly* in February 1953, Trevor-Roper vigorously addressed the matter. In his article he wrote: "Now he [Kersten] has been officially recognized by a government [the Netherlands], that was itself a victim of Nazi aggression, as one of the great benefactors of Mankind." He added that however incredible this history might seem, "the truth has at last triumphed, not only over natural doubt but also over certain obstacles," since the public release and publication of the Dutch inquiry and the recent nomination of Kersten by members of the Dutch government for the Nobel Peace Prize. One of the obstacles, in Trevor-Roper's opinion, had been the reticence of the Swedish government to make known in timely fashion all the facts known to it.[17] Perhaps because of the favorable report given Kersten by the Dutch commission, the Swedish government became more forthcoming in adopting a favorable posture toward him.

The Dutch Commission of Enquiry satisfied itself that charges made against Kersten alleging him to have been pro-Nazi and having profited from his rescue work in freeing countless foreign prisoners of the Nazis were completely unfounded. The commission concluded that Kersten had "saved thousands of lives of all nationalities at great risk to himself."

The former Swedish foreign minister, Christian Günther, saw fit to state publicly: "There can be no doubt that Dr. Kersten, during the closing stages of the War, saved the lives of thousands of people. As far as Sweden is concerned, among much else, special mention may be made of his decisive initiative on behalf of the jailed] 'Warsaw Swedes' and the planning of the rescue within Germany at the beginning of 1945 which was entrusted to the Red Cross and carried out under the leadership of Count Bernadotte."

While successfully practicing physical therapy in postwar Sweden, and finally having Swedish citizenship bestowed on him toward the end of 1953 after a spirited debate in the Swedish Riksdag (parliament) sparked by defenders of Kersten, there still remained a persistent cloud over his reputation caused by his wartime propinquity with Himmler. The cloud was not fully removed until April 26, 1956, with the publication of a Swedish Foreign Office "White Paper" (*1945 Ars Svenska Hjalpsexpedition till Tyskland*)[18] lauding Kersten specifically for his services during the War. The White Paper revealed additional details of the Bernadotte's 1945 Swedish Relief Expedition, admitting that Kersten's services at that time in saving the lives of many foreign citizens unjustly imprisoned and Jews from Germany and elsewhere scheduled for killing, were "incontestable, clear and important."[19] Thus the Swedish government, which had at first tended to disregard much of Kersten's story, finally gave him credit for his actions. And Trevor-Roper found satisfaction in the white paper's admission that the Swedish Red Cross expedition to transport remaining death camp inmates out of Germany had been made possible, and its success ensured, "by the indispensable secret work in Germany, at Himmler's court, of Felix Kersten."

Trevor-Roper's article, however, ignited an argument with the Swedish government when the Swedish Embassy in Washington, because of comments he had written, undertook to defend Bernadotte in the "Repartee" section of the April 1953 *Atlantic Monthly*. In summary, Trevor-Roper was provoked to cite evidence to the effect that Bernadotte had at first refused to include Jews in the Red Cross convoys bringing out Scandinavian prisoners in Nazi concentration camps, and that it took Kersten's intervention with Swedish foreign minister Günther to enable them to be included in the rescue operation. And with reference to the fateful meeting at Kersten's Gut Hartzwalde estate between Himmler and Norbert Masur of the World Jewish Congress on April 20–21, 1945, Trevor-Roper pointed out that the Reichsführer had formally agreed to the transport to Sweden of Jews held in the death camps. This was duly reported to the Swedish government on April 22, 1945, immediately after the meeting.

The Swedish ambassador to the United States, Erik Boheman, replying to Trevor-Roper in the April 1953 issue of *Atlantic Monthly*, did not question this, but he did deny that Bernadotte had initially refused to take Jews. It had been a misunderstanding, Boheman wrote; Bernadotte was not anti-Semitic. But, according to Kersten, the count had advised him in somewhat threatening tones to omit Jews from the operation on the grounds that he might otherwise "experience difficulties for himself and his family in Sweden." A less objectionable reply by Ambassador Boheman might have been predicated on the fear that Himmler, despite his agreement with Masur, might back out of so large an undertaking if it involved Jews and thus run the risk of having Hitler hear of it (which Hitler ultimately did, and sentenced Himmler to death for it).

Trevor-Roper, on his side, did make allowances for the possibility that Bernadotte "may have been unsure of his instructions" and may have genuinely believed that he was supposed to give priority to Scandinavian citizens. But he concluded in his April 1953 rebuttal to Ambassador Boheman's protests with this comment: "I think it unfortunate that this one officer [Bernadotte], by high-powered personal publicity and (to say no more) evident selection of evidence, should have done a personal injustice to a less fortunately placed man [Kersten] and a violence to historical truth."[20] Boheman probably found this offensive, but he certainly must have taken umbrage at Trevor-Roper's crack that Bernadotte's role in all of this was only that of a "transport officer"—implying that Bernadotte simply ran the trucks."[21]

Kersten was able to retrieve his reputation after the War not only because the Dutch Commission of Enquiry had lent prestige to his case and had perhaps influenced Sweden to issue the White Paper clearing his name, but because Foreign Minister Günther, with whom Kersten had enjoyed an effective relationship, spoke out in his behalf. In addition, a letter written on January 15, 1946, to Kersten by Goesta Engzell, chief legal adviser to the Swedish Ministry of Foreign Affairs, should be noted. Engzell wrote: "During the last years of the Nazi regime you gave notable and commendable help to the Swedish Government in saving victims of the Nazis. You were always ready to utilize your connections in Germany in furthering the wishes and endeavors of the Swedish Foreign Minister." This was a diplomatic way of saying that Kersten, in addition to having been involved in humanitarian activities in behalf of the Swedish government and the Red Cross, had served Sweden as an advocate and informant within Himmler's court.

Engzell went on to praise Kersten for his relief activities: "I know that it was due to you that the release was obtained of a large number of Swedes who had been sentenced to death or imprisonment because of their activities in Poland. . . . I especially remember the release of a great number of Jews and other persons from concentration camps, the transportation to Sweden of Jews interned in Norway, [and] the release, or at least the amelioration of conditions of political prisoners in Norway." Engzell closed his letter to Kersten, writing: "Since part of my work in the Swedish Ministry of Foreign Affairs consisted of trying to save human beings from the fangs of the Nazis, I should like to express my most sincere thanks for your assistance."[22]

Additionally, representatives of the World Jewish Congress, who were also in a position to know firsthand what Kersten had accomplished with regard to rescuing Jews, made known his successes. Norbert Masur wrote a memoir in which he described his epic meeting with Himmler, Kersten, and Schellenberg at Hartzwalde at which the Reichsführer after a long night's session signed an agreement permitting the Swedish Red Cross to transport Jews marked for extermination to Sweden.[23] And Hilel Storch, who requested the meeting arranged by Kersten and initially was to have been the World Jewish Congress's emissary to Himmler, wrote similarly on the subject. Of particular interest was an August 1955 report written by Storch that addressed several specific questions about Kersten and the events in which he took part. Like the British historian Trevor-Roper, the Swedish statesman Günther, and the Dutch historian Posthumus, Storch had a distinguished background he founded the Swedish Committee of the World Jewish Congress in 1942 and having also been a deputy of the Jewish Agency Rescue Committee of the Federation of Jewish Relief Organizations in London. By 1955, Storch had become a highly respected member of the Jewish World Executive.

Storch's efforts while working on behalf of the Jews of the Third Reich was technically separate from the WJC. His mission to Sweden and, very briefly, Germany would succeed or fail depending on his own ability to reach agreement with Himmler. Storch worked with Kersten in his own name, although Kersten was well aware of his official WJC position. By this formula the World Jewish Congress would, hopefully, be spared blame or criticism if double-crossed by the Reichsführer. In the event of failure, the question that might have been asked by some people would be "Why did you deal with a terrible person like Himmler in the first place?"

Storch's mission, thanks to Kersten, had been a success, however. Storch could also thank his good fortune not only for having the support of the

World Jewish Congress, but for having support from the Western Allies as well. He wrote in 1955 that the American envoy in Stockholm and even the U.S. secretary of state had been kept informed by him. He also saw to it that the Soviet ambassador to Sweden was informed of his activities related to freeing the Jews, and he received excellent cooperation from the Swedish government. Storch made it clear that he had been able to establish a close relationship with Foreign Minister Günther, "thanks to Kersten." Storch mentioned that he trusted Kersten and felt a special bond because of their mutual background in the Baltic states. He wrote, "I will never forget his [Kersten's] readiness to help," adding that "I am convinced that if I would have met him one year earlier, we could have prevented much human suffering and rescued the lives of many people of all nations."[24]

Storch summarized what he considered Kersten's accomplishments: Himmler's cancelation of Hitler's order to exterminate all half Jews and to arrest Jewish partners of mixed marriages. And, because of orders put out by Himmler at Kersten's instigation to hand over to the Allies all concentration camp inmates, an estimated sixty thousand Jews and a significant number of non-Jews were saved from Hitler's death sentence.

In most cases where Himmler's order was ignored, Ernst Kaltenbrunner could be blamed. Kaltenbrunner was egregiously guilty of moving the inmates of Buchenwald to avoid having to hand them over to the Allies. And had it not been for Kersten's rapid intervention with Himmler, the Bergen-Belsen camp would have been blown up on Kaltenbrunner's orders.

The Swedish Section of the World Jewish Congress sent a letter of thanks to Kersten after the War, as did the World Jewish Congress secretary-general of the executive in New York, A. Leon Kubowitzki. The text of Kubowitzki's letter, dated December 4, 1946, was generously worded:

Dear Mr. Kersten,

We consider it our duty to express to you our feelings of gratitude and appreciation for the valuable services which you have rendered our people in connection with our desperate attempts to save Jews during the tragic war years.

We have especially in mind your successful endeavors which have resulted in the liberation, before the end of the war, of some 3,500 Jews from German camps and their transfer to Sweden, as well as the surrender of a certain number of concentration camps by the German authorities to the Allies.

However trying the time, you never refused us your service. Our people remember your efforts and your achievements.

That more than sixty thousand Jews were spared brutal execution during the last days of the Third Reich must be attributed to the fateful meeting between Himmler and Norbert Masur of the World Jewish Congress secretly arranged by Kersten at his Gut Hartzwalde estate near Berlin. As we have seen, at this meeting Himmler agreed to issue orders to all Nazi death camp directors not to kill their inmates as earlier ordained by Hitler, but turn them over to the Allied enemy as their forces reached them. And earlier, in 1942, Kersten's persistent prodding of Himmler during a mission to Finland caused the Reichsführer to refrain from demanding that the Finnish government round up and turn over to the Nazis all Jews resident in Finland.

Kersten's reputation as a physical therapist of great talent assured him of success in his postwar career, although it took him seven years to be granted Swedish citizenship and thus provide him and his family with the security for which he had long struggled. Among other places where Kersten practiced his art was France, where he had made many friends who were grateful for the relief he had given them. Some of the most influential of them prevailed on President Charles de Gaulle to bestow upon Kersten France's Legion of Honor for having arranged the release of a considerable number of Frenchmen held by the Nazis during the War, including French Jews marked for death during the ravages of the Holocaust. In April 1960, some two hundred kilometers north of Düsseldorf, as Kersten and his wife were driving to Paris to receive this much-coveted award from de Gaulle, the couple stopped en route at a roadside shop for refreshments. Suddenly, Kersten fell ill and had to be rushed to a hospital. Three days later he died of a heart attack.[25]

Thus ended the life of an uncommonly talented man who was more than a survivor under the Nazis. At mortal risk to himself, Felix Kersten used his unique position of personal influence on Himmler to serve humanity.

Appendix 1

Reference: Chapter 2, "Kersten's Dutch Connection." This is a translation from the German of a memorandum of conversation written by Kersten for his files.

GUT HARTZWALDE   *Translation from the German*
bei Konigstadt uber Gransee
Tel. Schulzendorf Nr. 9 bei Gransee   September 10, 1942
i.d. Mark   Field Command Post

The Image of Europe

Still bewildered by the threatening statement by Himmler in the talks with Witting and Ryti in Finland in August–September 1942, I had a heart-to-heart talk with Berger on Himmler's designs against Sweden, on his ideas to move the peasant-soldiers forward to the Urals while simultaneously suppressing the native population. I reminded Berger of the intention to resettle Dutchmen by the millions to southeastern Europe, whereby Berger had faithfully supported me in forestalling this plan. All this made me ask Berger: "What is fantasy? What is genuine intention? Do they want to abnegate all human rights, destroy European culture and thus destroy Europe?"

Berger's answer was brusque, and astute at the same time: "Only people who in their youth got stuck in primitive heroic epics and Red-Indian stories can talk like this. Himmler is like a schoolboy who, sitting in front of a medieval atlas, and unaware that the world has changed in the meantime, distributes countries according to his wish dreams. Half a thousand years ago there were indeed only two dimensions in the formation of Europe: The princes as worldly power and the church as spiritual power with the pope. Both fought for the possession of countries in their play of war and politics without asking about the peoples. Since then a new dimension has been added, the peoples with their own way of life. Craft technology was superseded by machine technology, regional economy by international economy. The old power wielders who had not comprehended this had perished. Napoléon, the last one to want to unite Europe, had understood only half of it and failed. If we do not understand it and act accordingly, we also will perish. Himmler, despite being well-read in history, has not understood it."

(signed) Felix Kersten, etc.

A p p e n d i x   2

This is typical of the kind of memorandum of conversation made by Kersten for his own files after particularly interesting talks.

GUT HARTZWALDE
bei Konigstadt uber Gransee   December 18, 1942
Tel. Schulzendorf Nr. 9 bei Gransee   Field Command Post
i.d. Mark

Russia Wanted to Attack Poland together with Germany

Today, an hour before treatment went for a walk. Himmler had asked me to see him at 10 o'clock. He is very tired and weak. The stomach cramps are very strong. He is rather despairing. He keeps swearing at Italy and is embittered about Ciano. Today he said to me literally: "I'll see to it that this scoundrel will be sent to the gallows. I have proof that he is a traitor." I calm him and try to talk him out of this. He does calm down. We talk about women. Suddenly he asks me whether I have experience with Russian women. I said I still remembered from my young days that they were very vivacious. "Indeed?" asked Himmler. I suggested to him that if he wanted to know more, to find out from his SS "führer"s in the East. I expected them to have some experience with Russian women whereupon Himmler replied spontaneously: "Are you crazy, Kersten? Don't you know at all that any SS man is forbidden to become involved with enemy alien women. What should we come to if SS men were to beget children with enemy women? In 20 years we would have an army of self-begotten enemies against us." I broke out laughing and said: "Only two years ago, after all, you were allied with the Russians and together you invaded Poland." Himmler replied: "That would have suited the Russians to attack Poland together with us!"

"How so?" I asked. "It did happen after all." At this, Himmler with a furious look at me replied harshly: "No, this did not happen. The Russians had proposed to Ribbentrop to march into Poland simultaneously, on the same day and roll up Poland together. But the Führer did not want this under any circumstances so as not to let the Russians make it appear in later times that national-socialist Germany had not been able to do it by itself. It was therefore agreed upon that only after the destruction of the Polish army by our Wehrmacht the Russians were to be given the right to march into the abandoned Poland up to the limit set to them by the Führer. The Russians were not at all agreeable to not being allowed to march together with us. But they yielded to the iron will of the Führer. Now it is clear in the face of world history: it was the armies of the Führer that knocked out Poland." Thus Himmler's view.

[signed] F. Kersten

A p p e n d i x   3

Reference: Felix Kersten's talk with Himmler on March 4, 1943, protesting Himmler's intention to take custody of Dutch art treasures and store them in Germany—as written down by Kersten for inclusion in his personal file of memorandums of conversation.

GUT HARTZWALD   Berchtesgaden, March 4, 1943
Konigstadt uber Gransee
Tel. Schulzendorf Nr. 9 bei Gransee

The Dutch Art Treasures . . .

Dr. Brandt just told me that a conference on the Dutch art treasures had taken place here yesterday. They (Himmler) want to bring them over from Holland to the East since they now expect a landing of the English at the Dutch coast. The gentlemen did not, however, reach agreement; they will continue to confer tonight. There are some who want to store the art treasures in Austrian mines, others in the Warthegau. Brandt says Himmler had felt very rotten yesterday and not been able to make up his mind. It was good, Brandt said, that I had come today. I said the Dutch art treasures had to remain in Holland, especially if the English land there. They were Dutch national property. I thanked Brandt for his information.

Himmler is in very poor state. At 12 A.M. I was called to see him. He keeps groaning, saying he didn't know anymore where his mind was for all the work and conferences. Everything must be considered in detail so as not to be held guilty of mistakes by later historians. I ask him whether he had unfavorable news from Holland that maybe concerned him now? "No," he said, "at the moment there is nothing of importance. But I still had to attend to Holland again yesterday." "Really? Whatever is happening there again," I ask. "I want to bring the Dutch art treasures to safety," Himmler answers. "I don't quite understand," I said. "Could you give me some further explanation? As far as I am informed, everything there is stored bombproof." "Yes, that is true. But nevertheless, they cannot remain where they are now. Since yesterday I have some people here from my headquarters with whom I carefully consider the issue." After a while he continues: "We have reliable information that the English prepare a landing at the Dutch coast to push forward through Holland to Northern Germany in the direction of Bremen, Hamburg. Well, let them come. We'll make minced meat of them. All the same, it would be a shame if the valuable art values of the Dutch museums and private collections were damaged or stolen by the English. After all, they are Great-German property! I therefore decided to transfer these irreplaceable art treasures to the Warthegau. There they would be safe. Furthermore, he continued, he was thinking . . . of the most valuable objects in the Dutch palaces."

A p p e n d i x   4

Reference: Chapter 5, "Helsinki." Below is a memorandum of record written for his own files by Felix Kersten on October 25, 1943, regarding his journey to Finland, where he talked with Finnish foreign minister Ramsay.

FELIX KERSTEN   *Translation from the German*
Medicinalrd   Stockholm, October 25, 1943
STOCKHOLM

My Journey to Finland

From October 15 to 19 I was in Finland. The new Finnish foreign minister Ramsay had asked me to report. I explained to him that the German military situation was hopeless and that Germany could hold at the most one–two more years. In my opinion a total breakdown would follow. I considered it absolutely necessary for Finland to put out peace feelers now in order to extricate itself from the German clench which, I thought, was not weighing as heavily on Finland any more. Furthermore, I told Ramsay that, in case he wished to use it, I had a direct connection to Roosevelt. There was in Stockholm at present a special representative Mr. Hewitt, who was a patient of mine and whom I could use as a liaison. I told Ramsay that I, however, thought it advisable that the Finnish minister in Stockholm, Griepenberg, should conduct these negotiations. Ramsay was much pleased to learn about this connection and asked me to bring about the connection Griepenberg-Hewitt. I also told Ramsay that Himmler could still get over the matter of the Finnish Jews and has again asked me about it. He had orders from Hitler to investigate this question. I immediately offered myself to look into the matter so we can win time. Ramsay found my proposal appropriate. He asked me to calm down the people as far as possible when I came to Germany. I told him I would continue to treat the matter as before.

On October 16 I spent two hours with President Ryti over coffee. He is much concerned. The German pressure still weighs heavily on Finland. He too understands that Finland needs peace. But how get it. Thank God we are not at war with America. That is his hope.

(signed) Felix Kersten

Appendix 5

Reference: Chapter 12, "Enter the OSS." Goesta Engzell, chief legal adviser to the Swedish Ministry of Foreign Affairs, praises Kersten for obtaining the release of seven Swedish businessmen held in Poland by the Gestapo.
Source: Kersten's personal file of memorandums of conversation. Kersten family collection.

FELIX KERSTEN
Medicinalrad
STOCKHOLM   Stockholm, December 26, 1944

Final Report on the Deliverance of the Warsaw Men

During the whole summer I kept up an intensive fight for the five imprisoned Swedes. In this I was being supported by Schellenberg and Brandt in the most dependable way. We left out no opportunity to appeal to Himmler. Some months ago when I was going to Sweden, Himmler promised that he would send the gentlemen to Sweden even while I was still there. And indeed, on the first of November '44 he released two gentlemen, namely Director Carl Herslow and Diplomingenieur Einar Gerge. The Tandsticks A.B. gave a big dinner for the two to which Irmgard and I were also invited. But now I became furious about Himmler having kept only 40 percent of his promise. I myself had in the meantime settled in Stockholm. When at the beginning of December I went to Germany at the request of Excellency Günther, but also to resume the medical treatment of Himmler, Himmler and I got into a violent argument over the release of the last three Swedes. When he firmly refused—for reasons of prestige or retaining pawns as he called it—to release the gentlemen, I felt compelled to remind him that, under these circumstances, I would be forced to immediately break off his treatment. I was of course aware, I said, of the possible consequences of my action, being after all in Germany and in his power. But I advised him, I continued, to think of the consequences which a breakoff of my treatment might have for his health. Himmler flew into a temper, saying this was blackmail. I responded that this was a wrong view of the matter. My wish was only to help him fulfill his promise. Since Germanic "Führer"s always kept the promises they had given. Himmler said: "No, no, you are not to think badly of me." Some days later he asked me in a letter to take the last three gentlemen along with me on my plane as a Christmas present from him. On December 22, '44 I arrived with the last three gentlemen in Stockholm. From Director Brandin I received a somewhat funnily worded letter of appreciation.

(signed) Felix Kersten

A p p e n d i x   6

Reference: Chapter 12, "Enter the OSS."

FELIX KERSTEN: 486

Stockholm, November 1, 1943

Discussions on Peace with Mr. Hewitt

Mr. H [Hewitt] and I understand each other very well. We are both of the opinion that this dreadful war must be brought to an end. But Hewitt says, correctly: The world will make no peace with a Nazi Germany [i.e., *nationalsozialistischen*]. But I am thinking, first of all, of Finland. Between Finland and America there is no war. Hewitt believes it entirely possible that President Roosevelt would intervene to broker a peace between Russia and Finland, since there is great sympathy in America for Finland. I explained to Hewitt that Finland was absolutely not allied with Nazi Germany, and that in Finland National Socialism was thoroughly denied. We [i.e., the Finns] were only allied to Germany from doubts about the Russian alliance with Germany in the period of the Winter War (of 1939–1940). Hewitt stated that he understand that, and declared himself ready to undertake a mediation [*Vermittelung*] on this basis. [But] the initiative must come from Finland itself. I said to him that I would fly the next day to Finland, for the purpose of making a report on the German (situation there) and take this opportunity to pass on word of the conversation with him [i.e., with Hewitt]. For it was my honest wish that Finland should be freed from (its connection) with the Axis bloc, and that peace should be brought about. Probably I will be flying on October 15 to Helsinki [Helsingfors].

Felix Kersten

FELIX KERSTEN 490

Stockholm, November 1, 1943

Schellenberg Comes to Stockholm

The peace discussions with Hewitt and Graffman are making good progress [going well]. Both of them see the danger which threatens from the East [i.e., Russia]. Graffman says: "An economically destroyed and ruined Europe could become simply a games-counter for Russian Communism."

I have written to Himmler a few days ago that I had met with Hewitt, and that Himmler should incidentally [*umgehend*] send Schellenberg to Stockholm. I think it very important that Schellenberg speak with Hewitt. I do not wish as a Finn myself to interfere in the discussions of a German-American peace. I am excited by the prospect that Schellenberg will come.

Felix Kersten

Stockholm, November 9, 1943

Schellenberg is now in Stockholm. I have introduced him to Hewitt, and they find each other mutually sympathetic. It is my honest wish that out of this personal connection a peace agreement may be reached.

Felix Kersten

GUT HARZWALDE: 497
bei Konigstadt uber Gransee   Hochwald, December 4, 1943
Tel. Schulzendorf Nr. 9 bei Gransee
i.d. Mark

This morning I have begun to make Himmler aware that it is now time for him to make a decision and to take a position concerning my conversations with Hewitt and Graffman, which I have been conducting in Stockholm. I said to Himmler: "It is now time to bring this war to an end, which is not useful to any of the peoples of Europe." The moment has arrived for him to make a decision. *Himmler answered:* "Don't trouble yourself, leave me some time. I cannot simply set the Führer aside, to whom I owe everything. He," *Himmler continued,* "had placed me in this position. Should I now use my position as Reichsführer to set the Führer himself aside? That goes beyond my power, Kersten. Understand me clearly: Read what is inscribed on the badge on my belt. ["Meine Ehre heisst treu!"/"My honor is (stands for) absolute loyalty."] Should I declare all of this worthless, and become a traitor? By heavens, what are you demanding of me, Kersten?" I answered: "I personally don't demand anything of you, but the German people and Europe require that you make a decision now. You are the only one who can bring this about [*herbeiführer*]. And if you really wish to stand before history as the great Reichsführer, you must not hesitate to give Europe this peace. Mr. Hewitt awaits your decision in Stockholm to convey it to Rooseveldt [*sic*]. Use the hour, [because] it won't come again. *Himmler answered:* "The conditions which Schellenberg brought to me are virtually unacceptable. Just consider the sacrifices we have made [to reach this point]. Should all of these have been made in vain? How can I argue this at the highest levels of the party leadership." I responded: "You won't have to answer this in that setting because that party leadership will itself have ceased to exist. But the German people and all Europe will be thankful to you if you choose to go the path of peace." *Himmler said in response:* "I have studied with care the list of items which you sent me from Stockholm. The terms are frightful. But it might be possible to talk them over, if things come to that. But one condition is totally unacceptable, that we be compelled to accept the responsibility for specific war crimes, which are not such in our own eyes. For everything that has been done in Germany during the regime of the Führer has occurred on legal and lawful grounds." "Including the extermination of the Poles and the Jews?" I asked. "Certainly [*Jawohl*]," *said Himmler,* "that was in Breslau when the Führer ordered that the Jews should be exterminated. And the order of the Führer is the highest Führer. But that is a juridical question, and of juristic matters I have no understanding. It is therefore useless to talk further about these matters." I said that I had nonetheless to talk further with him about my conversations in Stockholm about the peace. At that point, Himmler took out of his briefcase the list [of terms] which I had sent to him from Stockholm [after talking with Hewitt], and which listed the terms of the [proposed] peace. *Himmler said:* "Hm, yes, evacuation of all occupied territories: a very hard condition. You must remember that the conquest of these lands has cost much noble German blood. But if it has to be: I could agree to it. Then, for example, you have written down, 'recognition of the boundaries in the east of 1914.' Your Mr. Hewitt is not asking for very much! We have to get a few hundred kilometers in the east to make the *Bogen* [bend, arch, circle] complete [to straighten out the boundaries]. Further," *said Himmler,* "'Free elections on a democratic base in Germany, under American and English control.' That, they can have notwithstanding that I am not in agreement with. 'Deposition of the Führer' and 'Abolition of the Party.' How can I do that?" I answered: "How you do it is your business, but it has to be done. Since the Allies will not negotiate either with the party or with the Führer." "Yes," *Himmler said,* "that is the most difficult point of all. I am asked to destroy the foundation of my own position." *He thought for a while, and then said, in great agitation:* "And then, the ultimate stupidity, I am asked to confess as a condition of the peace, that the Allies have a right to bring Germans to answer for war crimes which in their [i.e., the Allies] opinion have occurred. Such an idiocy!! Kersten. We are the most honest people [in the world?] and have conducted an honorable struggle. Isn't it perhaps a crime that the Allies have themselves for years been laying our cities in rubble and ruins? Don't they see that when Germany loses this war, Russia will have conquered Europe? And perhaps ten years later, America as well! In your paper stands a further condition: 'the complete reduction of the German army, so that it can never in the future be an instrument of aggression.' What does Mr. Hewitt mean by that? Perhaps he means the hundred-thousand-man-army [of the post-Versailles years?]. Germany requires an army of at least three million men to protect Europe from the [threat of] the east." After a few minutes, *Himmler said, with a tired voice:* "I can't make any decision [on these matters] today. Hewitt will certainly be in Stockholm for several more days. His conditions are not unacceptable for me, with the exception of that which relates to that referring to the answerability for war crimes." I asked Himmler if I could tell Hewitt and Graffman that he [Himmler] agreed in principle with the general idea otherwise. "Oh," *answered Himmler,* "wait for a few days, I have still to consider other aspects of the thing. I perceive that this war has been a misfortune for everyone. And if I can offer a helping hand to bring it to an end, I will do it. But I have to see from the American side, a corresponding readiness and good will."

This conversation between the Reichsführer-SS Heinrich Himmler and myself took place on December 4, 1943, at the Field Command Headquarters Hochwald in East Prussia. The conversation began early in the morning at 9:15, and ended at 10:55 A.M.

Gut Hartzwalde December 21, 1943

Felix Kersten

Appendix 7

Reference: Chapter 16, "Negotiations with the Devil." Source: U.S. National Archives, RG 226, Box 2, X-2, PTS 5.

An Account of Schellenberg's and Bernadotte's Efforts to Free Nazi Death Camp Victims

Part II.
Excerpts from the Annex Written by Hauptsturmführer Göring [Schellenberg's assistant] to Schellenberg's Report on His Transaction with Count Bernadotte, and Events in the Last Weeks of the German Reich—*Prepared while under Allied interrogation.*

Count Bernadotte, Chief of the Swedish Red Cross, who since February 1945 had been striving in common with General Schellenberg for the release of the Scandinavian detainees from German concentration camps, had, after overcoming endless difficulties, succeeded in being allowed to concentrate all Scandinavians in Camp Neuengamme, in North West Germany, and there to care for them through the Red Cross. As no transport was put at his disposal from the German side, he had brought a convoy of Swedish Red Cross lorries consisting of about 100 heavy vehicles, to Germany in order to bring the detainees to Neuengamme. This action was drawing to an end in the middle of April 1945. All Norwegians and Danes from the camp except for a small number who had meantime fallen into Russian or Allied hands, were in Camp Neuengamme. Only a group of about 450 Danish Jews were still in Theresienstadt, and Kaltenbrunner, making appeal to Hitler, vigorously resisted their transfer to Neuengamme. The fact that it was still possible to get these Jews out, at the last minute and in spite of their hopeless position, is to the credit solely and only of General Schellenberg. Medical Councillor Kersten also exercised a decisive influence on Himmler during his personal discussions with the latter and made it clear to him that at all costs the survivors must be spared from destruction. Germany, he said, could not answer for this before history. On this occasion Medical Councillor Kersten also reminded Himmler again of the promise he had already given him, Kersten, not to evacuate the camps [placing them beyond reach of Allied forces trying to liberate them], and demanded that this promise be adhered to.

When the last Swedish Red Cross convoy had left Theresienstadt on April 15, 1945, the Russian offensive had already advanced so far that on the following day there no longer existed any communication link between North and South Germany. Conditions in Germany became daily more hopeless, and one could feel the approach of complete collapse. Berlin had been declared a fortress and the Russians had almost closed the ring around the town. On April 21, 1945, I heard from General Schellenberg, who kept me informed by telephone of his conversations with Himmler, which he had had along with Count Bernadotte on the one hand and Kersten and Masur on the other, that transfers from the concentration camps were to be continued on the largest possible scale, even if there were other orders to the contrary. I also knew that in the course of the many discussions between Count Bernadotte and Himmler, this question had often been raised by Count Bernadotte. Through Himmler, it had been decided that all women from the concentration camp Ravensbrück might be evacuated provided they were immediately taken over by the Swedish Red Cross. Himmler had given Count Bernadotte assurances of this at his last interview. Since for the moment there was no transport available for the transfer of the women, but since there were prospects of more rapid release in view of the general situation, I stopped the Swedish Red Cross convoy which was on the point of leaving Germany.

On April 22, 1945, I left Berlin by night at the last minute, proceeding in a northerly direction. I stayed for a few hours at an estate some 90 km north of Berlin, where the news reached me from General Schellenberg that all women from the concentration camp Ravensbrück were to be set free. He gave me the mission of driving immediately to Ravensbrück in order to inform the Camp Commandant of Himmler's decision, and to make preparations for the removal of the women. On April 22, 1945, at about 12:00 o'clock I arrived at Camp Ravensbrück. I immediately had a fairly long discussion with the leader of the camp, Sturmbannführer Suhren. Detailed inquiries showed that the camp contained about 9,000 Polish women, 1,500 French women, Belgians, Dutch women and also about 3,000 Jewesses.

Several thousand prisoners of German, Russian and Italian nationality, who were also interned there, were unaffected by the arrangement. There also, the camp commandant and his colleagues showed a negative attitude towards the release of the detainees. Surhen always tried to evade precise questions and only gave vague answers. In every case he excused himself by saying that he had already destroyed all documentary material, registries and other evidence, stating that this had been done on the orders of the Führer. . . .

On my asking him [Suhren] why he had not kept to the agreement, he stated that he had received instructions from the Inspector of Concentration Camps, Gruppenführer Glucks, that in accordance with an order from the Führer the prisoners were to remain in the camp. I thereupon telephoned Sonderzug Steicmark from Suhren's room and in his presence, and had myself put through to Standartenführer Dr. Brandt, Himmler's personal referent. I described the situation to Dr. Brandt and asked for an immediate decision from Himmler. After a short time, Dr. Brandt rang back and gave Suhren the order to set the prisoners free for removal, as agreed. In this connection, Suhren then told me between ourselves that he no longer knew where he stood, for he had received the express order of the Führer via Kaltenbrunner to keep the prisoners in the camp and on the approach of enemy troops to liquidate them. Suhren now became very uncertain and, amongst other things, confided to me that he had a group of women in the camp whom he had also to kill, on express orders. The women in question were 54 Polish and 17 French women, on whom experiments had been made. When I asked him what kind of experiments he meant, he replied that the persons in question had been injected with bacilli which would develop into a disease which would in turn have been healed through operations, partly muscle and partly bone operations. I thereupon had brought before me and got proof of this affair. I at once drew Suhren's attention to the fact that under no circumstances was he to carry out Kaltenbrunner's order until a decision from Himmler was to hand. From Lübeck I again got into communication with Dr. Brandt and reported this incident to him, with the request that he obtain a decision from Himmler as soon as possible, pointing out to him also that on no account should these women be liquidated.

Appendix 8

Reference: Chapter 17, "Eleventh-Hour Rescue of Jewish Captives."

Text translated from German

The Reichsführer SS and Chief of German Police
Persoenlicher Referent

Berlin, April 20, 1945

Medizinalrat Felix Kersten is traveling to Sweden via Copenhagen. With him is a gentleman who, by the presentation of this certificate, shall be allowed to cross the border to Sweden without showing his papers.

The authorities in question are hereby requested to give these two gentlemen whatever help they may require. This certificate is to remain in the possession of Medizinalrat Felix Kersten.

[signed] R. Brandt

The above is a verbatim translation of the document signed by Rudolf Brandt, Himmler's adjutant, and carried by Felix Kersten as he escorted World Jewish Congress representative Norbert Masur from Stockholm to Germany for a secret meeting at Gut Hartzwalde with Himmler on April 20–21, 1945. The purpose of the meeting, to reach agreement on steps to be taken to rescue Jewish prisoners condemned to die in Nazi death camps, was successfully achieved.

Appendix 9

Reference: Epilogue. Below is an excerpt from American Legation, Stockholm Dispatch No. 5695, June 11, 1945, shortly after the end of the European war. Signed by American minister to Sweden Herschel V. Johnson and addressed to the secretary of state, this dispatch is a brief review of what the legation had been able to find and conclude about Felix Kersten, who apparently had drawn considerable local press commentary in Stockholm.

No. 5695

Stockholm,
Sweden June 11, 1945

CONFIDENTIAL

Subject: Activities of Dr. Felix Kersten, Stockholm, SAFEHAVEN

SIR:

In reference to the Legation's Confidential SAFEHAVEN report no 48, dated April 10, 1945 (sent to the department with copies for U.S. Embassy in London and certain Allied Missions in Stockholm), regarding Dr. Felix Kersten, I have the honor to report that the antecedents and wartime activities in Germany of this person have given occasion to considerable press comment in Sweden and Finland.

It appears from the press that Kersten, who is believed to be a Balt (one paper says Estonian) by birth, arrived in Finland in 1916, together with the German expeditionary force. Prior to this Kersten, according to one report, had been a minor film actor in Bucharest. He became a Finnish citizen by naturalization and is said to have tried his hand with little success at various jobs in his adopted country, his actual profession at the time being that of a masseur. Kersten did not pursue any medical studies during his sojourn in Finland and left the country in the early twenties. In 1924 he turned up in Berlin, becoming a nuisance for the staff at the Finnish Legation upon which he pressed his attentions. In Berlin Kersten presumably worked as a masseur, which apparently brought him into contact with certain influential persons and enabled him to acquire first the title of doctor and—in due time—that of Counselor of Medicine. The press refers to him as "*medicinalrat*," which title is also attached to his name in the Stockholm telephone register.

According to Kersten's recent statements to the Swedish press, he is a specialist on a method of treating neuralgia with massage and was called to attend Prince Consort Henry of the Netherlands, remaining his personal physician until the death of the Prince in 1934. After the German occupation of Holland in 1940 he moved to Berlin, where Heinrich Himmler became his patient. The result was that Himmler became dependent on Kersten's medical skill, which enabled Kersten to induce him to release a considerable number of people from concentration camps, to spare the lives of several persons and to save 2,500 Finnish Jews from deportation to Germany in August 1942.

Kersten reportedly came to Sweden in September 1943 and has filed an application for Swedish citizenship.

On May 28, 1945, GOTEBORG HANDELS-OCH SJOFARTSTIDNING reported that the Governor General of Stockholm had recommended that Kersten's naturalization application be granted, although he has not resided in Sweden the required time. The recommendation was motivated with the record of Kersten's activities in Germany. Among other things the paper mentioned, Kersten had succeeded in securing the release and repatriation of four Swedish Match Company representatives in Warsaw, three of whom had been condemned to death and the fourth sentenced to penal servitude for life. In 1944 he managed to have 50 Danish policemen and 50 Norwegian students freed from various concentration camps, and the same year he also achieved the reprieve of a friend of Swedish Bishop Bjorkquist, who had been condemned to death. In February 1945 Prime Minister Hansson approached Kersten through a Swedish Foreign Office official with the request that he should endeavor to have the lawsuit against the former Austrian Chancellor Seitz quashed, which he did accomplish. Last March, at the request of Foreign Minister Günther, Kersten mediated in the freeing of 77 individuals of various nationalities and confessions from German concentration camps. On April 19, Kersten went to Germany commissioned by Günther to try to achieve the release of 1,000 Jews, thirteen Swedes who had been interned in Norway, 50 married Dutch women, three French women, one Frenchman, 50 Norwegian and 50 Dutch Jews, as well as the reprieve of certain Swedes who had been sentenced to death. This he managed to do after negotiating with Himmler, from whom he also obtained permission for these persons to proceed to Sweden together with 5,000 interned Jewish women.

The paper quoted Kersten as stating that the releases were not achieved without considerable persuasion, and that Himmler's subordinates frequently tried to sabotage his orders. It was particularly difficult to save the Warsaw Swedes. The matter was complicated by Ribbentrop who, supported by Hitler, insisted that Sweden should deliver a very considerable quantity of iron ore in exchange for the four Swedes. Kersten, however, told Himmler that in the circumstances he felt that he could no longer offer Himmler his medical services. This threat, combined with the old antagonism between Himmler and Ribbentrop, produced the desired result.

SVEKSKA DAGBLADET wrote on May 28, 1945, that Count Folke Bernadotte testified to Kersten's "significant contribution to the work of obtaining the release of prisoners in Germany and that he therefore deserves the full appreciation of all those who have regarded this humanitarian work as a great humane achievement.". . .

Legation dispatch No. 5695, from which the above partial text has been quoted, is filed in the U.S. National Archives and Records Administration under RG 226, Entry 19, Box 157, XL Series.

Notes

Prologue

1. H. R. Trevor-Roper, Lord Dacre of Glanton, introduction to *The Kersten Memoirs, 1940–1945* (New York: Macmillan, 1957), p. 11.

Chapter 1. Felix Kersten: A Man of Influence

1. Herma Briffault, ed., *The Memoirs of Doctor Felix Kersten* (Garden City, N.Y.: Doubleday, 1947), p. 11.
2. Ibid., p. 13.
3. Ibid., p. 15.
4. Joseph Kessel, *The Man with the Miraculous Hands* (Freeport, N.Y.: Books for Libraries, 1971), pp. 7–11.
5. Ibid., p. 11.
6. Ibid., p. 18.
7. Felix Kersten, *The Kersten Memoirs, 1940–1945* (New York: Macmillan, 1957), p. 310.
8. H. R. Trevor-Roper, Lord Dacre of Glanton, introduction to *The Kersten Memoirs, 1940–1945*, p. 9. A noted British historian and a British Secret Intelligence Service (MI-6) officer in World War II, Trevor-Roper concluded his introduction to Kersten's memoirs with the statement: "Human memory and human judgment are always fallible, but as far as honesty of purpose and authenticity of documentation are concerned, I am pleased to support with such authority as I possess the accuracy of these memoirs of Felix Kersten" (p. 21).

9. H. R. Trevor-Roper, Lord Dacre of Glanton, "Kersten, Himmler and Count Bernadotte," *Atlantic Monthly* (February 1953): p. 13.

10. Ibid.

11. U. S. National Archives and Records Administration, RG 226, Entry 180, Roll 28, Donovan microfile A-3304; "Memorandum for the President [Roosevelt] from Donovan," March 20, 1944.

12. Kessel, *Man with the Miraculous Hands*, p. 52.

13. Kersten, *Memoirs*, p. 109.

14. Ibid., pp. 110, 111.

15. Briffault, *Memoirs of Felix Kersten*, p. 73.

16. Ibid.

17. Ibid., p. 77.

18. Ibid., pp. 77, 78. From Count Ciano's diary, October 7, 1942.

19. Briffault, *Memoirs of Felix Kersten*, p. 81. Also see *The Ciano Diaries, 1939–1943*, ed. Hugh Gibson (Garden City, N.Y.: Doubleday, 1946); Smyth, Howard, *Studies in Intelligence*. U.S. Central Intelligence Agency (unclassified). "The Ciano Papers, Rose Garden," Spring 1969 edition, Washington, D.C.

20. Kersten, *Memoirs*, p. 157.

21. Briffault, *Memoirs of Felix Kersten*, p. 81.

Chapter 2. Kersten's Dutch Connection

1. Joseph Kessel, *The Man with the Miraculous Hands* (Freeport, N.Y.: Books for Libraries, 1971), p. 94; Herma Briffault, ed., *The Memoirs of Doctor Felix Kersten* (Garden City, N.Y.: Doubleday, 1947), pp. 86–89; H. R. Trevor-Roper, Lord Dacre of Glanton, introduction to *The Kersten Memoirs, 1940–1945* (New York: Macmillan, 1957), p. 11.

2. Felix Kersten, *The Kersten Memoirs, 1940–1945* (New York: Macmillan, 1957), pp. 172, 173.

3. Briffault, *Memoirs of Doctor Felix Kersten*, p. 88.

4. Lucy S. Dawidowicz, *The War Against the Jews, 1933–1945* (1975; reprint, New York: Bantam, 1986), pp. 366–368.

5. Ibid.

6. Kersten, *Memoirs*, pp. 173, 174.

7. Kessel, *Man with the Miraculous Hands*, pp. 107–112; *Report of the Dutch Parliamentary Commission of Enquiry into the Government's Conduct of Affairs, 1940–1945, of the Second Chamber of the States General*, confirmed by depositions of Ludwig Pemsel, March 27, 1952, and General

Müller-Dachs, September 28, 1949 (The Hague: n.p., 1950). Hitler's project to colonize the Ukraine with Dutch in 1941 is suggested in *Hitler's Table Talk, 1941–1944*, ed. H. R. Trevor-Roper, Lord Dacre of Glanton (London: Weidenfeld and Nicolson, 1953), p. 25.

8. Regarding Kersten's account of the Dutch relocation plan, biographer Peter Padfield speculated in his excellent book *Himmler* (New York: Henry Holt, 1993, p. 323) that "it was an elaborate disinformation campaign to cover the imminent resettlement of the Jews, or the troop trains to the east, since it would have been plain madness to cripple the transport and administration systems and above all the war economy with the resettlement of an entire country at the very moment he was embarking on the greatest gamble of his life, the Russian campaign."

9. Kersten, *Memoirs,* p. 306.

10. Ibid.

11. Dawidowicz, *War Against the Jews,* pp. 129, 130.

12. Ibid., p. 129.

13. *Hitler's Table Talk,* pp. 24–25, 41–44.

14. Kersten, *Memoirs,* pp. 120–121.

15. Conversations with Felix Kersten's son Arno Kersten, August 2000; Briffault, *Memoirs of Doctor Felix Kersten,* pp. 115, 116.

16. Kessel, *Man with the Miraculous Hands,* p. 87.

17. Kersten, *Memoirs,* pp. 74–75.

18. Kessel, *Man with the Miraculous Hands,* pp. 74–75.

19. F. H. Hinsley and C.A.G. Simkins, *British Intelligence in the Second World War,* vol. 4, *Security and Counter-intelligence* (New York: Cambridge University Press, 1990), pp. 374, 375. This authoritative book, one of a series of semiofficial British World War II intelligence histories, makes mention (p. 375) of the "large scale penetration of [British] SOE activities in Holland," as exemplified in Appendix 14, "The Case of King Kong," and the German Abwehr (military intelligence) double agent Giskes, who featured in the North Pole case. Considering their penetrations of the Dutch resistance, it is little wonder that the German Abwehr would come to know of and have grave suspicions about Kersten. Himmler's Sicherheitsdienst (foreign intelligence and counterintelligence) could well have learned of Kersten's contacts with the Dutch underground either through the Abwehr or through its own agents in Holland.

20. Briffault, *Memoirs of Doctor Felix Kersten,* pp. 46–50.

21. Peter Padfield, *Himmler,* pp. 123, 308.

22. Ibid., p. 123.

23. After flying to the United Kingdom and there held as a prisioner of war, Hess was replaced by Martin Bormann as Hitler's deputy. Having worked closely with Hess, Bormann had his own insights as regards this strange flight to Scotland. According to Achim Besgen in his 1960 book, *Der Stille Befehl: Medizinalrat Kersten, Himmler und das Dritte Reich* (Munich: Nymphenburger Verlagshandlung, 1960, p. 181), Bormann went on record after the misbegotten flight, writing: "Rudolf Hess for years had himself treated for sexual impotence. . . . Hess believed that through this [flight] he could prove his masculinity to his wife, the Party and the people."

24. Briffault, *Memoirs of Doctor Felix Kersten*, p. 68.

25. Quoted in Alex Dejong, *Stalin and the Shaping of the Soviet Union* (New York: Morrow, 1986), p. 373.

26. Kessel, *Man with the Miraculous Hands*, pp. 116, 117.

27. Ibid., p. 117.

28. U.S. National Archives and Records Administration, RG 165, July 1945, declassified January 1995, "Report on the Case of Walter Friedrich Schellenberg," British-U.S. interrogation of Schellenberg, pp. 12–15, 20; U.S. National Archives and Records Administration, RG 319, IRR X-E 001752, Box 195, Folder 248, NND 837036, "Schellenberg Interrogation" with attachments.

Chapter 3. Walter Schellenberg: Senior Nazi Intelligence Officer

1. Walter Schellenberg, *The Labyrinth: Memoirs of Walter Schellenberg* (New York: Harper & Brothers, 1956), pp. 43–47.

2. Ibid., pp. 25–28.

3. U.S. National Archives and Records Administration, RG 165, July 1945, declassified January 1995, "Report on the Case of Walter Friedrich Schellenberg," British-U.S. interrogation of Schellenberg.

4. Ibid., p. 4.

5. Schellenberg, *Labyrinth*, pp. 17, 18.

6. Ibid., pp. 19, 20.

7. Ibid.

8. Ibid., p. 19.

9. For a book-length account of Salon Kitty, see Peter Norden, *Madam Kitty: A True Story* (London: Abelard-Schuman, 1973), specifically, see p. 146.

10. "Report on the Case of Walter Friedrich Schellenberg," p. 7.

11. Herma Briffault, ed., *The Memoirs of Doctor Felix Kersten* (Garden City, N.Y.: Doubleday, 1947), pp. 58, 59; Nigel West, introduction to *British Security Coordination: The Secret History of British Intelligence in the Americas, 1940–1945* (London: St. Ermin's Press, 1998), pp. 233, 234. According to Captain Fritz Wiedeman, the wartime German consul general in San Francisco, 1940, a German opposition group called Tatkreis, headed by a monarchist, Eustace Koch, planned the bombing.

12. John H. Waller, *The Unseen War in Europe* (New York: Random House, 1996), p. 115.

13. Ulrich von Hassell, *The von Hassell Diaries,* ed. Allen W. Dulles (New York: Doubleday, 1947), p. 88.

14. Waller, *Unseen War,* p. 116.

15. Wilhelm Hoettl, *The Secret Front: The Story of Nazi Political Espionage* (New York: Praeger, 1954), pp. 88–95.

16. Ibid., p. 45.

17. U.S. National Archives and Records Administration, RG 319, IRR X-E 001752, Box 195, Folder 14-B, NDD 837036, "Schellenberg Interrogation" with attachments, p. 7.

18. Schellenberg, *Labyrinth,* p. 111.

19. Ibid.

20. "Schellenberg Interrogation," pp. 9, 10.

21. Ibid., p. 10.

22. Ibid., p. 11.

23. Ibid.

Chapter 4. Rendezvous at Zhitomir: Genesis of High Treason

1. Felix Kersten, *The Kersten Memoirs, 1940–1945* (New York: Macmillan, 1957), p. 88.

2. Louis Kilzer, *Hitler's Traitor: Martin Bormann and the Defeat of the Reich* (Novato, Calif.: Presidio, 2000), p. 70.

3. Ibid.

4. B. H. Liddell Hart, *The German Generals Talk* (New York: Morrow, 1979), pp. 146, 147.

5. Noel Annan, *Changing Enemies* (London: HarperCollins, 1995), pp. 61, 62.

6. Kersten, *Memoirs,* p. 237.

7. The U.S. Office of Strategic Services sent a warning to certain of its European stations that Hohenlohe was not to be trusted. Carleton Hayes, the U.S. ambassador to Spain, who had been approached by Hohenlohe, sent a report to Washington and the OSS station chief in Bern, Switzerland, who also knew Hohenlohe, that the German was "utterly without scruples, lying to anyone without hesitation, including his German chiefs." (U.S. National Archives and Records Administration, Document 2-60, Telegram 1023–28, November 9, 1943, Box 341, from OSS Washington; Telegram 853, November 18, 1943, Box 165, from Carleton Hayes.

8. U.S. National Archives and Records Administration, OSS telegram from Allen Dulles in Bern to OSS Washington, November 21, 1943, Box 341.

9. Minute by Frank Roberts regarding the Burckhardt and Hohenlohe telegrams, July 16, 1940, British Public Record Office, FO 371/2440 7; John H. Waller, *The Unseen War in Europe* (New York: Random House, 1996), pp. 165, 166.

10. U.S. National Archives and Records Administration, RG 165, July 1945, declassified January 1995, "Report on the Case of Walter Friedrich Schellenberg," British-U.S. interrogation of Schellenberg, pp. 29, 30, paragraph headed "Preliminary Peace Feelers."

11. It is interesting to note that in April 1945, as the War was rapidly winding down, Schellenberg tried to frighten the United States into joining with Germany against the USSR by sending word through OSS station chief Allen Dulles that the rapid advance on Germany by the Russians had been made possible by a secret deal between Hitler and Stalin. The deal supposedly called for German troops to hold firm against the Allied advance in the West, but permit Red troops to advance without serious opposition from the East. Schellenberg's eleventh-hour offer was that the Germans would be willing to agree with the Western Allies to a cease-fire on the Western Front, thus turning the tables on the Russians. Dulles rejected the overture, considering it phony as well as dangerous to discuss, and replied negatively to Schellenberg, dismissing the Germans as already on the run and doomed to imminent defeat. U.S. National Archives and Records Administration, RG 226, Box 2, Entry 110, telegram from OSS Bern No. 8139, April 5, 1945.

12. Walter Schellenberg, *Hitler's Secret Service: The Memoirs of Walter Schellenberg*, 2nd ed., ed. Louis Hagen (New York: Pyramid, 1968), p. 153.

13. Peter Padfield, *Himmler* (New York: Henry Holt, 1993), p. 294 n. 79.

14. Karl E. Myer and Shareen Blair Brysac, *Tournament of Shadows: The*

Great Game and the Race for Empire in Central Asia (Washington, D.C.: Counterpoint, 1999), pp. 512, 513.

15. Brooke Dolan, "Across Tibet: Excerpts from the Journal of Captain Brooke Dolan, 1942–1943," *Frontiers* (annual of the Academy of National Science, Philadelphia) 2 (1980).

16. U.S. National Archives and Records Administration, RG 165, Entry 79, P. File, dated February 15, 1943, OSS Project SADDLE: Report by Major Tolstoy.

17. Ilya Tolstoy, "Across Tibet from India to China," *National Geographic* (August 1946).

18. Myer and Brysac, *Tournament of Shadows,* p. 519.

19. U.S. National Archives and Records Administration, RG 338, OLFIR No. 32, February 12, 1946, "Ernst Schaefer's Interrogation at Nuremberg; Final Interrogation Report."

20. Walter Schellenberg, *The Labyrinth: Memoirs of Walter Schellenberg* (New York: Harper & Brothers, 1956), pp. 310, 311.

21. U.S. National Archives and Records Administration, RG 226, Entry 125-A, Box 2, Folder 21, OSS, X-2, Stockholm, PTS 5, "Interrogation of Schellenberg, 16 July, 1945."

22. Schellenberg, *Hitler's Secret Service,* pp. 156–157.

23. Ibid.

24. Ibid.

25. U.S. National Archives and Records Administration, RG 226, Entry 125-A, Box 2, Folder 21, OSS, X-2, Stockholm, PTS-5, "Schellenberg Statement no. 6, July 16, 1945."

26. Kersten, *Memoirs,* p. 93.

27. Ibid., p. 159.

28. Schellenberg, *Hitler's Secret Service,* p. 159.

29. Kersten, *Memoirs,* p. 86.

30. Schellenberg, *Hitler's Secret Service,* pp. 161, 162.

31. Ibid.

32. Ibid.

33. "Report on the Case of Walter Friedrich Schellenberg," Attachment 17, p. 1.

34. Ibid., p. 2.

35. "Schellenberg's Statement no. 6."

36. Anthony Cave Brown, *"C": The Secret Life of Sir Stewart Menzies, Spymaster to Winston Churchill* (1987; reprint, New York: Collier, 1989), p. 564.

37. "Report on the Case of Walter Friedrich Schellenberg," Attachment 17, p. 3.
38. Ibid.
39. Martin Gilbert, *The Second World War*, rev. ed. (New York: Henry Holt, 1989), p. 341.

Chapter 5. Helsinki

1. U.S. National Archives and Records Administration, RG 226, Entry 125-A, Box 29, Folder 404, "Canaris," message to "Saint Amazon" (X-2, or counterespionage, OSS, Washington HQ code designation) from "Saint" (X-2) London, Subject: Admiral Canaris, Hans Lunding et al.
2. Felix Kersten, *The Kersten Memoirs, 1940–1945* (New York: Macmillan, 1957), p. 143.
3. Bernd Wegner, "Hitler's Visit to Finland," *Vierteljah Resheft fur Zeiggeschidite* 43, no. 1 (Munich: Aldenberg Verlag, 1993): pp. 117–137, reprinted in *Command* 38 (July 1996): pp. 12–14.
4. Churchill's attitude toward the Soviet Union at this critical point bearing on the survival of Great Britain can be seen in the well-known statement he made the day Hitler invaded Soviet Russia: "I knew we would not lose the War." See John H. Waller, *The Unseen War in Europe* (New York: Random House, 1996), p. 211.
5. Franz Halder, *The Halder War Diary, 1939–1942*, ed. Charles B. Burdick and Hans-Adolf Jacobsen (Novato, Calif.: Presidio, 1988), p. 104.
6. British House of Lords Record Office, No. 313, File 48 (1943), Diaries of Robert Bruce Lockhart.
7. John Lukacs, *The Duel* (New York: Ticknor & Fields, 1990), p. 29.
8. Kersten, *Memoirs*, p. 144.
9. Ibid., pp. 143, 144.
10. U.S. National Archives and Records Administration, RG 226; Entry 19, Box 157, XL Series, Stockholm Embassy dispatch number 5695, June 11, 1945, p. 2.
11. Lucy S. Dawidowicz, *The War Against the Jews, 1933–1945* (1975; reprint, New York: Bantam, 1986), p. 374, Appendix A.
12. British Public Record Office, Kew, File HW-I, no. 929.
13. Ulrich Blenneman, "German-Soviet Peace Talks, 1942–1944," *Command* 22 (May–June 1993): p. 9.
14. David Kahn, "Finland's Codebreaking in World War II," in *In the Name of Intelligence*, ed. Samuel Halpern and Hayden Peake (Washington, D.C.: NIBC Press, 1994), pp. 339, 340.

15. U.S. National Archives and Records Administration, RG 59, Box 2955; *Foreign Relations of the U.S. [FRUS], Diplomatic Papers, 1943* (Washington, D.C.: U.S. Government Printing Office, 1963), pp. 269–277, 340 n. 34.

16. FRUS, *Diplomatic Papers, 1943*, pp. 269–277, 340 n. 34.

Chapter 6. Searching for Contacts with the West

1. U.S. National Archives and Records Administration, RG 165, July 1945, declassified January 1995, "Report on the Case of Walter Schellenberg," British-U.S. interrogation of Walter Schellenberg, pp. 30, 31; U.S. National Archives and Records Administration, RG 319, IRR X-E 001752, Box 195, NND 837036, "Schellenberg's interrogation," with attachments.

2. "Report on the Case of Walter Schellenberg," Attachment 17, pp. 2, 3.

3. Peter Padfield, *Himmler* (New York: Henry Holt, 1993), p. 123.

4. Jacob Wallenberg, a friend of Hermann Göring's, visited London in his behalf during December 1941 to test the attitude of the British toward making a separate peace with the Germans.

5. "Report on the Case of Walter Schellenberg," p. 36.

6. Ibid., pp. 44, 45.

7. Joseph E. Persico, *Piercing the Reich* (New York: Viking, 1979), p. 316; Klemens von Klemperer, *German Resistance Against Hitler: The Search for Allies Abroad, 1938–1945* (Oxford, U.K.: Clarenden Press, 1992), p. 326.

8. R. Harris Smith, *OSS: The Secret History of America's First Central Intelligence Agency* (Berkeley: University of California Press, 1972), p. 202.

9. British House of Lords Record Office, No. 313, File 48 (1943), Diaries of Robert Bruce Lockhart, entry for March 24, 1943.

Chapter 7. Saving Switzerland

1. U.S. National Archives and Records Administration, RG 226, Entry 125-A, Box 2, Folder "Schellenberg," OSS, X-2, Stockholm, PTS-5, "Brigadenführer Schellenberg, Amtscheff VI, June 1945. Schellenberg wrote this "autobiography" during his temporary stay near Stockholm at the village of Troza under the protection of Swedish Red Cross official Count Folke Bernadotte as World War II ended; it was then given to Allied Intelligence, prior to his being taken into custody. This document, sometimes referred to as the "Troza [or Trosa] Memorandum," was used as a basis

for interrogation and was considered by the Allied interrogators to be "more chronologically and factually" accurate than subsequent statements made by Schellenberg under interrogation. (A Soviet version of the "Troza Memorandum" came into the hands of Soviet Intelligence: H.P. 1637, UD's Arkiv [Russian Archives]).

2. Ibid., p. 3.

3. U.S. National Archives and Records Administration, RG 165, July 1945, declassified January 1995, "Report on the Case of Walter Friedrich Schellenberg," British-U.S. interrogation of Schellenberg, p. 45.

4. Telegram from the Office of the U.S. Chief of Counsel, signed by Robert H. Jackson, U.S. representative to the International Conference preparing the U.S. cases for the War Crimes Trial, to USFET MAIN, December 8, 1945, Ref. No. 1787.

5. "Report on the Case of Walter Friedrich Schellenberg," p. 35.

6. Ibid., p. 41; Jon Kimche, *Spying for Peace* (New York: Roy Publishers, 1961), p. 97.

7. "Report on the Case of Walter Friedrich Schellenberg," p. 45.

8. Kimche, *Spying for Peace*, pp. 100, 101.

9. Ibid., pp. 102, 103.

10. "Report on the Case of Walter Friedrich Schellenberg," p. 45.

11. Kimche, *Spying for Peace*, pp. 52, 53, 54; Stephen P. Halbrook, *Target Switzerland* (Rockville Centre, N.Y.: Sarpedon, 1988), pp. 1–21. Guisan had always felt strongly about the need for a strong military defense of Switzerland. On October 9, 1939, then Colonel Guisan delivered a lecture titled "Our People and Its Army" to the Federal Institute of Technology in Zurich in which he said, "A people defends itself in two ways: by its moral force, expressed by its patriotism, and by its material force, represented by its army."

12. Kimche, *Spying for Peace*, p. 104; Stephen P. Halbrook, *Target Switzerland*, p. 179.

13. Allen W. Dulles, *The Secret Surrender* (New York: Harper & Row, 1966), pp. 25–27.

14. U.S. National Archives and Records Administration, OSS telegram, Bern to Washington, no. 2181, April 7, 1943.

15. Ibid.

16. Neal H. Petersen, *From Hitler's Doorstep* (University Park: Pennsylvania State University Press, 1996), p. 94; U.S. National Archives and Records Administration, OSS Bern telegram no. 534-36, August 2, 1943, Doc 1-103.

17. U.S. National Archives and Records Administration, RG 226, Entry 19, XL 48910, enclosure to U.S. Legation in Bern, Switzerland, dispatch no. 13612, March 25, 1946.
18. Ibid.
19. Ibid.
20. Ibid.

Chapter 8. Turkey and the Balkans

1. Howard McGrath Smyth, "The Ciano Papers: Rose Garden," *Studies in Intelligence* (U.S. Central Intelligence Agency) (spring 1969); John H. Waller, *The Unseen War in Europe* (New York: Random House, 1996), p. 314.
2. Wilhelm Hoettl, *The Secret Front: The Story of Nazi Political Espionage* (New York: Praeger, 1954), p. 224.
3. Walter Schellenberg, *The Labyrinth: Memoirs of Walter Schellenberg* (New York: Harper & Brothers, 1956), pp. 350, 354, 355; Andre Brissaud, *Canaris: The Biography of Admiral Canaris, Chief of German Intelligence in the Second World War* (New York: Grosset & Dunlap, 1974), p. 309; Waller, *Unseen War,* pp. 315–316.
4. U.S. National Archives and Records Administration, RG 226, Entry 124, Box 22, July 3, 1945, "OSS HQ. Detachment 2677, Regt. Italian Division, SI—MEDTO."
5. Ibid.; Brissaud, *Canaris,* p. 312; Waller, *Unseen War,* p. 316; Ian Colvin, *Canaris, Chief of Intelligence* (Maidstone, U.K: George Mann, 1973).
6. U.S. National Archives and Records Administration, RG 165, July 1945, declassified January 1995, "Report on the Case of Walter Friedrich Schellenberg," British-U.S. interrogation of Schellenberg, p. 50.
7. Ibid.
8. U.S. National Archives and Records Administration, RG 226, Entry 134, Box 251, Folder 1519, OSS Cairo to HQ, April 18, 1953; Folder OSS/Donovan, 1941–1943, PSF, Box 167, Franklin D. Roosevelt Library, Hyde Park, New York.
9. U.S. National Archives and Records Administration, RG 319, Box 195, Folder 7, pp. 50, 52–54.
10. Ibid., p. 50.
11. Combined Services Detailed Interrogation Centre, PW Paper 19, "Recent German Pressure on Hungary," p. 2.

12. Ibid., pp. 2, 3.
13. Hoettl, *Secret Front,* pp. 196–207.
14. Ibid., p. 165.
15. Ibid., p. 166; Noel Malcolm, *Bosnia: A Short History* (New York: New York University Press, 1994), p. 182: "The main reason why the Germans decided to clear Tito's forces out of north-western Bosnia in early 1943 was that they feared an Allied landing on the Dalmatian coast, and therefore wanted to strengthen their control over the strategically important hinterland."

"As for Tito, he sent three of his senior officials to negotiate with the Germans in March 1943, first in the Bosnian town of Gornji Vakuf and then in Zagreb: they informed the Germans that 'Tito in the event of an Anglo-American landing was prepared to cooperate with the German divisions in Croatia in common operations against the invaders.' Tito knew that an Allied occupation of Yugoslavia would mean the restoration of the King and his government, and the end of all dreams of an immediate Communist takeover. Such fears continued to plague him even after he had begun to receive direct support from the Allies in the late summer of 1943. As one senior German official in Yugoslavia noted, 'In 1944 there were moments when Partisans worried less about the Germans than about the Allied landing'"(p. 183).

Walter R. Roberts, *Tito, Mihailovic and the Allies, 1941–1945* (Durham, N.C.: Duke University Press, 1987), p. 100: "On April 5, Churchill sent Roosevelt a cable in which he commented on Eden's discussions in Washington and the general war situation. With regard to Yugoslavia, Churchill considered it an important objective to get a 'footing' on the Dalmatian coast so that the 'insurgents can be fomented by weapons, supplies and possibly commandos.'"

"The content of this German memorandum of conversation is confirmed by a document which the Partisan delegation left behind and which bears the signatures of the three Partisan emissaries. In it Djilas, Velebit and Popovic proposed not only further prisoner exchanges and German recognition of the right of the Partisans as combatants but, what was more important, the cessation of hostilities between German forces and the Partisans. The three delegates confirmed in writing that the Partisans 'regarded the Cetniks as their main enemy'" (pp. 108, 109).
16. Hoettl, *Secret Front,* p. 167.
17. John H. Waller, "The Devil's Doctor: Felix Kersten," *International Journal of Intelligence and Counterintelligence* 2, no. 3 (Fall 1998): p. 134; U.S.

National Archives and Records Administration, RG 226, Entry 109, Box 35, July 1945, "Re: Wirsing."

18. Barry Rubin, *Istanbul Intrigues* (New York: McGraw-Hill, 1989), pp. 233–235, 241–247, 259; Richard Wires, *The Cicero Spy Affair: German Access to British Secrets in World War II* (Westport, Conn.: Praeger, 1999).

19. "Report on the Case of Walter Friedrich Schellenberg," pp. 52, 53.

20. Ibid.

21. Richard Breitman, "Himmler's Alleged Peace Emissaries: Autumn 1943," *Journal of Contemporary History* 30 (1995): pp. 415, 416.

Chapter 9. Hitler: Unfit to Rule

1. Felix Kersten, *The Kersten Memoirs* (New York: Macmillan, 1957), pp. 165, 166.

2. Ibid., pp. 167, 168, 169.

3. U.S. National Archives and Records Administration, Intelligence Report, March 21, 1943, prepared by a Naval Intelligence officer at NGB Iceland, issued by the Intelligence Division, Office of Chief of Naval Operations, "Hitler Psychiatric Study," disseminated by OSS, CID No. 31963, evaluation B-3.

4. Walter C. Langer, *The Mind of Adolf Hitler: The Secret Wartime Report* (New York: Basic Books, 1972), p. 27.

5. Birger Dahlerus, *The Last Attempt* (London: Hutchinson, 1945), pp. viii, 62.

6. Ibid., p. vii.

7. Ulrich von Hassell, *The von Hassell Diaries,* ed. Allen W. Dulles (New York: Doubleday, 1947), p. 84.

8. Ibid., pp. 173, 174.

9. Ibid., p. 293.

10. *Civilization* (U.S. Library of Congress) (March–April 1995): p. 54.

11. Langer, *Mind of Hitler,* p. 106.

12. Document CSDIC, Report SRGG 1219 (e), "Interrogation of General Friedrich Dollman," Joseph Mark Lauinger Library, Special Collections Department, Anthony Cave Brown Papers, Box 4, Georgetown University.

13. John Weitz, *Hitler's Diplomat: The Life and Times of Joachim von Ribbentrop* (New York: Ticknor & Fields, 1992), p. 313.

14. Allen W. Dulles, *Germany's Underground* (New York: Macmillan, 1947), p. 4.

15. U.S. National Archives and Records Administration, RG 226, OSS dispatch from Bern, March 6, 1944.
16. Albert Speer, *Inside the Third Reich* (London: Orion Books, 1995), pp. 159, 160, 163.
17. Langer, *Mind of Adolf Hitler,* p. 237.
18. Ibid., p. 162.
19. Ibid., pp. 318, 319.
20. Ernst Hanfstaengl, *Hitler: The Missing Years* (1957; reprint, New York: Arcade, 1994), p. 52.
21. Ibid., chap. 15.
22. U.S. National Archives and Records Administration, RG 226, OSS Files. Entry 139, Box 107, Folder 1496, Henry A. Murray, "Analysis of the Personality of Adolph Hitler."
23. Ibid., p. 24.
24. Ibid., p. 3.
25. Ibid., p. 18.
26. Ibid., p. 22.
27. John H. Waller, *The Unseen War in Europe* (New York: Random House, 1996), p. 71; Dahlerus, *Last Attempt,* pp. 18, 19.
28. Kersten, *Memoirs,* p. 167.
29. Ibid., p. 168.
30. Murray, "Personality of Adolph Hitler," p. 28.
31. Ibid., p. 29.

Chapter 10. The Astrologer

1. U.S. National Archives and Records Administration, RG 319, IRR X-E 001752, Box 195, NND 873036, "Schellenberg Interrogation," pp. 52–55, with attachments.
2. Wilhelm Wulff, *Zodiac and Swastika* (New York: Coward, McCann & Geoghegan, 1973).
3. Ibid., p. 79.
4. Ibid., p. 78.
5. Ibid., p. 81.
6. Ibid., p. 83.
7. Ibid., p. 92.
8. Ibid., p. 94.
9. Ibid., p. 98.
10. Ibid., p. 101.

11. Ibid., p. 106.
12. Ibid., p. 111.
13. Ibid., p. 114.
14. John H. Waller, *The Unseen War in Europe* (New York: Random House, 1996), pp. 48–51, 72, 121–123, 176, 244, 278–281, 340.
15. Wulff, *Zodiac and Swastika*, p. 131 n.
16. Waller, *Unseen War,* pp. 339, 341, 347.
17. Neal H. Petersen, *From Hitler's Doorstep* (University Park: Pennsylvania State University Press, 1996), p. 434, Doc. 5–17, Telegram 4039, January 24, 1945, and p. 629 n., Doc. 5–17; Hans Bernd Gisevius, *To the Bitter End* (Boston: Houghton Mifflin, 1947), pp. 592, 593, 597, 598. In hiding near Berlin for more than six months, Gisevius was becoming desperate. By January 1, 1945, help had not arrived, and he had almost given up hope when a package arrived at his doorstep. In the package were a badge, worn by Gestapo officers, and an official German passport with a photo of himself and an alias.

These forged documents had been made in London by the OSS and given to Henry Goverts to deliver. This was a hazardous mission at best, but became even more unnerving when, by sheer coincidence, Goverts suddenly encountered his superior officer, the new chief of Abwehr, SS General Schellenberg, in his hotel lobby in Constance, Switzerland. Schellenberg knew Goverts well as an Abwehr officer whose duties frequently took him abroad on liaison tasks, so nothing untoward happened. But Goverts was becoming increasingly nervous to have on his person such compromising documents, so he cut a few security corners to catch the fastest train to Berlin. With relief, he dropped off the material for Gisevius at the latter's refuge house. Gisevius then made his way to safety to Switzerland, where he called on his American contact, Allen Dulles, in Bern, to express his heartfelt appreciation. Gisevius, *To the Bitter End,* pp. 592, 593, 597, 598. It should be noted that Goverts had long been a good friend of Dulles's German-American OSS assistant, Gero von Gaevernitz. (NARA, RG-84, file 1940–1944, Box 24, 820.02 540.6 U.S. Legation Memo of October 16, 1945.)
18. Wulff, *Zodiac and Swastika*, pp. 116–117.
19. Ibid.

Chapter 11. Himmler, the Man

1. Felix Kersten, *The Kersten Memoirs, 1940–1945* (New York: Macmillan, 1957), p. 75.

2. Ibid., p. 76.
3. Peter Padfield, *Himmler* (New York: Henry Holt, 1993), p. 319. The mistress taken by Himmler was his personal secretary, Haschen Potthast (p. 320).
4. Kersten, *Memoirs,* p. 150.
5. Ibid., p. 151.
6. Ibid., p. 152.
7. Ibid., p. 153.
8. Wilhelm Hoettl, *The Secret Front: The Story of Nazi Political Espionage* (New York: Praeger, 1954), pp. 49–55.
9. Kersten, *Memoirs,* pp. 160, 161.
10. Ibid., p. 163.
11. Ibid., p. 164.
12. Ibid., pp. 119, 120.
13. Ibid.

Chapter 12. Enter the OSS

1. Felix Kersten, *The Kersten Memoirs, 1940–1945* (New York: Macmillan, 1957), p. 187.
2. Anders Frankson, "Spared Sweden During the Second World War," *Command* 39 (September 1996): p. 38.
3. "Gist of the 'Report of the Dutch Parliamentary Commission [of Enquiry],' Consisting of Jonkheer A. M. Snouck Hurgronje, LL.D., Professor A. J. C. Rutter, and C. J. van Schelle, LL.D., on Mr. E. A. F. Kersten," in *Who Was Felix Kersten? Documents Issued by Persons and Organisations Confirming Medicinalrådet Felix Kersten's Involvement and Achievements During the Second World War,* ed. and comp. Arno Kersten (Stockholm: privately published, 2000), p. 3. Arno Kersten published this booklet to complement a documentary film produced by Mandart Production, Helsinki, Finland, concerning his father's involvement in saving the victims of SS brutality and persecution in Nazi Germany.
4. Kersten, *Memoirs,* p. 188.
5. John H. Waller, "The Devil's Doctor: Felix Kersten," *International Journal of Intelligence and Counterintelligence* 2, no. 3 (Fall 1998): p. 314; British Public Record Office, Kew, File HW-1, no. 929.
6. Ulrich Blenneman, "German Soviet Peace Talks, 1942–1944," *Command* 22 (May–June 1993): p. 9.
7. R. Harris Smith, *OSS: The Secret History of America's First Central Intelligence Agency* (Berkeley: University of California Press, 1972), p. 201.
8. Kersten, *Memoirs,* p. 188.

9. Felix Kersten's original diary, October 8, 1943 (not published in verbatim form).

10. Ibid., October 25, 1943.

11. Kersten, *Memoirs*, pp. 188, 189.

12. R. Harris Smith, *OSS*, pp. 198, 199.

13. Stanton Griffis, *Lying in State* (New York: Doubleday, 1957).

14. David Kahn, "Finland's Code Breaking During the Second World War," in *In the Name of Intelligence*, ed. Samuel Halpern and Hayden Peake (Washington, D.C.: NBC Press, 1994), pp. 339, 340.

15. *Foreign Relations of the U.S. [FRUS], Diplomatic Papers, 1943* (Washington, D.C.: U.S. Government Printing Office, 1963), pp. 269–277.

16. Kersten, *Memoirs*, pp. 188, 189.

17. Aide-mémoire from the U.S. Department of State, British Public Record Office, Kew, FO 371/29085, January 22, 1944; seven-point agreement also published in Kersten, *Memoirs*, pp. 190, 191.

18. Kersten, *Memoirs*, p. 189.

19. Ibid.

20. Allen W. Dulles, *Germany's Underground* (New York: Macmillan, 1947), pp. 142, 143.

21. Richard Breitman, "Himmler's Alleged Peace Emissaries," *Journal of Contemporary History* 30 (1995): p. 415.

22. Kersten, *Memoirs*, pp. 192, 193.

23. U.S. National Archives and Records Administration, RG 226, Entry 25-A, Box 2, Schellenberg Folder, X-2 (OSS Counterespionage), Nr. PTS-5 to "Saint" (X-2, or Counterespionage, OSS, Washington HQ code designation), "J.C.-Land Information in SHAEF [Allied headquarters in Europe] Summaries."

24. Ibid., pp. 1, 2.

25. Kersten, *Memoirs*, pp. 195, 196.

26. Ibid., p. 165.

27. Walter Schellenberg, *Hitler's Secret Service: The Memoirs of Walter Schellenberg*, 2nd ed., ed. Louis Hagen (New York: Pyramid, 1968), p. 338; U.S. National Archives and Records Administration, RG 226, Entry 125-A, Box 2, Folder 21, "Schellenberg's Statement of 6 August 1945."

28. Kersten, *Memoirs*, p. 195.

Chapter 13. Hewitt Reports to President Roosevelt

1. All quotations from Hewitt are taken verbatim from his report, "Contact with Himmler," attached to William Donovan's "Memorandum for the

President," March 20, 1944, U.S. National Archives and Records Administration, RG 226, Microfilm 1642, Roll 23, Frames 782–800, declassified 1978.

2. In the spring of 1942, preceding Hewitt, the Office of Coordinator of Information Agency (COI), predecessor of the OSS, placed Bruce Hopper in Stockholm. In a May 7, 1942, message Hopper gave an opinion as to the Swedish situation vis-à-vis Germany gleaned from "a man of excellent authority." In response to the question asked by Hopper— would "the wounded Teutonic dragon . . . lash out at Sweden if it were foiled in Libya and the Caucasus?"—the source replied, "The *Führer* is very irritated against Sweden (so says the *Führer's* doctor), but there are indications of preparation for an attack on Sweden (German Sources). While the Red Army can keep striking back, the minute the *Wehrmacht* lets up, Hitler cannot spare the 500,000 men needed to handle Sweden. . . . Sweden will never let Nazi units be routed through the country again, even if unarmed, but might let military equipment and supplies thru to Finland under pressure because of sympathy for the Finns' struggle against Communism. . . ." U.S. National Archives and Records Administration, RG 226, Entry 92, Box 4-D, Folder 20, Interoffice Memo of Coordinator of Information (COI), May 11, 1942, S. W. Morgan to F. L. Belin, Reporting Board.

3. Allen W. Dulles, *Germany's Underground* (New York: Macmillan, 1947), pp. 142, 143.

4. John H. Waller, *The Unseen War in Europe* (New York: Random House, 1996), pp. 299, 301.

5. An OSS Bern report of December 20, 1943, described indications that Germany was developing biological weapons. Sources mentioned were Dr. Paul Scherrer, a well-known Swiss scientist; another scientist, Professor Mooser; and Allen Dulles's assistant in Bern, Gero von Schulze-Gaevernitz. U.S. National Archives and Records Administration, RG 226, OSS Records, Box 274, Tel 138185.

6. H. R. Trevor-Roper, introduction to Felix Kersten, *The Kersten Memoirs, 1940–1945* (New York: Macmillan, 1957), p. 11.

7. See note 1 above.

8. Aide-mémoire from the U.S. Department of State, British Public Record Office, Kew, FO 371/29085, January 22, 1944.

9. See note 1 above.

10. Felix Kersten, *The Kersten Memoirs, 1940–1945* (New York: Macmillan, 1957), p. 191.

11. H. R. Trevor-Roper, Lord Dacre of Glanton, *The Philby Affair* (London: William Kimber, 1968), pp. 78, 79.
12. Aide-mémoire from the U.S. Department of State, January 24, 1944; U.S. National Archives and Records Administration, RG 84, Stockholm Legation, Box 1, Folder 6, 1943, "Hewitt's Report," December 20, 1943.
13. Walter Schellenberg, *The Labyrinth: Memoirs of Walter Schellenberg* (New York: Harper & Brothers, 1956), p. 371.
14. Calvin Hoover, *Memoirs of Capitalism, Communism and Nazism* (Durham, N.C.: Duke University Press, 1965), p. 217.
15. Achim Besgen, *Der Stille Befehl: Medizinalrat Kersten, Himmler und das Dritte Reich* (Munich: Nymphenburger Verlagshandlung, 1960), pp. 33, 34.
16. Anthony Cave Brown, ed., *The Secret War Report of the OSS* (New York: Berkley, 1976), p. 309.
17. U.S. National Archives and Research Administration, RG 226, Entry 125-A, Box 2, Folder "Schellenberg," OSS, X-2, Stockholm, PTS-5, "Brigadenführer Schellenberg, Amtscheff VI," June 1945, p. 2.
18. *Foreign Relations of the U.S. [FRUS] 1944*, vol. 1 (Washington, D.C.: U.S. Government Printing Office, 1965), p. 490.
19. Ibid., pp. 489–493, 496.
20. Ibid., p. 494.
21. Ibid., p. 495.
22. Ibid., p. 491. The aide-mémoire referred to was in accordance with item 13 of a secret protocol signed by the U.S., Britain, and the USSR on November 1, 1943, at the Tripartite Conference of Allied Foreign Ministers.
23. Ibid., p. 493.
24. Ibid., p. 494.
25. British House of Lords Record Office, No. 313, File 60 (1945), Diaries of Robert Bruce Lockhart, entry for January 19, 1945.
26. U.S. National Archives and Records Administration, RG 319, IRR X-E 001752, Box 195, NND 837036, "Schellenberg Interrogation," with attachments, p. 53.

Chapter 14. Murder Plot Puts Kersten at Risk

1. Heinz Hohne, *Canaris: Hitler's Master Spy* (Garden City, N.Y.: Doubleday, 1979), p. 568.
2. Original handwritten diary of Kersten, seen by the author in Stockholm.

3. Joseph Kessel, *The Man with the Miraculous Hands* (Freeport, N.Y.: Books for Libraries, 1971), p. 181.
4. U.S. National Archives and Records Administration, RG 165, July 1945, declassified January 1995, "Report on the Case of Walter Friedrich Schellenberg," British-U.S. interrogation of Schellenberg.
5. Ibid., pp. 72, 73.
6. "Gist of the 'Report of the Dutch Parliamentary Commission [of Enquiry],' consisting of Jonkheer A. M. Snouck, Hurgronje, LL.D., Professor A. J. C. Rutter, and C. J. van Schelle, LL. D., on Mr. E. A. F. Kersten," in *Who Was Felix Kersten? Documents Issued by Persons and Organisations Confirming Medicinalrådet Felix Kersten's Involvement and Achievements During the Second World War*, ed. and comp. Arno Kersten (Stockholm: privately published, 2000), p. 3; note from Schellenberg to Felix Kersten, August 2, 1944, Kersten family personal collection.
7. Herma Briffault, ed., *The Memoirs of Doctor Felix Kersten* (Garden City, N.Y.: Doubleday, 1947), pp. 194, 243–244.
8. Ibid., p. 245.

Chapter 15. Jews in Jeopardy

1. Peter Black, *Ernst Kaltenbrunner: Ideological Soldier of the Third Reich* (Princeton, N.J.: Princeton University Press, 1984), pp. 230, 231; John H. Waller, *The Unseen War in Europe* (New York: Random House, 1996), p. 293.
2. U.S. National Archives and Records Administration, RG 165, July 1945, declassified January 1995, "Report on the Case of Walter Friedrich Schellenberg," British-U.S. interrogation of Schellenberg, p. 79.
3. Ibid.
4. Monty Noam Penkower, *The Jews Were Expendable* (Urbana: University of Illinois Press, 1983), pp. 260–265.
5. Walter Schellenberg, *Hitler's Secret Service: The Memoirs of Walter Schellenberg*, 2nd ed., ed. Louis Hagen (New York: Pyramid, 1968), p. 199.
6. Felix Kersten, *The Kersten Memoirs, 1940–1945* (New York: Macmillan, 1957), pp. 275–276.

Chapter 16. Negotiations with the Devil

1. Felix Kersten, *The Kersten Memoirs, 1940–1945* (New York: Macmillan, 1957), p. 277; John Toland, *The Last 100 Days* (New York: Bantam,

1967), p. 181; Peter Padfield, *Himmler* (New York: Henry Holt, 1993), pp. 545, 546.

2. U.S. National Archives and Records Administration, RG 319, Box 195, Germany, Folder 348, File X-E 0011752, "Report on the Case of Walter Friedrich Schellenberg."

3. Ibid., p. 87.

4. Count Folke Bernadotte, *The Fall of the Curtain* (London: Cassell, 1945), p. 8.

5. Wilhelm Wulff, *Zodiac and Swastika* (New York: Coward, McCann & Geoghegan, 1973), pp. 134, 135.

6. H. R. Trevor-Roper, introduction to Kersten, *Memoirs,* p. 13.

7. Kersten, *Memoirs,* p. 274.

8. Walter Schellenberg, *The Labyrinth: Memoirs of Walter Schellenberg* (New York: Harper & Brothers, 1956), p. 383.

9. "Report on the Case of Walter Friedrich Schellenberg," p. 87; Schellenberg, *Labyrinth,* p. 384.

10. Ibid.

11. Bernadotte, *Fall of the Curtain,* p. 11.

12. Wulff, *Zodiac and Swastika,* p. 135.

13. Ibid., p. 136.

14. Ibid.

15. "Report on the Case of Walter Friedrich Schellenberg," p. 88.

16. Perhaps discouraged by Wehrmacht defeats on the Eastern Front, particularly a critical defeat at the Battle of Kursk, Ribbentrop had sent Peter Kleist to Stockholm as early as September 1943 in an effort to make contact with the Soviets. The foreign minister was oblivious to the fact that Kleist was a Resistance activist in Admiral Wilhelm Canaris's Abwehr Resistance circle. Roger Manvell and Heinrich Fraenkel, *The Canaris Conspiracy* (New York: David McKay, 1969), p. 174.

17. Bernadotte, *Fall of the Curtain,* pp. 18, 19.

18. Ibid., p. 21.

19. "Report on the Case of Wilhelm Friedrich Schellenberg," p. 89.

Chapter 17. Eleventh-Hour Rescue
of Jewish Captives

1. Based on a letter dated August 1, 1955, from Hilel Storch to Professor N. W. Posthumus, a prominent Dutch scholar who conducted, after World

War II, an official investigation concerning Kersten's actions on behalf of anti-Nazi activities in the Netherlands and elsewhere in Europe. See Arno Kersten, ed. and comp., *Who Was Felix Kersten? Documents Issued by Persons and Organisations Confirming Medicinålradet Felix Kersten's Involvement and Achievements During the Second World War* (Stockholm: privately published, 2000), Para. 5.

2. Walter Schellenberg, *The Labyrinth: Memoirs of Walter Schellenberg* (New York: Harper & Brothers, 1956), p. 391.

3. Felix Kersten, *The Kersten Memoirs, 1940–1945* (New York: Macmillan, 1957), p. 286.

4. Ibid., p. 289.

5. An article written by Shmuel Krakowski, director of archives, at the Holocaust Martyrs and Heroes Rememberance Authority in Sweden, quoting Kersten's diary, was described in a letter dated August 2, 1988, from Moshe Erell, Israeli ambassador in Stockholm, to Kersten's widow, Irmgard Kersten. Kersten's diary described a four-point agreement. Schellenberg, *Labyrinth*, pp. 393–394. See also U.S. National Archives and Records Administration, RG 226, Entry 125-A, Box 2, Folder "Schellenberg," X-2, Stockholm, OSS, PTS-5, "Brigadenführer Schellenberg, Amtscheff VI," p. 116.

6. Norbert Masur, *En Jude Talar Med Himmler* (Stockholm: Albert Bonniers Förlag, 1945); H. R. Trevor-Roper, introduction to Kersten, *Memoirs*, p. 15.

7. Peter Padfield, *Himmler* (New York: Henry Holt, 1993), pp. 592, 593.

8. "Brigadenführer Schellenberg, Amtscheff VI," p. 21.

9. Ibid.

10. Wilhelm Wulff, *Zodiac and Swastika* (New York: Coward, McCann & Geoghegan, 1973), p. 142.

11. Ibid., p. 147.

12. "Brigadenführer Schellenberg, Amtscheff VI," p. 20.

13. Walter Schellenberg, *Hitler's Secret Service: The Memoirs of Walter Schellenberg*, 2nd ed., ed. Louis Hagen (New York: Pyramid, 1968), p. 205.

14. Ibid., pp. 206, 207.

15. Ibid., p. 207.

16. Wilhelm Hoettl, *The Secret Front: The Story of Nazi Political Espionage* (New York: Praeger, 1954), pp. 55, 56.

17. U.S. National Archives and Records Administration, RG 165, July 1945, declassified January 1995, "Report on the Case of Walter Friedrich Schellenberg," British-U.S. interrogation of Schellenberg.

18. Ibid.

19. Hoettl, *The Secret Front,* p. 56.

20. Ibid.

21. Ibid.

22. Count Folke Bernadotte, *The Fall of the Curtain* (London: Cassell, 1945), pp. 54, 55, 56.

23. Ibid.

24. H. R. Trevor-Roper, *The Last Days of Hitler,* 6th ed. (Chicago: University of Chicago Press, 1987), p. 204.

25. Padfield, *Himmler,* p. 598.

26. Joachim Kramarz, *Stauffenberg: The Architect of the Famous July 20th Conspiracy to Assassinate Hitler* (New York: Macmillan, 1967), p. 176.

27. Allen W. Dulles, *Germany's Underground* (New York: Macmillan, 1947), pp. 145, 146.

28. Wulff, *Zodiac and Swastika,* pp. 182, 183.

29. Ibid., pp. 185, 186.

30. "Statements of Erna Flegel, R. W. Red Cross Nurse from the Training School, Markisches Haus," *Studies in Intelligence* (U.S. Central Intelligence Agency) (Fall 1981): p. 34.

Chapter 18. Schellenberg Tries to Negotiate Surrender in Scandinavia

1. U.S. National Archives and Records Administration, RG 226, Entry 125-A, Box 2, Folder "Schellenberg," OSS, X-2, Stockholm, PTS-5, "Brigadenführer Schellenberg, Amtscheff IV," p. 27.

2. Ibid.

3. Ibid., p. 32.

4. Ibid., pp. 33, 34.

5. Ibid. The Allied interrogation report that included Schellenberg's autobiographical memorandum, was introduced by the following introductory comment:

On the 7th of July 1945, a German who gave his name as Walter Friedrich Schellenberg was admitted for purposes of interrogation to Camp 020.

Schellenberg's name was known to have received a certain prominence in the World Press, not only because of the important position in the G.I.S. [German Intelligence Service] that he had held during the greater part of the war, but also on account of the leading part he had played in certain peace negotiations.

Some few days before the capitulation of Germany, Schellenberg had in fact been empowered by the new German Government under Admiral Doenitz to open negotiations with the Swedish Government with the intention of arranging the surrender of the German forces in the Northern Zone and the opening of peace negotiations with the Western Powers. But Schellenberg's efforts to fulfill his mission were without result as the general capitulation of Germany, including the northern area, took place before the conclusion of negotiations.

After the cessation of hostilities Schellenberg remained in Sweden and was, at the beginning of June 1945, approached by the American authorities with a view to supplying certain information. It was then put to him that he should place himself at the disposal of the Allies and furnish them with all the information in his possession to which proposal he agreed. On the morning of the 17th of June, therefore, he flew in a Dakota to Frankfort on Main where he was taken in charge by the Allied authorities. On the 7th of July, he was flown to London.

6. The evidence given by Schellenberg is in *The Trial of German Major Criminals*, pt. 3 (London: H.M.S.O., 1946–1952), pp. 290–298.
7. *Trials of War Criminals before the Nuremberg Military Tribunal under Control Council*, no. 10, vols. 12–14 (London: H.M.S.O., 1947–1949).
8. Walter Schellenberg, *The Labyrinth: Memoirs of Walter Schellenberg* (New York: Harper & Brothers, 1956), pp. 261–276.

Chapter 19. Himmler's Demise

1. H. R. Trevor-Roper, *The Last Days of Hitler* (London: Pan, 1973), pp. 225, 226.
2. Willi Frischauer, *Himmler* (New York: Belmont Books, 1962), pp. 170, 171.
3. Ibid., p. 212.
4. Roger Manvell and Heinrich Fraenkel, *Heinrich Himmler* (London: Heineman, 1965), p. 245.
5. Peter Padfield, *Himmler* (New York: Henry Holt, 1993), p. 610.
6. Felix Kersten, *The Kersten Memoirs, 1940–1945* (New York: Macmillan, 1957), pp. 306, 307.

7. Charles G. Cogan, *Charles de Gaulle: A Brief Biography with Documents* (New York: St. Martin's Press, 1999), p. 6.

8. Kersten, *Memoirs,* pp. 306, 307.

Epilogue

1. *Report of the Dutch Parliamentary Commission of Enquiry into the Government's Conduct of Affairs, 1940–1945,* of the Second Chamber of the States General, confirmed by depositions of Ludwig Pemsel, March 27, 1952, and General Müller-Dachs, September 28, 1949 (The Hague: n.p., 1950).

2. Declarations made after the War, May 1, 1949, by a Finnish Legation secretary, Mr. E. Lundstrom, and by H. Ramsay, Finnish minister of foreign affairs from 1943–1944, June 13, 1949, in ibid.

3. Former Finnish minister in Berlin, T. M. Kivimäkki to Felix Kersten, December 1948, in *Who Was Felix Kersten? Documents Issued by Persons and Organisations Confirming Medicinålradet Felix Kersten's Involvement and Achievements During the Second World War,* ed. and comp. Arno Kersten (Stockholm: privately published, 2000).

4. Memorandum of October 25, 1946, from Mrs. J. E. H. Van Nagell-Van Haersolte, "Gist of the 'Report of the Dutch Parliamentary Commission [of Enquiry],' consisting of Jonkheer A. M. Snouck Hurgronje, LL.D., Professor A. J. C. Rutter, and C. J. van Schelle, LL.D., on Mr. E. A. F. Kersten," in *Who Was Felix Kersten?,* p.5.

5. Based on notes taken by Martin Bormann, in *Hitler's Table Talk, 1941–1944,* ed. H. R. Trevor-Roper, Lord Dacre of Glanton (London: Weidenfeld & Nicolson, 1953), p. 25.

6. "Gist of the 'Report of the Dutch Parliamentary Commission,'" p. 22.

7. H. R. Trevor-Roper, Lord Dacre of Glanton, introduction to *The Kersten Memoirs, 1940-1945* (New York: Macmillan, 1957), pp. 19, 20.

8. Professor N. W. Posthumus to Norske Stortings Nobel Komitee, Oslo, Norway, January 20, 1960 in *Who Was Felix Kersten?*

9. John H. Waller, *The Unseen War in Europe* (New York: Random House, 1996), pp. 366–390.

10. H. R. Trevor-Roper, Lord Dacre of Glanton, "Kersten, Himmler and Count Bernadotte," *Atlantic Monthly* (February 1953): pp. 43, 44.

11. Achim Besgen, *Der Stille Befehl: Medizinalrat Kersten, Himmler und das Dritte Reich* (Munich: Nymphenburger Verlagshandlung, 1960), pp. 33, 34.

12. Official letter from the Embassy of Israel in Stockholm to Mrs. I. Kersten, August 2, 1988 in *Who Was Felix Kersten?*

13. Count Folke Bernadotte, *The Fall of the Curtain* (London: Cassell, 1945).

14. U.S. National Archives and Records Administration, RG 165, July 1945, declassified January 1995, "Report on the Case of Walter Friedrich Schellenberg," British-U.S. interrogation of Schellenberg, Appendix II, "Schellenberg's Relations with the Swedish Intelligence Service."

15. Ibid.

16. H. R. Trevor-Roper, *The Last Days of Hitler* (London: Pan, 1947).

17. Trevor-Roper, "Kersten, Himmler and Count Bernadotte," pp. 13–15.

18. Foreign Ministry of Sweden, 1945 *Ars Svenska Hjalpsexpedition till Tyskland*, April 26, 1956 (Hoover Institution on War, Revolution and Peace, Stanford University, Palo Alto, California).

19. Ibid.

20. Trevor-Roper, "Kersten, Himmler and Count Bernadotte," pp. 24–26.

21. Ibid.

22. Herma Briffault, ed., *The Memoirs of Doctor Felix Kersten* (Garden City, N.Y.: Doubleday, 1947), pp. 4, 5.

23. Norbert Masur, *En Jude Talar Med Himmler* (Stockholm: Albert Bonniers Förlag, 1945).

24. Brief sent to Professor N. W. Posthumus in Leiden, Holland, by Hilel Storch, World Jewish Congress, Relief and Rehabilitation Department, Stockholm, Sweden, January 8, 1955, paras. 2, 3.

25. Arno Kersten, son of Felix Kersten, in *Who Was Felix Kersten?*

Bibliography

Archives

Joseph Mark Lauinger Library, Special Collection, Georgetown University, Washington, D.C.

    Russell J. Bowen Collection, Intelligence Literature

Military History Institute, U.S. Army War College, Carlisle Barracks, Carlisle, Pennsylvania

    William J. Donovan Papers

U.S. National Archives and Records Administration

    RG 226: Records of the Office of Strategic Services

    Records of the German Armed Forces High Command (microfilmed)

    Modern Military Reference Division

    RG 59: Records of the U.S. Department of State

    RG 84: Records of U.S. Foreign Legations

Key Archival Documents

Documents Relating to Felix Kersten

1945 Ars Svenska Hjalpsexpedition Till Tyskland (Swedish White Paper, including an analysis of Felix Kersten's role in World War II), Stockholm, April 26, 1956.

U.S. Department of State Records, U.S. National Archives and Records Administration, RG 59, European War (EW) Files.

U.S. National Archives and Records Administration, RG 226, OSS, Entry 63, Stockholm Correspondence, 1942-1945, Box 1.

U.S. National Archives and Records Administration, RG Entry 125-A, Stockholm X-2 documents, Box 59.

U.S. National Archives and Records Administration, RG 226, Entry 180, Microfilm 1642, Microfilm A-3304, Roll 28, Frames 782-800, declassified 1978, "Contact with Himmler," written by OSS officer Abram Hewitt, Stockholm, attached to OSS chief William Donovan's Memorandum for the President, March 20, 1944.

Documents Relating to Walter Schellenberg

U.S. National Archives and Records Administration, RG 226, Entry 125-A, Box 2, Folder "Schellenberg," OSS, X-2, Stockholm, PTS-5, "Brigadenführer Schellenberg, Amtscheff VI," June 1945.

U.S. National Archives and Records Administration, RG 319, IRR X-E 001752, Box 195, NND 837036, "Schellenberg Interrogation," with attachments.

U.S. National Archives and Records Administration, RG 165, July 1945, declassified January 1995, "Report on the Case of Walter Friedrich Schellenberg," British-U.S. interrogation of Schellenberg.

Selected Bibliography

Aarons, Mark, and John Loftus. *Unholy Trinity.* New York: St. Martin's, 1991.

Abshagan, Karl Heinz. *Canaris.* London: Hutchinson, 1956.

Allen, Peter. *The Crown and the Swastika.* London: Robert Hale, 1991.

Andrew, Christopher. *Secret Service: The Making of the British Intelligence Community.* London: Heinemann, 1985.

Andrew, Christopher, and David Dilks, eds. *The Mission Dimensions: Governments and Intelligence Communities in the Twentieth Century.* London: Macmillan, 1984.

Andrew, Christopher, and Oleg Gordiekvsky. *KGB: The Inside Story of Its Foreign Operations from Lenin to Gorbachev.* New York: HarperCollins, 1990.

Andrew, Christopher, and Vasili Mitrokhin. *The Sword and the Shield.* New York: Basic Books, 1999.

Andrew, Christopher, and Jeremy Noakes, eds. *Intelligence and International Relations, 1900-1945.* Exeter, U.K.: Exeter University Publications, 1987.

Annan, Noel. *Changing Enemies.* London: HarperCollins, 1995.

Bailey, Geoffrey. *The Conspirators.* New York: Harpers, 1960.

Balfour, Michael. *Withstanding Hitler in Germany, 1933-1944.* London: Routledge, 1988.

Barnett, Corelli, ed. *Hitler's Generals.* New York: Grove & Weidenfeld, 1989.

Bartz, Karl. *The Downfall of the German Secret Service.* London: William Kimber, 1956.

Bazna, Elyesa, with Hans Nogly. *I Was Cicero.* New York: Harper & Row, 1962.

Bernadotte, Count Folke. *The Fall of the Curtain.* London: Cassell, 1945.

Bertrand, Gustave. *Enigma ou La Plus Grande Enigme de la Guerre, 1939-1945.* Paris: Librairie Plon, 1973.

Besgen, Achim. *Der Stille Befehl: Medizinalrat Kersten, Himmler und das Dritte Reich.* Munich: Nymphenburger Verlagshandlung, 1960.

Best, S. Payne. *The Venlo Incident.* London: Hutchinson, 1950.

Bethell, Nicholas. *The Last Secret.* New York: Basic Books, 1974.

Black, Peter R. *Ernst Kaltenbrunner: Ideological Soldier of the Third Reich.* Princeton, N.J.: Princeton University Press, 1984.

Blackstock, Paul. *The Secret Road to World War II.* Chicago: Quadrangle, 1969.

Bloch, Michael. *Operation Willi.* London: Weidenfeld & Nicolson, 1984.

———. *Ribbentrop: A Biography.* New York: Crown, 1992.

Blum, William. *The CIA: A Forgotten History.* London: Zed, 1986.

Bonhoeffer, Dietrich. *Letters and Papers from Prison.* London: S.C.M. Press, 1953.

Bonhoeffer Family. *Last Letter of Resistance.* Philadelphia: Fortress, 1986.

Boorstin, Daniel J. *Hidden History.* New York: Random House, 1989.

Borovik, Genrikh. *The Philby Files.* Boston: Little, Brown, 1994.

Boveri, Margaret. *Treason in the Twentieth Century.* New York: Putnam, 1963.

Bowen, Russell J. *Scholar's Guide to Intelligence Literature: Bibliography of the Russell J. Bowen Collection* (Washington, D.C.: Joseph Mark Lauinger Library, Georgetown University). Frederick, Md.: Publications of America, 1983.

Boyd, Carl. *Hitler's Japanese Confidant.* Lawrence: University of Kansas Press, 1993.

Boyle, Andrew. *The Fourth Man.* New York: Dial, 1979.

Breitman, Richard. "Hitler's Alleged Peace Emissaries." *Journal of Contemporary History* 30 (1995).

Breuer, William B. *Hoodwinking Hitler: The Normandy Deception.* Westport, Conn.: Praeger, 1993.

————. *Top Secrets of World War II.* New York: John Wiley & Sons, 2000.

————. *Unexplained Mysteries of World War II.* New York: John Wiley & Sons, 1997.

Briffault, Herma, ed. *The Memoirs of Doctor Felix Kersten.* Garden City, N.Y.: Doubleday, 1947.

Brissaud, Andre. *Canaris: The Biography of Admiral Canaris, Chief of German Military Intelligence in the Second World War.* New York: Grosset & Dunlap, 1974.

————. *The Nazi Secret Service.* New York: W.W. Norton, 1974.

Bristow, Desmond. *A Game of Moles: The Deceptions of an MI-6 Officer.* London: Little, Brown, 1993.

Bross, John. *Special Operations.* Washington, D.C.: privately published, 1992.

Brown, Anthony Cave. *Bodyguard of Lies.* New York: Morrow, 1975.

————. *"C": The Secret Life of Sir Stewart Menzies, Spymaster to Winston Churchill.* 1987. Reprint, New York: Collier, 1989.

————. *The Last Hero: Wild Bill Donovan.* New York: Times Books, 1982.

————. *Treason in the Blood.* Boston: Houghton Mifflin, 1994.

————. ed. *The Secret War Report of the OSS.* New York: Berkley, 1976.

Bullock, Alan. *Hitler and Stalin: Parallel Lives.* New York: Random House, 1993.

Buranelli, Vincent, and Nan Buranelli. *Spy, Counterspy: An Encyclopedia of Espionage.* New York: McGraw-Hill, 1982.

Burdick, Charles, and Hans-Adolf Jacobsen. *The Halder War Diaries, 1939-1942.* Novato, Calif.: Presidio, 1988.

Butler, Rohan, and Ernest L. Woodward, eds. *Documents on British Policy Overseas, 1919-1939.* Ser. 2. 1947. Reprint, London: Her Majesty's Stationery Office, 1984.

Cadogan, Sir Alexander. *The Diaries of Sir Alexander Cadogan, 1938-1945.* New York: Putnam, 1972.

Calvocoressi, Peter. *Top Secret Ultra.* New York: Pantheon, 1980.

Carley, Michael Jabara. *The Alliance That Never Was and the Coming of World War Two.* Chicago: Ivan R. Dee, 1939.

Carsten, F. L. *Reichswehr and Politics, 1918-1933.* Oxford, U.K.: Oxford University Press, 1966.

Central Intelligence Agency, Counterintelligence Staff. *The Rote Kapelle: The CIA's History of Soviet Intelligence Networks in Western Europe, 1936-1945.* Washington, D.C.: University Publications of America, 1979.

Chalow, George C., ed. *The Secret War: The Office of Strategic Services.* Washington, D.C.: U.S. National Archives, 1992.

Charmley, John. *Churchill: The End of Glory.* New York: Harcourt Brace, 1993.

Churchill, Winston. *The Second World War.* Vol. 1, *The Gathering Storm.* London: Reprint Society, 1954.

Clark, Alan. *Barbarossa: The Russian-German Conflict, 1941-1945.* New York: Morrow, 1985.

Clark, Mark Wayne. *Calculated Risk.* New York: Harper & Brothers, 1950.

Clifford, Alexander. *Conquest of North Africa, 1940-1943.* Boston: Little, Brown, 1943.

Colville, John. *The Fringes of Power: 10 Downing Street Diaries.* New York: W.W. Norton, 1986.

Colvin, Ian. *Canaris, Chief of Intelligence.* Maidstone, U.K.: George Mann, 1973.

———. *The Chamberlain Cabinet.* New York: Taplinger, 1971.

Conot, Robert E. *Justice at Nuremberg.* New York: Carron & Graf, 1983.

Conquest, Robert. *The Great Terror: A Reassessment.* New York: Oxford University Press, 1990.

———. *The Great Terror: Stalin's Purge of the Thirties.* New York: Macmillan, 1968.

Constantinides, George C. *Intelligence and Espionage: An Analytical Bibliography.* Boulder, Colo.: Westview, 1983.

Coon, Carleton S. *A North African Story.* Ipswich, Mass.: Gambit, 1980.

Costello, John. *Mask of Treachery.* London: Collins, 1988.

———. *Ten Days to Destiny.* New York: Morrow, 1991.

Costello, John, and Oleg Tsarev. *Deadly Illusions.* New York: Crown, 1993.

Cross, Robin. *Fallen Eagle.* New York: John Wiley & Sons, 1995.

Cumberlege, Geoffrey. *A German of the Resistance.* London: Oxford University Press, 1948.

Dahlerus, Birger. *The Last Attempt.* London: Hutchinson, 1945.

Dawidoff, Nicholas. *The Catcher Was a Spy.* New York: Pantheon, 1994.

Dawidowicz, Lucy S. *The War Against the Jews, 1933–1945.* 1975. Reprint, New York: Bantam, 1986.

Deacon, Richard. *"C": A Biography of Sir Maurice Oldfield, Head of MI-6.* London: Macdonald, 1985.

———. *A History of the British Secret Service.* London: Panther/Grenada, 1980.

Deane, John R. *The Strange Alliance: The Story of Our Efforts at Wartime Cooperation with Russia.* New York: Viking, 1947.

Degras, Jane, ed. *Soviet Documents,* vol. 3. London: Oxford University Press, 1953.

Deighton, Len. *Blood, Tears and Folly.* New York: HarperCollins, 1993.

DeJong, Alex. *Stalin and the Shaping of the Soviet Union.* New York: Morrow, 1986.

DeLarue, Jacques. *The Gestapo.* New York: Morrow, 1964.

DeLaunay, Jacques. *Secret Diplomacy of World War II.* New York: Simmons-Boardman, 1963.

Denham, Henry. *Inside the Nazi Ring. A Naval Attaché in Sweden, 1940-1945.* New York: Holmes & Meier, 1984.

Deutsch, Harold C. *The Conspiracy Against Hitler in the Twilight War.* Minneapolis: University of Minnesota Press, 1968.

———. "The Matter of Records." *Journal of Military History* 59, no. 1 (January 1995): p. 135.

Dilks, David. "Appeasement and Intelligence." In *Retreat from Power: Studies in Britain's Foreign Policy of the 20th Century.* London: Macmillan, 1981.

———, ed. *The Diaries of Sir Alexander Cadogan, 1938-1945.* New York: Putnam, 1971.

Dolan, Brooke. "Across Tibet: Excerpts from the Journal of Captain Brooke Dolan, 1942-1943." *Frontiers* (annual of the Academy of National Science, Philadelphia) 2 (1980).

Donhoff, Countess Marion. *Before the Storm in Old Prussia.* New York: Knopf, 1990.

Douglas-Hamilton, James. *Motive for a Mission.* New York: Aragon, 1986.

———. *The Truth about Rudolf Hess.* Edinburgh: Mainstreet Publishing, 1993.

Downes, Donald. *The Scarlet Thread: Adventures in Wartime Espionage.* New York: British Book Center, 1953.

Duffy, James P., and Vincent L. Ricci. *Target Hitler.* Westport, Conn.: Praeger, 1992.

Dulles, Allen W. *The Craft of Intelligence.* New York: Harper & Row, 1968.

———. *Germany's Underground.* New York: Macmillan, 1947.

———. *The Secret Surrender.* New York: Harper & Row, 1966.

Dunlop, Richard. *Donovan, America's Master Spy.* New York: Rand McNally, 1982.

Eisenhower, Dwight D. *Crusade in Europe.* New York: Doubleday, 1948.

Erickson, John. *The Soviet High Command.* London: Macmillan, 1962.

Farago, Ladislas. *The Game of the Foxes.* New York: Bantam, 1973.

Feis, Herbert. *Churchill, Roosevelt, Stalin.* Princeton, N.J.: Princeton University Press, 1957.

Fest, Joachim. *The Face of the Third Reich.* San Francisco: Da Capo, 1999.

———. *Plotting Hitler's Death: The Story of German Resistance.* New York: Metropolitan Books, 1996.

Fischer, Klaus P. *Nazi Germany: A New History.* New York: Continuum, 1995.

Fleming, Peter. *Operation Sea Lion.* New York: Simon & Schuster, 1957.

Flicke, Wilhelm F. *War Secrets in the Ether.* 2 vols. Laguna Hills, Calif.: Aegean Park Press, 1977.

Foltz, Charles. *The Masquerade in Spain.* Boston: Houghton Mifflin, 1948.

Foote, Alexander. *Handbook for Spies.* New York: Doubleday, 1949.

Ford, Corey. *Donovan of OSS.* Boston: Little, Brown, 1970.

Foreign Relations of the U.S. [FRUS], 1944, vol. 1. Washington, D.C.: U.S. Government Printing Office, 1965.

Foreign Relations of the U.S. [FRUS], Diplomatic Papers, 1943. Washington, D.C.: U.S. Government Printing Office, 1963.

Friedhoff, Herman. *Requiem for the Resistance.* London: Bloomsbury Press, 1993.

Friedlander, Saul. *Nazi Germany and the Jews, 1933-1939.* Vol. 1. New York: HarperCollins, 1997.

Frolik, Josef. *The Frolik Defection: The Memoirs of an Intelligence Agent.* London: Leo Cooper, 1975.

Galante, Pierre. *Operation Valkyrie: The German Generals Plot Against Hitler.* New York: Harper & Row, 1981.

Garlinski, Jozef. *The Swiss Corridor.* London: J. M. Dent, 1959.

Gehlen, Reinhard. *The Service: The Memoirs of General Reinhard Gehlen.* New York: World Publishing, 1972.

Gelb, Norman. *Dunkirk.* New York: Morrow, 1989.

Gellman, Irwin F. *Secret Affairs: Franklin Roosevelt, Cordell Hull, Sumner Welles.* Baltimore: Johns Hopkins University Press, 1995.

Gilbert, Felix, ed. and annot. *Hitler Directs His War.* New York: Oxford University Press, 1950.

Gilbert, G. M. *Nuremberg Diary.* New York: Da Capo, 1995.

Gilbert, Martin. *Churchill: A Life.* New York: Henry Holt, 1991.

———. *The Second World War.* Rev. ed. New York: Henry Holt, 1989.

Gill, Anthony. *An Honorable Defeat.* New York: Henry Holt, 1994.

Gisevius, Hans Bernd. *To the Bitter End.* Boston: Houghton Mifflin, 1947.

Giskes, Herman J. *London Calling North Pole.* New York: British Book Center, 1953.

"Gist of the 'Report of the Dutch Parliamentary Commission [of Enquiry],' consisting of Jonkheer A. M. Snouck Hurgronje, LL.D., Professor A. J. C. Rutter, and C. J. van Schelle, LL. D., on Mr. E. A. F. Kersten," in *Who Was Felix Kersten? Documents Issued by Persons and Organisations Confirming Medicinalrådet Felix Kersten's Involvement and Achievements During the Second World War.* Ed. and comp. Arno Kersten. Stockholm: privately published, 2000.

Glantz, David M. *The Role of Intelligence in Soviet Military Strategy in World War II.* Novato, Calif.: Presidio, 1990.

Goebbels, Joseph. *The Goebbels Diaries.* Ed. by Louis Lochner. Garden City, N.Y.: Doubleday, 1948.

Goodrick-Clarke, Nicholas. *Hitler's Priestess.* New York: NYU Press, 1998.

Grose, Peter. *Gentleman Spy: The Life of Allen Dulles.* Boston: Houghton Mifflin, 1994.

Gun, Nerin E. *Hitler's Mistress: Eva Braun.* New York: Bantam, 1969.

Halder, Franz. *Hitler as Warlord.* London: Putnam, 1950.

Halpern, Samuel, and Hayden Peake. *In the Name of Intelligence.* Washington, D.C.: NIBC Press, 1994.

Hamerow, Theodore S. *On the Road to the Wolf's Lair.* Cambridge, Mass.: Belknap/Harvard University Press, 1997.

Hanfstaengl, Ernst. *Hitler: The Missing Years.* 1957. Reprint, New York: Arcade, 1994.

Hassell, Fey von (Pirzio-Biroli). *Hostage of the Third Reich.* New York: Scribner's, 1989.

Hassell, Ulrich von. *The von Hassell Diaries.* Ed. Allen W. Dulles. New York: Doubleday, 1947.

Hayes, Carlton J. H. *Wartime Mission in Spain, 1942–1945.* New York: Macmillan, 1946.

Hayman, Ronald. *Hitler and Geli.* New York: Bloomsbury, 1997.

Heiber, Helmut. *The Early Goebbels Diaries, 1925–1926.* New York: Praeger, 1963.

Heideking, Jurgen, and Christof Mauch. *The USA and the German Resistance: Analysis and Operations of the American Secret Service in World War II.* Tübingen: A. Franke Verlag, 1993.

Henderson, Sir Neville. *Failure of a Mission.* New York: Putnam, 1940.

Henhoeffer, William. *The Intelligence War in 1941: A 50th Anniversary Perspective.* Doc. no. TE/CSI/92/002. Washington, D.C.: U.S. Central Intelligence Agency, 1992.

Hersh, Burton. *Old Boys.* New York: Scribner's, 1992.

Higham, Charles. *Wallis.* London: Sidgwick & Jackson, 1988.

Hinsley, F. H., and Alan Stripp, eds. *Codebreakers.* Oxford, U.K.: Oxford University Press, 1993.

Hinsley, F. H., E. E. Thomas, C. A. G. Simkins, C. G. Ransom, and Michael Howard. *British Intelligence in the Second World War, Its Influence on Strategy and Operations: History of the Second World War.* 5 vols. London: Her Majesty's Stationery Office, 1979-1990.

Hoare, Sir Samuel. *Ambassadeur en Mission Speciale, 1946.* Paris: Vent du Large, 1946.

Hoettl, Wilhelm. *The Secret Front: The Story of Nazi Political Espionage.* New York: Praeger, 1954.

Hoffman, Peter. *Claus Schenk Graf von Stauffenberg und Sein Bruder.* Stuttgart: DVA, 1993.

———. *The History of German Resistance, 1933–1945.* Cambridge, Mass.: MIT Press, 1977.

Höhne, Heinz. *Canaris: Hitler's Master Spy.* New York: Doubleday, 1979.

———. *Codeword: Direktor: The Story of the Red Orchestra.* New York: Coward, McCann & Geoghegan, 1971.

———. *The Order of the Death's Head: The Story of Hitler's SS.* London: Martin Secker & Warburg, 1969.

Holbrook, Stephan P. *Target Switzerland: Swiss Neutrality in World War II.* New York: Sarpedon, 1998.

Hoover, Calvin. *Memoirs of Capitalism, Communism and Nazism.* Durham, N.C.: Duke University Press, 1965.

Hopkirk, Peter. *Like Hidden Fire.* New York: Kodansha, 1994.

Howard, Michael. *Studies in War and Peace.* New York: Viking, 1971.

Hull, Cordell. *Memoirs of Cordell Hull.* 2 vols. New York: Macmillan, 1948.

Hyde, H. Montgomery. *Room 3603: The Story of the British Intelligence Center in New York During World War II.* New York: Farrar, Strauss, 1963.

———. *Secret Intelligence Agent: British Espionage in America and the Creation of the OSS.* New York: St. Martin's, 1982.

"Interrogation of General Friedrich Dollman." Document CSDIC, Report SRGG 1219 (e). Anthony Cave Brown Papers, Box 4. Special Collections Department, Joseph Mark Lauinger Library, Georgetown University.

Ivanov, Miroslav. *Target: Heydrich.* New York: Macmillan, 1972.

Jaggers, R. C. "The Assassination of Reinhard Heydrich." *Studies in Intelligence* (Central Intelligence Agency) (Winter 1960).

Jansen, Jon B., and Stefan Weyl. *The Silent War: The Underground Movement in Germany.* Philadelphia: Lippincott, 1943.

John, Otto. *Twice Through the Lines: The Autobiography of Otto John.* New York: Harper & Row, 1972.

Kahn, David. *Hitler's Spies: German Military Intelligence in World War II.* New York: Macmillan, 1978.

Kalugin, Oleg. *The First Directorate; My Thirty-two Years in Intelligence and Espionage Against the West.* New York: St. Martin's, 1994.

Katz, Barry M. *Foreign Intelligence Research and Analysis in the Office of Strategic Services, 1942–1945.* Cambridge, Mass.: Harvard University Press, 1989.

Keegan, John. *The Second World War.* New York: Viking, 1989.

Kennan, George. *From Prague after Munich.* Princeton, N.J.: Princeton University Press, 1968.

———. *Russia and the West under Lenin and Stalin.* Boston: Little, Brown, 1968.

Kent, Sherman. *Strategic Intelligence for American World Policy.* Princeton, N.J.: Princeton University Press, 1949.

Kershaw, Ian. *Hitler: Nemesis: 1936–1945.* New York: W.W. Norton, 2000.

———. Foreward to *Operation Foxley: The British Plan to Kill Hitler.* London: Kew United Kingdom Public Record Office Publications, 1999.

Kersten, Arno, ed. and comp. *Who Was Felix Kersten? Documents Issued by Persons and Organisations Confirming Medicinalrådet Felix Kersten's Involvement and Achievements During the Second World War.* Stockholm: privately published, 2000

Kersten, Felix. *The Kersten Memoirs, 1940–1945.* New York: Macmillan, 1957.

Kessel, Joseph. *The Man with the Miraculous Hands.* Freeport, N.Y.: Books for Libraries, 1971.

Kessler, Leo. *Betrayal at Venlo.* London: Leo Cooper, 1991.

Kilzer, Louis C. *Churchill's Deception.* New York: Simon & Schuster, 1994.

———. *Hitler's Traitor: Martin Bormann and the Defeat of the Reich.* Novato, Calif.: Presidio, 2000.

Kimball, Warren F. *Forged in War.* New York: Morrow, 1997.

———. *The Juggler: Franklin Roosevelt as Wartime Statesman.* Princeton, N.J.: Princeton University Press, 1991.

Kimche, Jon. *Spying for Peace.* New York: Roy Publishers, 1961.

Klehr, Harvey, John Earl Hayes, and Fridrikh Igorevich Firsov. *The Secret World of American Communism.* New Haven, Conn.: Yale University Press, 1995.

Klemperer, Klemens von. *German Resistance Against Hitler: The Search for Allies Abroad, 1938–1945.* Oxford, U.K.: Clarendon Press, 1995.

Knightly, Phillip. *The Master Spy.* New York: Knopf, 1989.

————. *The Second Oldest Profession.* New York: W. W. Norton, 1986.

Korbel, Joseph. *The Communist Subversion of Czechoslovakia, 1938–1948.* Princeton, N.J.: Princeton University Press, 1959.

Kozaczuk, Wladyslaw. *Enigma: How the German Machine Cipher Was Broken and How It Was Read by the Allies in World War II.* Frederick, Md.: University Publications of America, 1984.

Kramarz, Joachim. *Stauffenberg: The Architect of the Famous July 20th Conspiracy to Assassinate Hitler.* New York: Macmillan, 1967.

Kuusinen, Aino. *The Rings of Destiny: Inside Soviet Russia, from Lenin to Brezhnev.* New York: Morrow, 1974.

Lamb, Richard. *War in Italy: 1943–1945: A Brutal Story.* New York: St. Martin's, 1993.

Lane, Peter B. *The U.S. and the Balkan Crisis of 1940–1941.* New York: Garland, 1988.

Langer, Walter C. *The Mind of Adolf Hitler: The Secret Wartime Report.* New York: Basic Books, 1972.

Langer, William L. *Our Vichy Gamble.* New York: Knopf, 1947.

Lankford, Nelson, ed. *OSS Against the Reich: The World War II Diaries of Colonel David K. E. Bruce.* Kent, Ohio: Kent State University.

Laqueur, Walter. *The Terrible Secret.* Boston: Little, Brown, 1980.

Lattimer, John K., M.D. *Hitler's Fatal Sickness and Other Secrets of the Nazi Leaders.* New York: Hippocrene, 1999.

Leber, Annedore, ed., reedited by Karl Bracher. *The Conscience in Revolt.* Mainz: V. Hase & Koehler, 1994.

Lebor, Adam. *Hitler's Secret Bankers; Myth of Swiss Neutrality.* Secaucus, N.J.: Carol Publishing Group, 1997.

Lee, Bruce. *Marching Orders.* New York: Crown, 1995.

"*The Legacy of Alexander Orlov.*" As considered by the U.S. Senate, Congressional Record, 93rd Cong. 1st sess., August 1973.

Leutze (Lütz), James, ed. *The London Journal of General Raymond E. Lee, 1940–1941.* Boston: Little, Brown, 1971.

Leverkuehn, Paul. *German Military Intelligence.* New York: Praeger, 1954.

Lewin, Ronald. *Hitler's Mistakes.* New York: Morrow, 1984.

————. *Ultra Goes to War: The First Account of World War II's Greatest Secret Based on Official Documents.* New York: McGraw-Hill, 1978.

Lewis, Adrian R. "Failure of Allied Planning and Doctrine for Operation Overlord." *Journal of Military History* 62, no. 4 (1998).

Liddell-Hart, B. H. *The German Generals Talk.* New York: Morrow, 1979.

———. *History of the Second World War.* New York: Putnam, 1982.

Lifton, Robert Jay. *The Nazi Doctors.* New York: Basic Books, 1986.

Lockhart, R. H. Bruce. *Comes the Reckoning.* London: Putnam, 1947.

Lockhart, Robin Bruce. *Reilly, Ace of Spies.* Middlesex, U.K.: Penguin, 1967.

Loftus, John, and Mark Aaron. *The Secret War Against the Jews.* New York: St. Martin's, 1994.

Lovell, Mary S. *Cast No Shadow: The Life of the American Spy Who Changed the Course of World War II.* New York: Pantheon, 1992.

Lukacs, John. *The Duel.* New York: Ticknor & Fields, 1991.

———. *Five Days in London: May 1940.* New Haven, Conn.: Yale University Press, 1999.

———. *The Hitler of History.* New York: Knopf, 1997.

MacDonald, Callum. *The Killing of SS Obergruppenführer Reinhard Heydrich.* New York: Free Press, 1989.

Mahl, Thomas E. *Desperate Deception: The British Covert Operations in the United States, 1939–1944.* Washington, D.C.: Brassey's, 1998.

Manvell, Roger, and Heinrich Fraenkel. *The Canaris Conspiracy.* New York: David McKay, 1969.

Maser, Werner. *Hitler: Legend, Myth and Reality.* New York: Harper & Row, 1971.

Masterman, J. C. *The Doublecross System in the War of 1939–1945.* New Haven, Conn.: Yale University Press, 1972.

Masur, Norbert. *En Jude Talar Med Himmler.* Stockholm: Albert Bonniers Förlag, 1945.

Mauch, Christof, and Jurgen Heideking. *American Intelligence and the German Resistance to Hitler: A Documentary History.* Boulder, Colo.: Westview, 1996.

May, Ernest, ed. *Knowing One's Enemies.* Princeton, N.J.: Princeton University Press, 1984.

McCormich, Donald. See Deacon, Richard.

McGovern, James. *Martin Bormann.* New York: Morrow, 1968.

McIntosh, Elizabeth P. *Sisterhood of Spies.* Annapolis, Md.: Naval Institute Press, 1998.

McKale, Donald M., ed. *Rewriting History: The Original and Revised World War II Diaries of Curt Prufer, Nazi Diplomat.* Kent, Ohio: Kent State University Press, 1998.

McLachland, Donald. *Room 39.* New York: Atheneum, 1968.

Melchior, Ib, and Frank Brandenburg. *Quest: Searching for Germany's Nazi Past.* Novato, Calif.: Presidio, 1990.

Montagu, Ewen. *Beyond Top Secret Ultra.* New York: Coward, McCann & Geoghegan, 1978.

Moravec, General Frantisek. *Master of Spies.* Garden City, N.Y.: Doubleday, 1975.

Mosley, Leonard. *Dulles.* New York: Dial, 1978.

Moyzisch, L. C. *Operation Cicero.* New York: Coward-McCann, 1950.

Myer, Karl E., and Shareen Blair Brysac. *Tournament of Shadows: The Great Game and the Race for Empire in Central Asia.* Washington, D.C.: Counterpoint, 1999.

Neilson, Keith, and B. J. C. McKerchor, eds. *Go Spy the Land.* Westport, Conn.: Praeger, 1992.

Nicolai, Colonel W. *The German Secret Service.* London: Stanley Paul, 1924.

Nicolson, Harold. *Diaries and Letters, 1939–1945.* Ed. Nigel Nicolson. London: Collins, 1967.

Nicosia, Francis R., and Lawrence Stokes, eds. *Germans Against Nazism.* Oxford, U.K.: Oxford University Press, 1992.

Norden, Peter. *Madam Kitty: A True Story.* London: Abelard-Schuman, 1973.

O'Toole, G. J. A. *The Encyclopedia of American Intelligence and Espionage.* New York: Facts on File, 1988.

———. *Honorable Treachery.* New York: Atlantic Monthly Press, 1991.

Padfield, Peter. *Hess: Flight for the Führer.* London: Weidenfeld & Nicolson, 1991.

———. *Himmler.* New York: Henry Holt, 1993.

Paillat, Claude. *Le Désastre de 1940: La Guerre Éclair.* Paris: Laffont, 1985.

Paillole, Paul. *Notre Espion chez Hitler.* Paris: Laffont, 1985.

———. *Services Speciaux, 1935–1946.* Paris: Laffont, 1975.

Paine, Lauren. *The Abwehr: German Intelligence in World War II.* London: Robert Hale, 1980.

Palmer, Raymond. "Felix Kersten and Count Bernadotte: A Question of Rescue." *Journal of Contemporary History* 29, no. 1 (January 1994).

Parrish, Thomas. *The Ultra Americans: The U.S. Role in Breaking the Nazi Codes.* New York: Stein & Day, 1986.

Perrault, Gilles. *The Red Orchestra.* New York: Schocken, 1969.

Persico, Joseph E. *Nuremberg: Infamy on Trial.* New York: Viking, 1994.

———. *Piercing the Reich.* New York: Viking, 1979.

Petersen, Neal H. *From Hitler's Doorstep.* University Park: Pennsylvania State University Press, 1996.

Pforzheimer, Walter, ed. *Bibliography of Intelligence Literature.* 8th ed. Washington, D.C.: U.S. Defense Intelligence College, 1985.

Philby, Harold Adrian Russell (Kim). *My Silent War.* London: Granada, 1969.

Piekalkiewicz, Janusz. *Secret Agents, Spies and Saboteurs.* New York: Morrow, 1973.

Pincher, Chapman. *Top Secret Too Long.* New York: St. Martin's, 1984.

Ponting, Clive. *Armageddon: Reality behind Distortions, Myths, Bias and Illusion of World War II.* New York: Random House, 1995.

Pool, James. *Hitler and His Secret Partners.* New York: Pocket Books, 1997.

Popov, Dusko. *Spy/Counterspy.* London: Weidenfeld & Nicolson, 1974.

Powers, Thomas. *Heisenberg's War: The Secret History of the German Bomb.* New York: Knopf, 1993.

Presser, Jacob. *The Destruction of the Dutch Jews.* New York: Dutton, 1969.

Preston, Paul. *Franco.* New York: Basic Books, 1994.

Prittie, Terrence. *Germans Against Hitler.* London: Hutchinson, 1964.

Prochazka, Theodore. *The Second Republic: The Disintegration of Post-Munich Czechoslovakia (October 1938–March 1939).* Boulder, Colo.: East European Monographs, 1981.

Pujol, Juan. *Garbo.* London: Weidenfeld & Nicolson, 1985.

Putlitz, Wolfgang zu. *The Putlitz Dossier.* London: Allan Wingate, 1975.

Raad, R. C. "Stalin Plans His Post-War Germany." *International History Project from the Russian Archives.* (Smithsonian Institution, Woodrow Wilson Center) (Fall 1993).

Redlick, Fritz. *Hitler: Diagnosis of a Destructive Prophet.* New York: Oxford University Press, 1999.

Reese, Mary Ellen. *General Reinhard Gehlen: The CIA Connection.* Fairfax, Va.: George Mason University Press, 1990.

Reilly, Sidney George. *The Adventures of Sidney Reilly, Britain's Master Spy.* London: Elkin, Matthews & Marrot, 1931.

Rejewski, Marian. "How Polish Mathematicians Deciphered the Enigma." *Annals of the History of Computing* 3, no. 3 (July 1981).

Report of the Dutch Parliamentary Commission of Enquiry into the Government's Conduct of Affairs, 1940–1945, of the Second Chamber of the States General. Confirmed by depositions of Ludwig Pemsel, March 27, 1952, and General Müller-Dachs, September 28, 1949. The Hague: n.p., 1950.

Reuth, Ralf George. *Goebbels.* New York: Harcourt Brace, 1990.

Reynolds, Nicholas E. *Treason Was No Crime: Ludwig Beck, Chief of the German General Staff.* London: William Kimber, 1976.

Ritter, Gerhard. *The German Resistance: Carl Goerdeler's Struggle Against Tyranny.* New York: Praeger, 1959.

Rogers, James. *The Secret War: Espionage in World War II.* New York: Facts on File, 1991.

Rommetveit, Karl, ed. *Narvik, 1940: Five Nations War in the High North.* Oslo: Norwegian Institute for Defense Studies, 1991.

Roosevelt, Kermit. *The Overseas Targets: War Report of the OSS.* Vol. 2. New York: Walker, 1976.

Royce, Hans. *20 July 1944.* Bonn: Berto, 1961.

Rubin, Barry. *Istanbul Intrigues.* New York: McGraw-Hill, 1989.

Schechtman, Joseph B. *The Mufti and the Führer.* New York: Thomas Yoseloff, 1965.

Schecter, Jerrold L., and Vyacheslav Luchkov. *Khrushchev Remembers: The Glasnost Tapes.* Boston: Little, Brown, 1990.

Schell, Orville. *Virtual Tibet.* New York: Henry Holt, 2000.

Schellenberg, Walter. *Hitler's Secret Service: The Memoirs of Walter Schellenberg,* 2nd ed. Ed. Louis Hagen. New York: Harper Brothers, 1957; Pyramid, 1968.

———. *The Labyrinth: Memoirs of Walter Schellenberg.* New York: Harper & Brothers, 1956.

Schulze-Holthus. *Day Break in Iran.* London: Staples Press, 1954.

Semelin, Jacques. *Unarmed Against Hitler.* Westport, Conn.: Praeger, 1993.

Sereny, Gitta. *Albert Speer: His Battle with Truth.* New York: Knopf, 1995.

Sheymon, Victor. *Tower of Secrets*. Annapolis, Md.: Naval Institute Press, 1994.

Shirer, William L. *The Nightmare Years*. Vol. 2 of *Twentieth Century Journey*. New York: Bantam, 1992.

Shulsky, Abram N. *Silent Warfare: Understanding the World of Intelligence*. Washington, D.C.: Brassey's, 1991.

Sklar, D. *The Nazis and the Occult*. New York: Dorset, 1989.

Smith, Bradley F. "Admiral Godfrey's Mission to America, June, July, 1941." *Intelligence and National Security* 1, no. 3 (September 1986): pp. 441–450.

———. *The Shadow Warriors: OSS and the Origins of the CIA*. New York: Basic Books, 1983.

———. *The ULTRA-MAGIC Deals and the Most Secret Special Relationship, 1940–1946*. Novato, Calif.: Presidio, 1993.

Smith, Bradley F., and Elena Agarossi. *Operation Sunrise: The Secret Surrender*. New York: Basic Books, 1979.

Smith, Gaddis. *American Diplomacy During the Second World War, 1941–1945*. New York: John Wiley & Sons, 1966.

Smith, Paul A., Jr. *On Political War*. Washington, D.C.: National Defense University Press, 1989.

Smith, R. Harris. *OSS: The Secret History of America's First Central Intelligence Agency*. Berkeley: University of California Press, 1972.

Smith, Walter Bedell. *Eisenhower's Six Great Decisions, 1944–45*. London: Longmans, Green, 1956.

Smyth, Howard McGrath. "The Ciano Papers: Rose Garden." *Studies in Intelligence* (U.S. Central Intelligence Agency) (Spring 1969).

Snyder, Louis L. *Hitler's German Enemies*. New York: Berkley, 1992.

Speer, Albert. *Inside the Third Reich*. London: Orion Books, 1995.

Spitzy, Reinhard. *How We Squandered the Reich*. Wilby, U.K.: Michael Russell, 1997.

Srodes, James. *Allen Dulles: Master of Spies*. Washington, D.C.: Regnery, 1999.

Stead, John Phillip. *Second Bureau*. London: Evans Brothers, 1959.

Stevenson, William. *The Bormann Brotherhood*. New York: Harcourt Brace Jovanovich, 1973.

———. *Intrepid's Last Case*. New York: Villard, 1983.

————. *A Man Called Intrepid: The Secret War.* New York: Harcourt Brace Jovanovich, 1976.

Stoltzfus, Nathan. "Dissent in Nazi Germany." *Atlantic Monthly* 270, no. 3 (September 1992): pp. 86–94.

Strong, Major General Sir Kenneth W. D. *Intelligence at the Top: The Recollections of Our Intelligence Officers.* Garden City, N.Y.: Doubleday, 1969.

Sudoplatov, Peter, and Anatoli Sudoplatov. *The Memoirs of an Unwanted Witness: A Soviet Spymaster.* Boston: Little, Brown, 1994.

Swedish Foreign Office. 1945 *Ars Svenska Hjalpsexpedition Till Tyskland.* Hoover Institution on War, Revolution and Peace, Stanford University, Palo Alto, California. Eng. lang. ed. Stockholm: 1956.

Sykes, Christopher. *Troubled Loyalty: A Biography of Adam von Trott zu Solz.* London: Collins, 1968.

Taylor, Telford. *The Anatomy of the Nuremberg Trials.* New York: Knopf, 1992.

Thomas, Hugh. *The Murder of Adolf Hitler.* New York: St. Martin's, 1995.

Thomsett, Michael C. *The German Opposition of Hitler.* Jefferson, N.C.: McFarland, 1997.

Toland, John. *Adolf Hitler.* Abr. ed. New York: Ballantine, 1976.

————. *Captured by History.* New York: St. Martin's, 1997.

————. *The Last 100 Days.* New York: Bantam Book, 1967.

Tompkins, Peter. *A Spy in Rome.* New York: Simon & Schuster, 1962.

Trepper, Leopold. *The Great Game: Memoirs of the Spy Hitler Couldn't Silence.* New York: McGraw-Hill, 1977.

Trevor-Roper, H. R., Lord Dacre of Glanton. *The Diaries of Joseph Goebbels.* Trans. Richard Barry. New York: Putnam's, 1978.

————. *Hitler's Table Talk, 1941–1944.* London: Weidenfeld & Nicolson, 1953.

————. *Introduction to The Kersten Memoirs, 1940–1945.* New York: Macmillan, 1957.

————. "Kersten, Himmler and Count Bernadotte." *Atlantic Monthly* (February 1953).

————. *The Philby Affair.* London: William Kimber, 1968.

————, ed. *Blitzkrieg to Defeat: Hitler's War Directive, 1939–45.* New York: Holt, Rinehart & Winston, 1964.

Troy, Thomas F. *Donovan and the CIA: A History of the Establishment of the Central Intelligence Agency.* Foreign Intelligence Book Series, ed. Thomas F. Troy. Frederick, Md.: University Publications of America, 1984.

Tuchman, Barbara W. *The Zimmerman Telegram.* New York: Viking, 1958.

Turner, Stansfield. *Secrecy and Democracy.* Boston: Houghton Mifflin, 1985.

———. *Terrorism and Democracy.* Boston: Houghton Mifflin, 1991.

U.S. Department of State. "The British Commonwealth." In *Foreign Relations of the U.S.* [FRUS], *1944.* Vol. 3. Washington, D.C.: U.S. Government Printing Office, 1965.

Van der Vat, Dan. *The Good Nazi: The Life and Lies of Albert Speer.* Boston: Houghton Mifflin, 1997.

Vassiltchikov, Marie. *Berlin Diaries, 1940–1945.* New York: Vintage, 1988.

Volkman, Ernest. *Spies: The Agents Who Changed the Course of History.* New York: John Wiley & Sons, 1994.

Volkogonov, Dmitri. *Lenin.* New York: Free Press, 1994.

Waller, John H. "The Devil's Doctor: Felix Kersten." *International Journal of Intelligence and Counterintelligence* 2, no. 3 (Fall 1998).

———. *The Unseen War in Europe.* New York: Random House, 1996.

Wark, Wesley K. *The Ultimate Enemy: British Intelligence and Nazi Germany.* Ithaca, N.Y.: Cornell University Press, 1985.

Warlimont, Walter. *Inside Hitler's Headquarters, 1939–45.* Novato, Calif.: Presidio, 1964.

Watt, Donald Cameron. "British Intelligence and the Coming of the Second World War in Europe." Chap. 9 in *Knowing One's Enemies,* ed. Ernest May. Princeton, N.J.: Princeton University Press, 1984.

Weinstein, Allen, and Alexander Vassiliev. *The Haunted Wood.* New York: Random House, 1999.

Weitz, John. *Hitler's Diplomat: The Life and Times of Joachim von Ribbentrop.* New York: Ticknor & Fields, 1992.

Welles, Sumner. *The Time for Decision.* New York: Harper & Brothers, 1944.

West, Nigel. *MI-5: British Security Service Operations, 1909–1945.* London: Weidenfeld & Nicolson, 1981.

———. Introduction to *British Security Coordination: The Secret History of British Intelligence in the Americas, 1940–1945.* London: St. Ermin's Press, 1998.

————. *MI-6.* New York: Random House, 1983.

————. *Seven Spies Who Changed the World.* London: Secker & Warburg, 1991.

————. *A Thread of Deceit: Espionage Myths and World War II.* New York: Random House, 1985.

West, Nigel, and Oleg Tsarev. *The Crown Jewels.* New Haven, Conn.: Yale University Press, 1999.

Westerfield, H. Bradford, ed. *Inside CIA's Private World.* New Haven, Conn.: Yale University Press, 1995.

Whaley, Barton. *Codeword Barbarossa.* Cambridge, Mass.: MIT Press, 1973.

Wheeler-Bennett, John W. *The Nemesis of Power.* London: Macmillan, 1953.

Whiting, Charles. *The Spymasters.* New York: Dutton, 1976.

Wiener, Jan, *The Assassination of Heydrich.* New York: Grossman, 1969.

Wighton, Charles, and Günter Peis. *Hitler's Spies and Saboteurs.* New York: Henry Holt, 1958.

Williams, Charles. *The Last Great Frenchman.* New York: John Wiley & Sons, 1995.

Winks, Robin. *Cloak and Gown: Scholars in the Secret War, 1939–1965.* New York: Morrow, 1987.

Winterbotham, F.W. *The Ultra Secret.* London: Weidenfeld & Nicolson, 1974.

————. *The Ultra Spy.* London: Macmillan, 1989.

Wires, Richard. *The Cicero Spy Affair: German Access to British Secrets in World War II.* Westport Conn.: Praeger, 1999.

Wohlstetter, Roberta. *Pearl Harbor: Warning and Decision.* Palo Alto, Calif.: Stanford University Press, 1962.

Woytak, Richard A. *On the Border of War and Peace: Polish Intelligence and Diplomacy in 1937–1939 and the Origins of the Ultra Secret.* New York: Columbia University Press, 1979.

Wright, Peter. *Spycatcher: The Candid Autobiography of a Senior Intelligence Officer.* New York: Viking, 1987.

Wulff, Wilhelm. *Zodiac and Swastika.* New York: Coward, McCann & Geoghegan, 1973.

Index